Uncommon Common Ground

THE AMERICAN ASSEMBLY was established by Dwight D. Eisenhower at Columbia University in 1950. It holds nonpartisan meetings that give rise to authoritative books, which illuminate issues of United States policy.

An affiliate of Columbia University, the Assembly is a national, educational institution incorporated in the state of New York.

The Assembly seeks to provide information, stimulate discussion, and evoke independent conclusions on matters of vital public interest.

THE AMERICAN ASSEMBLY
Columbia University

Uncommon Common Ground

Race and America's Future

Angela Glover Blackwell
Stewart Kwoh
Manuel Pastor

W. W. Norton & Company
New York · London

For information about permission to reproduce selections from this book, write to Permissions, W. W. Norton & Company, Inc., 500 Fifth Avenue, New York, NY 10110

For information about special discounts for bulk purchases, please contact W. W. Norton Special Sales at specialsales@wwnorton.com or 800-233-4830

Manufacturing by Courier Westford
Production manager: Devon Zahn

Library of Congress Cataloging-in-Publication Data

Blackwell, Angela Glover.
Uncommon common ground : race and America's future / Angela Glover Blackwell, Stewart Kwoh, Manuel Pastor.
p. cm.
"The American Assembly, Columbia University."
Previous ed.: New York : W.W. Norton, c2002, under title Searching for the uncommon common ground.
Includes bibliographical references and index.
ISBN 978-0-393-33685-6 (pbk.)
1. United States—Race relations. 2. United States—
Ethnic relations. 3. Cultural pluralism—United States.
I. Kwoh, Stewart. II. Pastor, Manuel, 1956–
III. Blackwell, Angela Glover. Searching for the uncommon common ground. IV. American Assembly. V. Title.
E184.A1B5545 2010
305.800973—dc22

2010001899

W. W. Norton & Company, Inc.
500 Fifth Avenue, New York, N.Y. 10110
www.wwnorton.com

W. W. Norton & Company Ltd.
Castle House, 75/76 Wells Street, London W1T 3QT

2 3 4 5 6 7 8 9 0

"I have never been so naïve as to believe that we can get beyond our racial divisions in a single election cycle, or with a single candidacy—particularly a candidacy as imperfect as my own."

—Presidential candidate Barack Obama

Contents

Preface

Race has been identified as the most divisive issue of the U.S. domestic agenda. Its tendrils have reached into and shadowed a myriad of critical public policy issues, the study of which The American Assembly has undertaken over its sixty-year history. With this in mind, in 1999 the Assembly sponsored a multiyear project entitled "Uniting America: Toward Common Purpose" designed to address some of the most difficult and complex forces in our society, with race identified as a pernicious, disuniting issue for the nation. Angela Glover Blackwell, Stewart Kwoh, and Manuel Pastor served as codirectors of the 2001 project, which included a four-day meeting of seventy leading authorities on race relations and the publication of the report *Racial Equality: Public Policy for the Twenty-first Century*.

The project directors also wrote the book *Searching for the Uncommon Common Ground* (2002), which was extremely well received and in the intervening years went into additional printings as it was used by policymakers and lawmakers, academicians, and concerned citizens. It addressed a new vision with new strategies and stressed the need for new leadership. The scholarship and stirring call to action by the authors made the volume a leading text during a period not generally recognized for fostering social equity. It provided encouragement to those who believed the promise of opportunity made America the beacon to the world but had grown concerned that its inability to effectively address racial equity issues had dulled the nation's promise to itself. The book also became one of the most popular volumes in The American Assembly book series.

Impressed by the reception of the first edition, The American Assembly and its publisher, W. W. Norton & Company, noted how the authors' prescient and persuasive thesis matched the fresh era of change before the nation and with it a renewed sense of hope about race, inclusion, and equity. The timing was ideal for the authors to revisit their earlier work, to build upon those insights, and to present current empirical data. *Uncommon Common Ground: Race and America's Future*, though a second edition, was almost entirely rewritten and recognized as deserving a new title.

In the first decade of the twenty-first century, America is at a demographic, economic, and environmental crossroads. While the national election in the fall of 2008 has been used as a signal of change in equality of opportunity, the authors provide the most perceptive new data on the reality of our national landscape. It would be ideal to believe that racial equity issues were behind us, but the authors prove that this is far from a reality and that tough challenges remain.

Race issues in America continue to be contentious and complicated, but the authors have brought a reasoned clarity to many of the most troubling aspects. They provide strategies and approaches for the country to commit to in order to constructively address these problems. They also examine our most entrenched and divisive institutions and policies. They demonstrate persuasively that as the nation restructures for a more balanced, sustainable future it must address the existence of inequality and invest in all members of an increasingly diverse society. This nation is at its best when it creates better opportunities for everyone, and the broad, equity framework proposed by the authors will result in an America in which more people are able to contribute to their communities, their metropolitan areas, and their nation. With this book, Angela Glover Blackwell, Stewart Kwoh, and Manuel Pastor create the climate necessary to usher in an era of change for racial justice and equity as they call for a new generation of leaders prepared to lead across constituencies and toward uncommon ground.

The original "Uniting America" project, for which the first edition of this volume was commissioned, was conceived by my predecessor Daniel A. Sharp with the advice of a distinguished national steering committee and directed by Deborah Burns Melican.

Uncommon Common Ground: Race and America's Future was supported by Bank of America, the Annie E. Casey Foundation, the Ford Foundation, and the California Community Foundation. As in all our publications, the views expressed in this volume are those of its authors, and do not necessarily reflect the views of The American Assembly or its supporters.

David H. Mortimer
President
The American Assembly

Acknowledgments

Uncommon Common Ground, the second edition of *Searching for the Uncommon Common Ground*, would not have happened without the urging and encouragement of The American Assembly. We are indebted to the Assembly and especially to David Mortimer for his determination and vision.

The authors collectively generated the themes, book structure, and writing tasks in a series of meetings and discussions, then took primary responsibility for specific chapters, sharing complementary research and critical commentary from each other to inform the work. All three contributed to shaping and editing the final product. Manuel Pastor, with the research assistance of Vanessa Carter, Lauren Ng, Jennifer Orlick, Justin Scoggins, and Jennifer Tran, provided the charts, tables, and most of the data analysis used throughout the book.

Heather Bent Tamir of PolicyLink coordinated the project, arranging planning meetings and conference calls and contributing her own considerable writing and editing skills. Her constant attention to detail was invaluable.

A book of this sort is a collaboration in the finest sense of the word. The authors could not have produced this document without the colleagues and staffs of our respective organizations, and we thank them for their extraordinary efforts. In addition to those already cited, we would like to acknowledge the writing contributions of Van Jones, James Allen Crouch, Robin Toma, and Dwayne Marsh, along with those who worked with the Asian Pacific American Legal Center—Diana Jou, Ryan Khamkongsay, Karin Wang, Carmen Morgan, Julie Su, and Daniel Ichinose; the writing and editing efforts of Vanessa Carter and Jennifer Tran of the Program for Environmental and Regional Equity (PERE) at the University of Southern California; and the editorial and writing team of Jon Jeter and Milly Hawk Daniel of PolicyLink, along with editorial and research assistance from Jennifer Pinto and Erika Bernabei.

Uncommon Common Ground

1

Are We Postracial Yet?

The presidency of Barack Obama defies simple analyses of racial progress in America. At precisely the same
moment that a black man leads the wealthiest and most
powerful nation in the world, African Americans and Latinos are grappling with their greatest loss of wealth in modern U.S. history. With ties to Islam and the Ivy League,
Obama, the son of an immigrant Kenyan father and a
midwestern white mother, is the unquestioned and popular leader of a broad-based multiethnic coalition. Yet as we
reflect on his historic electoral victory, we can't help but
wonder what Martin Luther King, Jr., would have thought
of an America that elects a black man to lead it but still fails
to graduate over one-quarter of its young black men from
high school.*

---

*The more popular figure in the press is that half of young black men
fail to "graduate" from high school. See, for example, the report from
the Schott Foundation entitled *Given Half a Chance: The Schott 50 State
Report on Public Education and Black Males*, available at http://www.black
boysreport.org. However, this figure refers to "on-time" graduation

So what is to be made of this conundrum? Was "the last racial barrier in American politics"[1] swept away by Obama's election, as some pundits have suggested, ushering in, finally, the nation's long-overdue postracial phase? Or, have Americans merely watched one remarkably gifted and fortunate person of color vault spectacularly over a wall and concluded, mistakenly, that the wall is no longer there? And, just as important, what does a black man's success have to do with the growing Latino and Asian Pacific communities, particularly at a time when immigration has emerged as a preeminent civil rights issue and is fueling a stark demographic transformation that before midcentury will result in a new American majority in which people of color outnumber whites?

This book seeks to address the issue of race and the future of the United States and to illustrate why one depends on the other. In the midst of an epic financial crisis, dealing squarely with the question of racial justice, and narrowing significantly the gap between the affluent and the poor, is the only way America gets out of its jam—and stays out.

Consider, as one example, the subprime mortgage debacle and resulting foreclosures. In the San Francisco Bay Area, for example, the top 20 percent of zip codes with the highest foreclosure rates have a population that is nearly three-quarters minority—largely Latino—while zip codes with a minority population of little more than a third, have the fewest foreclosures (Pastor, 2008). This racial character, repeated nationwide, is the result of financial systems that have been segmented, with lenders more often making high interest—or subprime—home loans to more minor-

---

within four years, a metric that does not account for later completion and one that is also affected by a methodology that can tend to overstate the initial ninth-grade enrollment on which it is based. For a discussion of the methodological issues and an attempt to generate more accurate rates using longitudinal data (that track students over time), see Mishel and Roy, 2006, and Heckman and LaFontaine, 2007.

ity borrowers than to whites—even when respective income levels suggest that such treatment makes little economic sense (ACORN, 2007).

The damage, as the nation quickly discovered, was not limited to communities of color, as the housing bubble that was inflated largely by risky home loans burst, pummeling home values across the nation, sending the construction industry and then the entire economy into a tailspin. To be sure, African Americans and Latinos have borne the brunt of the foreclosures and layoffs produced by the housing crisis, but whites have hardly been insulated from the soaring rates of unemployment, the drop in consumer spending, and depleted tax revenues.

So, how might policymakers have lessened the pain of recession if they had intervened when African American and Latino borrowers in outlying areas first began losing their homes? Imagine how much better off the country would be had our failing education system been addressed early, when test scores and dropout rates made it clear that something was going terribly wrong for black and brown kids. How much cleaner would our air and water supplies be if there had been an immediate and concerted response to the elevated levels of environmental toxins in the primarily Latino corridors of industrial Los Angeles or the refinery-rich "Cancer Alley" in Louisiana's heavily black neighborhoods? And consider what New Orleans might look like today had decision-makers understood that shoring up the levees would protect from catastrophic damage not just the mostly black Lower Ninth Ward, but the entire city.

These examples represent the promise of constructing public policy around what academics and advocates have come to call an "equity" framework. As a nation, we are only as strong as our weakest link, as Jed Horne makes clear in his book *Breach of Faith* (excerpted in Box 1-1). And when communities choose to leave some of their own behind, the safety, security, and prosperity of everyone is compromised. The principles of equity and inclusion are even more critical given America's approaching demographic tsunami, a tidal

Box 1-1. An Excerpt from *Breach of Faith**

Katrina tore up lives as well as landscapes. A city below sea level was churned suddenly and convulsively by the hurricane that struck New Orleans in late August 2005. Rich people died along with the indigent. The pricey homes of the professional classes, both black and white, were destroyed, as were rickety cottages owned or rented by the poor. Millionaires and high-flying politicians were undone by Katrina, while other survivors found opportunity in the ruins of the city. That did not make Katrina an "equal opportunity destroyer," as some hastened to call it. Poor blacks did disproportionately more of the dying. And as engines of recovery creaked into gear, people of means enjoyed advantages that had been theirs all along.

There is a comforting fatalism in thinking of Katrina as a natural disaster, or as God's will—whether that God is seen as a wrathful deity visiting retribution on a famously hedonistic part of the world or as the savior who once again spared New Orleans.

Katrina was an unnatural disaster—unnatural in its scale and destructiveness, but also unnatural in the sense that it was not limited causally to the forces of nature, to weather and geography and tides. (Of course, in an age of ominously rising temperatures and oceans, it may be that nothing about the weather is entirely a natural phenomenon anymore. I leave that debate to more knowledgeable writers.)

Both in its destructiveness—most of it tied to flooding—and throughout the early phases of the recovery . . . Katrina has been essentially a man-made disaster. The levees that failed New Orleans were artifacts that, as much as the ruin of a Maya temple or the Great Wall of China, reflected the dreams and skills and politics of the society that built them. The relief effort and recov-

ery now under way have been only more obviously a
manifestation of human agency—at a particular time
and place in the lengthening history of a still-powerful
nation.

Katrina taught us much about ourselves here in southeast Louisiana. It taught the rest of America a bit about
Louisiana. . . . But as a whole, these stories provide a
lesson for America about itself. Because, for all that New
Orleans lays claim to eccentric ways and a special place
in our culture, it is at heart an American city now testing
the greatness of America to save it—for and from itself
(Horne, 2006).

*From *Breach of Faith: Hurricane Katrina and the Near Death of a
Great American City* by Jed Horne.

wave that will eventually replace 78 million baby boomers
with a new wave of workers, many of them people of color.
The very future of the country will turn on how well it prepares that next generation of workers.

Racial justice was once the nation's rallying cry, and
social movements in the 1950s and 1960s went to work
tearing down codified discrimination that blocked—by
force of law—the path to full citizenship for people of
color. Racial "equality" is not the same as racial "equity." As
a result of the antidiscrimination laws, people of color can,
in theory at least, buy a home anywhere. But here's the
rub: most blacks can't afford to buy in predominantly white
neighborhoods, and even if they can, they are unlikely
to be able to sign a comparable home loan. So an equity
framework addresses race-based challenges by advancing
policies and practices that consciously ask who might be left
behind and crafting approaches that will include all. As one
of us has written (and all three of us agree), "Equal-rights
legislation is rendered hollow without policies that compre-
hensively address those practical barriers to economic and

social parity. Equity, in essence, makes real the promise of equality" (Blackwell, 2007: 245).

This book does not abandon racial justice as a concept—it still maintains a currency and relevance—but equity more precisely describes the modern-day challenge of expanding opportunity in America.

Our own consideration of these issues—and our passion about the hope and promise of America—has driven us to return to a volume we published in 2002 for The American Assembly entitled *Searching for the Uncommon Common Ground: New Dimensions on Race in America*. That book was part of a Uniting America series organized by the Assembly, an organization founded by Dwight Eisenhower to create a space for leaders to discuss critical national and international issues. That book laid bare America's racial challenges and argued for a new approach to reaching "uncommon common ground." What we meant is that America needs to go beyond the lowest common denominator, either in the form of racial scapegoating, or the well-meaning but ultimately naïve call for everyone to "just get along." If the nation is to progress, we said, then Americans had to fight through their discomfort with open and honest public discussions about racial grievances and keep going, until they reached some understanding—some uncommon common ground—on how to move ahead together.

Eight years later, mired in a deep recession, yet celebrating the election of the first African American president, the country is positioned at a curious intersection, at once beleaguered and hopeful, united in a desire to create a tomorrow that is better than today, but polarized over the means to achieve that end. America needs to find uncommon common ground now more than ever, and so we have altered the title—and as readers of the first volume will quickly notice—much of the content from the first book as well.

Over the years since *Searching*, it has not become any easier to talk about race: many whites cast their vote for Obama but still sense that things are not settled and worry that they may say the wrong thing in mixed company; people of color worry even more that legitimate grievances will be trivialized as "political correctness" or worse, summarily dismissed as "playing the race card." Obama's ascendancy to the White House, in that regard, actually dampens racial dialogue by convincing far too many whites (and a fair number of blacks, Latinos, and Asians as well) that America has slain the dragon, and racism is, at best, a trumped-up charge conveniently pulled out whenever someone wants to qualify their personal failing.

Similarly, many younger leaders, often of color, think race is important but stress that "class" is the new marker. Surely, they argue, the priorities now must be economic recovery, not economic equity; climate change not climate justice. To this, we warn that the last attempt to address a financial crisis of this magnitude—the New Deal during the Great Depression—represents a profound lesson on how even the grandest plan can fall short of the mark if it doesn't specifically address racial equity.

In fact, far from seizing an opportunity to reform long-standing disparities in the American economy, parts of the New Deal reinforced and even deepened this enduring racial hierarchy, according to Ira Katznelson's analysis in *When Affirmative Action Was White* (2005). To appease powerful southern lawmakers who were determined to protect the "southern way of life," Roosevelt's administration allowed key pieces of New Deal legislation to largely exclude blacks and minorities. From its inception in 1935 until it was amended in 1954, Social Security insurance exempted agricultural and domestic workers, leaving 40 percent of all white retirees and 65 percent of blacks without access to the government pension plan. Similarly, the Wagner Act recognized workers' right to unionize, and the unions' right to negotiate wages and working conditions on behalf of employees, unless they were farm or domestic workers. The GI Bill cut black servicemen in on the deal, but left it up to local governments to dole out the benefits, all but guaranteeing that African American veterans, particularly in the Deep South, received less generous subsidies than white veterans.

This played out in fairly predictable ways. Buoyed by the postwar industrial expansion and the availability of unionized manufacturing jobs that expanded America's middle class, Americans of color, on the whole, managed to make up some economic ground at first. But the gains were relatively small and short-lived, and the New Deal's failure to address racism left intact the country's design flaw—systemic and crippling inequality—that is the wobbly cornerstone of America's current economic collapse. With the nation hemorrhaging jobs, families losing their homes, the gap between rich and poor growing ever wider, and an integrated global economy that does not wait for stragglers, America is once again confronted with its nagging Achilles' heel. Class matters. But so does race.

In fact, any conversation about race today is, by necessity, more complicated than in the past, its racial fissures more nuanced. Many Asians more closely resemble whites in their socioeconomic standing. In addition to the present occupant of the White House and several CEOs in Fortune 500 companies, there are many black superstars in entertainment and sports, and hip-hop's commercial appeal is strongest in suburban communities. Latinos are building their own middle class, and immigrants are revitalizing aging neighborhoods across the country.

Yet racism still segregates our inner-city schools, still turns down black applicants for jobs in the private sector, still racially profiles black and Latino motorists, and funnels both blacks and Latinos into the broken criminal justice system at rates astronomically higher than whites (or Asians). And imagine how Obama would have fared in the campaign if he really had been a Muslim.[2] We aren't postracial. We aren't even close.

Under these circumstances, a new style of leadership is required that transcends race, culture, and class yet is grounded in the goal of equity—just and fair inclusion for everyone. Equity, in fact, is the uncommon common ground that we seek. To get there we do need different ways to talk about race. And the country has, in Obama, perhaps a model for how to talk about race and racism. Obama doesn't wear his race on his sleeve, but it never seems far away either. Many argue that one of the moments when he rescued his campaign was his Philadelphia speech on race. It was powerful, nuanced, and complicated—it did not tiptoe around the issues nor did it dwell on them, arguing that racism was real *and* that it should not be used as a distraction.

Change in America*

The new leaders of America will have to understand race, if for no other reason than that the future of our country is a multicultural one. The U.S. Census Bureau recently (but unofficially) projected that America would become a " majority-minority" country—that is, a population with no single racial group as the majority—in 2050. While the *official* estimate remains 2042, the new estimate acknowledges that lower immigration may delay the turning point.

By November of 2008, America's white majority had dropped from 83 percent in 1970 to 65 percent of the population. Latinos' share of the population increased to 15.5 percent, surpassing African Americans—who hover

---

* As the face of America changes, so does the language to mirror those changes. People within racial groups sometimes refer to themselves as one type—"Hispanic," for example—while others (both within *and* outside the group) may prefer to call themselves "Latino." Consequently, throughout this book, the authors have deliberately chosen to use ethnic and racial terms *interchangeably*, unless a differentiation is required for specificity within a segment of that population: "Mexican Americans," "Puerto Ricans." For Americans of African descent, we interchange "African Americans" and "blacks." For those of Asian descent, we may use "Asian Americans," "Asian Pacific Americans," or "Asian Pacific Islanders." We also interchange "Native Americans" with "American Indians" and sometimes sprinkle our discussion with "America's First Peoples." Finally, we interchange white with non-Hispanic white, Anglos, and Caucasian. Unless noted otherwise, all ethnic and racial terms other than Latino refer only to non-Latino members of that group to avoid double counting.

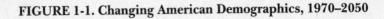

FIGURE 1-1. Changing American Demographics, 1970–2050

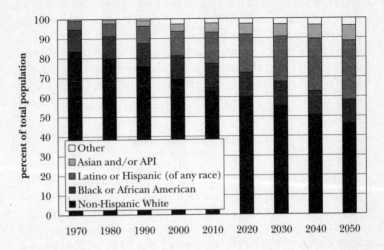

at around 12 percent of the population—as the nation's largest minority group. (See Box 1-2 for an analysis of how demographic changes influenced the election.) Asian groups have grown to 4 percent of the national total.[3] The Latino population will exceed that of all of the other minority groups combined before 2030 (see Figure 1-1).

The relative increases in the Latino and Asian population stem partly from immigration, a topic that has often generated more heat than light. At this point, however, the higher birth rates for Latinos and Asians, compared to that of whites, is playing an instrumental role in America's demographic makeover. While immigration policy does need review, and new immigrants do drive much of these demographic shifts, the higher birth rates for Latinos and Asians, compared to that of whites, also play a role. As Figure 1-2 shows, the minority population is much younger than the white population, indicating that even if immigration was stemmed, the demographic trend is likely to continue. In places like Los Angeles, where two-thirds of those

Box 1-2. How Demographic Change Influenced the 2008 Presidential Election

During the 2008 presidential election, Barack Obama headed into the home stretch with a clear advantage but also a cloud of uncertainty hanging over his head. Would he fall prey to the Bradley effect (so named after Tom Bradley, a 1982 black gubernatorial candidate in California whose actual votes were well below polling estimates and who hence lost his bid to be California's first black governor)? After Obama's victory, the Bradley effect was relegated to history. The nation had changed since 1982. In winning 43 percent of the white vote, Obama did better among white voters than did his predecessors Massachusetts Senator John Kerry and Vice President Al Gore. Obama did especially well among white men (Tilove, 2008), a more traditionally reliable Republican base, winning 41 percent of that constituency's vote and trimming the Democratic deficit by nine percentage points.

Still, he couldn't have won without getting sizable portions of the African American and Latino vote. In 2008, 5 million more blacks, Hispanics, and Asian Americans voted than in 2004. A decreased proportion of whites turned out to vote between 2004 and 2008 but blacks, Hispanics, and Asians all increased their turnout in 2008. Young blacks (eighteen to twenty-nine years old) also turned out more than young whites, at a rate of 58 percent and 52 percent, respectively. Other demographic details reveal that fast-growing "purple" states (those that aren't clearly Democratic or Republican and have become battleground states) now have the highest percentage of minority voters, at more than one-quarter of voters. Obama, the candidate of change, benefited from change and rode that wave straight into the White House (Frey, 2009).

FIGURE 1-2. Percent Distribution of U.S. Resident Population by Age and Ethnic Origin Status for 2007

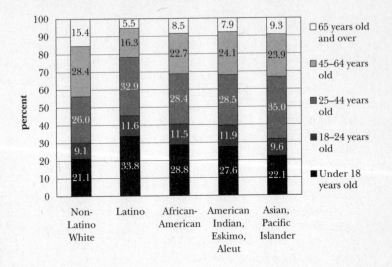

under eighteen are the children of immigrants—and 90 percent of those are U.S.-born—we are seeing the lasting impacts of what was initially a wave of foreign-born residents (Pastor and Ortiz, 2009: 1).

The mismatched age profile extends further: minorities constitute a much larger share of the young than they do the old. Nearly half of those younger than eighteen are people of color, while about 80 percent of those of retirement age are white (see Figure 1-3). This is what we term "America's generation gap"—the demographic divergence between the old and the young. It's not just a cultural distance. A study done for the Public Policy Institute of California concluded that in the states where the demographic generation gap is widest, the level of state capital outlays—essentially public investments for the future—are the lowest (Pastor and Reed, 2005). This disconnect can only be addressed by bridging the racial divide.

FIGURE 1-3. U.S. Resident Population by Age and Ethnic Origin Status for 2007

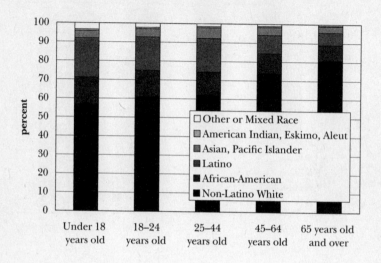

As David Hayes-Bautista and coauthors in *The Burden of Support* (1988), and more recently Dowell Myers in *Immigrants and Boomers* (2007), have pointed out, it is exactly these youths whom baby boomers will be relying on to help finance their retirement. In an already cash-strapped country, the long-run health of Social Security, Medicare, and other social supports will be bolstered by the prosperity of ethnic and racial minorities, particularly immigrants and their children. As a result, Myers—himself an Anglo baby boomer—argues for a new "social compact" in which older white Americans and younger minorities work together to ensure mutual success.

Blacks and Latinos, unfortunately, historically, earn less and are poorer than whites. A robust economy has sometimes narrowed that gap slightly, but the financial crisis and recession have wiped away the small gains from the booming late 1990s, with its soaring rates of unemploy-

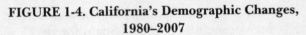

FIGURE 1-4. California's Demographic Changes, 1980–2007

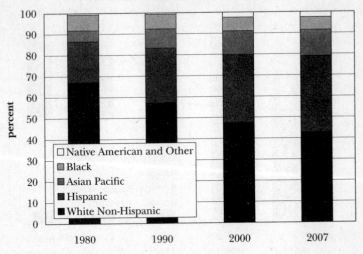

ment and foreclosures. This persistent—and perhaps worsening—disparity has obviously been particularly hard on minority Americans, but, as Myers and others point out, the nation's dependence on an increasingly minority workforce means that healthy communities of color are vital to the nation's economic fortunes.

Home to nearly one of every ten Americans, California's missteps in dealing with its changing demographics may be a harbinger of things to come for the nation as a whole if it doesn't refocus its sights on equity. Figure 1-4 shows the pattern of demographic change in California from 1980 to 2007, with the change over that period roughly parallel to—but even more pronounced than—the change the U.S. is projected to experience between 2000 and 2050.

Throughout the 1990s, for example, the state struggled with affirmative action policies and immigration, one racially charged trial after another, and the riots that were the aftermath of one of those trials. Yet it wasn't all bad news. In

2005, Los Angeles' large Latino community produced the election of the city's first Latino mayor since 1872. And in 2006, the groundswell of resistance in the Latino community against federal immigration policies led to historic demonstrations, attracting more than 600,000 protesters at a single rally.[4] And while African Americans have seen a relative decline in their political influence, Latino support at the polls helped Los Angeles County elect black politician Mark Ridley-Thomas as county supervisor, signaling perhaps a consolidation of ethnic political interests.

The shifting demographics have triggered tensions between California's ethnic groups, and when the media raises the issue of race relations in California, it's often referring to the black-brown divide more than the black-white one. Overshadowed in press reports are the burgeoning relationships between black and brown in campus politics or a resurgence of California's labor unions that is spearheaded by budding alliances between immigrant janitors and African American security guards. The interethnic cooperation around securing community benefits agreements from major private developments—although it produces real jobs and helps real families—is not as compelling to the media as looming ethnic conflicts over scarce public dollars in a recession-plagued state.

Not all of the country is faced with these challenges that come with demographic change—or at least not at the pace and scale that have confronted California. But, to varying degrees, they will be. As Figure 1-5 illustrates, the proportion of minority populations varies significantly from one state to the next. In 2007, California, Hawaii, New Mexico, and Texas had the highest concentrations of minorities, followed by Nevada and Arizona (but change is coming: see Figure 1-6 for the 2025 projections). While some states, such as North Dakota, will remain overwhelmingly white, it's clear that, on the coasts and in the Deep South, America is returning to its early roots as a panethnic nation.

Consequently, minority concerns are no longer strictly minority concerns. As our multicultural future nears, the

FIGURE 1-5. Minority Population of the United States for 2007, as a Percentage of the Total Population by State

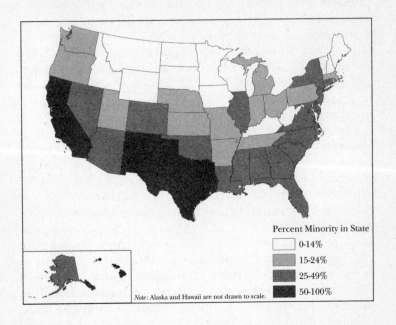

Percent Minority in State

	0-14%
	15-24%
	25-49%
	50-100%

Note: Alaska and Hawaii are not drawn to scale.

challenge of becoming one America—that is, seeing all Americans as part of a whole—grows more urgent even as it becomes more difficult. Healing racial wounds through conversation or photo ops will not be enough. Progress will be measured in large part by material gains and economic and social indices on the ground. In this volume, we challenge the reader to set their sights high and to aim for the uncommon common ground.

Stories of America: How We Came to Update This Book

Writing a book about race is a daunting task, further complicated by the collaboration of three authors, each with different perspectives and trajectories. Weaving our work

FIGURE 1-6. Minority Population of the United States for 2025, as a Percentage of the Total Population by State

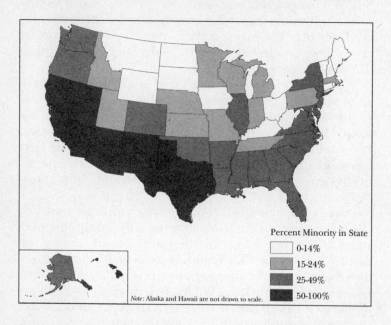

Percent Minority in State

☐ 0-14%

▨ 15-24%

▨ 25-49%

■ 50-100%

Note: Alaska and Hawaii are not drawn to scale.

and worldviews into a single narrative, however, is in some ways taking a dose of the very medicine we prescribe.

While our work ranges from scholarship to policy advocacy to legal protection, we have agreed to "play it as it lays," following our lines of inquiry to their empirical conclusion and exploring the truth, no matter how uncomfortable.

One inconvenient truth is this: there is a disconnect between what Americans say about race in public, and what they think in private. Nothing else explains the lack of public will to tackle issues as toxic as rising incarceration rates, teen dropouts, labor market discrimination, segregation and isolation, immigrant exclusion, and environmental injustice.

We decided just a few weeks after Obama's election that we should revisit this volume, the first edition of which was published eight years ago. In reexamining what we wrote, we thought some of it still seemed useful, which we attribute not to any great wisdom of our own, but rather to that of the communities we have turned to for strength and guidance over the years. At the same time, we realized that much had changed and much needed to be reworked to suit our current era.

What you hold in your hands now is not quite a sequel—although we did build from our earlier version and much of the basic framework for the book is similar. Nor is it a simple update—new graphs, old words, simple epilogue. It's somewhere in between—a sort of a 2.0 upgrade that has some similar features but is adapted for a new operating system, in our case, a new administration and a new beginning.

Despite the new approach, one basic principle remains. We believe that race is a deeply lived and profoundly personal experience. In our writing of this book and in our other work together in support of racial understanding, we have been struck by the way our personal journeys have influenced our thinking. We have decided to bring those journeys forth, so that the reader can better understand the lens through which we view the world—and think about their own.

Angela Glover Blackwell

I grew up in a segregated St. Louis, Missouri, during the 1950s and early 1960s. From talking to my parents, reading, and interviewing people about St. Louis during those years, I know that racism there was harsh. My personal experience there as a child, however, was almost completely devoid of any awareness of racism. For I had the benefit of a web of caring adults who must have spent twenty-four hours a day figuring out ways to protect their children from racism. Part of their job was made easy by the complete separation of the races. The schools, churches, social events, service organizations, and neigh-

borhoods where we played and volunteered were all black.
But separation from whites did not satisfy these adults;
their aim was higher. They wanted their children to have
exposure to the best that St. Louis had to offer without
coming into contact with those who would seek to diminish
us. What's amazing is that they succeeded.

When I was growing up, St. Louis (then the ninth-largest
city in the United States) was known for its outdoor opera,
its wonderful museum (with the steep hill behind used for
sledding in the snow), its world-class zoo, its magnificent
city park, and its symphony orchestra. While all of these
attractions did not hold my interest equally, they were all
a regular part of my life. These determined black adults
would take us to enjoy these activities, literally shielded
from the rest of the world. At the outdoor opera, for
instance, the children sat on the inside seats and the adults
sat on the perimeter, shooting stares and threatening ges-
tures at any child who might embarrass them or us. When
there was a special exhibit at the museum, we were taken
as a group to explore the arts with our own private docent.
And so it was; racism all around and the children of the
black middle class in St. Louis oblivious to its sting and
burn, playing in St. Louis as if it were ours.

When we weren't on reconnaissance missions, we were
having a grand time within the community: Sunday school
picnics, block parties, activities at the Phillis Wheatley Y
(this, too, was all-black), hayrides and apple picking in the
fall, neighborhood trick or treat and Christmas caroling,
social clubs, dances, and church, church, church.

Of course, it has taken the benefit of hindsight for me to
appreciate the richness of the community that surrounded
me as a child. At the time, I felt constrained and watched.
I have come to understand that for black people growing
up in America during those and earlier years, community was the scaffolding around the mainstream of society
that allowed us to move up. We were locked out, but we
were not locked in. Through ingenuity and collaboration my black community created a parallel universe that

took from the outer world what it needed to expand my horizons and make me feel that I could do anything. That strong, caring, resourceful, creative, demanding community shaped me, and its values and expectations continue to nurture me.

It was not until I went to college that I began to understand the racism that had surrounded me in St. Louis. Few of my classmates went to college, because not all black children in St. Louis had the experience that I did. Our group of middle-class children, while large for a social group, represented a tiny minority of black children in St. Louis. Most of the black children were poor and were not protected. Segregation and racism hit them with full force. And those proud black adults I described were disrespected and beaten down daily as they tried to earn livings, shop, buy homes, and generally provide for their families. In fact, every good thing I experienced had an ugly flip side. For example, I received a great education in St. Louis's segregated public schools partly because the well-educated, well-trained teachers that I had were not allowed to do anything else. Then, I never thought about how frustrating it must have been for the journalists, scientists, actors, singers, athletes, mathematicians, and would-be senators who taught me to spend their entire professional lives in the only careers available to them.

After college I became an organizer, a public interest lawyer, a community builder, a foundation executive, and a policy advocate. I've had many jobs, but only one project—to do something about racism, injustice, and inequality; to help build a society in which all people can thrive, contribute, and participate fully—socially and economically. In searching for solutions, I never forget that community matters.

Stewart Kwoh

I was once asked by a white waitress who was taking my restaurant order where my family was from. I answered that

on my mother's side of the family, my great-grandfather
was a miner in New Mexico; my grandfather was a tai-
lor in Oakland and Stockton, California; and that my
mother was born in Stockton. The waitress interrupted
me without hesitation and asked, "And how do you like
your new country?" Although both of my sons were born
in Los Angeles, I am willing to bet that they will be asked
the same question during their lifetimes. Although the
stereotype of the model minority has most recently been
applied to Asian Americans and Pacific Islanders (APIs),
the most enduring image of APIs is that of the foreigner.
No matter that the first Chinese came in large immigrant
waves in the 1840s to California, U.S. society still knows
very little about the API community, although it is now
over 12 million strong.

My own evolution into a civil rights advocate actually did
not begin with concerns over Asian Americans and Pacific
Islanders. It came as a result of growing up in Los Angeles—although I was born in Nanjing, China, because my
parents were teaching there at the time—and experiencing the civil rights movement in the 1960s. I was certainly
influenced by my parents, who are dedicated Christians
and givers to the community. In the early 1960s, I also vividly recall the debates in my Presbyterian church. Our minister went to march in the civil rights demonstrations in the
Deep South and came back to a partially hostile congre-
gation in Los Angeles. That eye-opening experience led to
my participation in the National Conference of Christians
and Jews (NCCJ), now the National Conference for Communities and Justice, and its brotherhood camp (now the
brotherhood and sisterhood camp). Although I grew up in
a racially integrated, moderate-income community of Echo
Park and Silver Lake in Los Angeles, the NCCJ camp widened my interracial connections and understandings.

While I saw the Asian American and Pacific Islander
student population in high school grow due to the 1965
changes in the immigration laws that changed decades of
exclusion and restrictions for Asian immigrants, I did not

become familiar with racism against Asians until I attended UCLA in 1966. Becoming a student activist after a stint in an Asian fraternity, I became part of the movement to begin the Asian American Studies Center and later became president of the Asian American Student Alliance. It was only through my involvement in Asian American studies that I began to understand the harsh racism against Asians, including immigration exclusion and World War II concentration camps for Japanese Americans. I have been the best man in three Japanese American weddings, and the parents of my friends never told me about their experiences in the internment camps. Stigmatization has long kept Asian Americans from looking at their own histories. My student organization helped to set up community service programs in communities like Chinatown and later organized demonstrations against the war in Vietnam and Cambodia.

The rest is history. I had to explain to my parents that, instead of going to medical school, I was going to law school because I was so influenced by helping to bail out some of my fellow students who were accused of throwing rocks at the police as they invaded the UCLA campus after an antiwar protest. I had to explain that I decided not to participate in law review because I needed to help an undocumented Buddhist monk who had come to a legal service program that I had established. I had to explain that I rejected a number of job offers after law school because I volunteered to start a law collective that paid a salary of $500 per month.

In my work on civil rights cases dealing with Asian Americans, African Americans, and Latinos, it is always the valiant struggles of individuals and communities that continue to inspire me. In 1983, just as the Asian Pacific American Legal Center was established, I heard about the tragic killing of Vincent Chin in Detroit. Actually, Vincent, who was celebrating his upcoming marriage, was killed in 1982 by two white autoworkers in what I believe was a racially motivated killing. In 1983 his two killers received sentences of probation and $3,000 fines for manslaughter. This case galvanized the Asian American community and many others. I met the family and supporters of Vincent and got involved in a campaign for federal civil rights charges to be filed against the two killers. Vincent would be the first Asian American to be covered by the civil rights law that authorized such federal charges. But it was his mother, Lily Chin, who truly inspired me. After the sentence, she decided that she needed to speak out to get support for a more just sentence against the killers. I remember she came to Los Angeles and, in a crowded Chinatown restaurant, she asked the crowd to help get justice for her son. Then she fainted. A few of us helped to revive her. Later that evening during her stay at my home, I asked her if she was okay. She said, "Stewart, there's nothing I can do to bring back Vincent, but I don't want any other mother to go through what I've been going through." While there eventually was a federal prosecution and a conviction in the first trial, an appellate reversal led to a second trial and acquittals. Mrs. Chin, whose husband died six months before Vincent was killed, decided to leave the United States and return to China. In 2002 she returned to the United States, gravely ill, and passed away that same year.

It was that experience and the failures of our justice system that have led me to provide leadership to build the Asian Pacific American Legal Center into the largest API legal organization in the United States today, and to cofound the Asian American Justice Center, the first national pan-Asian civil rights legal organization in the history of this nation.

Manuel Pastor

Like many sons of immigrants, my story began long before my birth. My dad came to the United States in the 1930s, a young man fleeing economic despair in Cuba. His documentation was, shall we say, imperfect. But World War II came and the fervor to fill the ranks of the army eventually presented him with a stark choice: be deported to the island or go fight in Europe. He couldn't decide and so asked my cousin Carlitos to flip a coin. That coin traveled with him to the war; both returned safely.

My mom was born in Tampa, Florida, where her mother, an immigrant cigar roller in a sweaty factory, had been swept off her feet by my grandfather, Joaquín, a sometime singer and sometime janitor. They headed north for economic opportunity, and my mother grew up in Spanish Harlem. The prosperity of the North did not pan out, and she eventually dropped out of her first year of high school to help support a struggling family. This put her ahead of my father, who had completed only sixth grade in his homeland. They met; they married; they never quite clawed their way to the middle class. But they were hardworking, earnest, and curious about the way the world worked—and a generation later their son is a professor at one of the premier private universities in the country.

It is an immigrant story, the sort Americans often celebrate by pointing to individual initiative and drive. But it is not just our story. I grew up in a racially mixed neighborhood in Southern California, our home purchase made possible by federally sponsored loans for veterans. My father—who began his American work life as a busboy, a cook, and a janitor—moved from cleaning buildings to repairing air conditioners by virtue of a community college willing to take all comers, including those lacking strong English or the usual educational credentials. Our family income soared from poor to working-class because my father's union negotiated well and occasionally struck to back up its demands. With just two books in our house—one an autobiography of Sammy Davis, Jr., entitled *Yes I Can* that I probably read more times than any other American—my passage to the university relied on strong public schools, affirmative action programs, and financial aid scholarships. In my success I stand not alone but in the shadow of my parents' history and in debt to the social policies that helped all of our hard work pay off—and I have always felt an obligation to keep those opportunities alive.

Recognizing that you don't just make it on your own has also driven me to multiethnic alliances and coalition building. This desire to bridge also stems from my own history as both an insider and an outsider. I am Cuban American, but as low-income immigrants from an earlier era, my family never fit into the conservative, anti-Castro ethos of that community. I am a survivor of the usual problems of discrimination and educational tracking, but I came of political age in the context of a highly nationalist Chicano movement that was sometimes wary of other Latinos. I am an oft-published university professor, but my working-class sensibilities have caused me to pursue research and writing that reflects the stories of those who lack voice.

Never quite fitting in can be a source of discomfort, but it can also generate skills of translation and accommodation. Building one America, after all, requires recognition of our new multicultural stew—a fact I used to remember every Thanksgiving when my family sat down for the traditional meal (at least for us) of roast turkey and *arroz con frijoles negros*. It involves more than acceptance of the "other"; it includes the ability to negotiate one's own contradictions, to truly listen to another person's stories and values, to respect difference but speak for the common good. I see this in the colleagues with whom I wrote this book; I strive for it in myself.

Like Angela and Stewart, my professional life has been devoted to social justice, sometimes through research and teaching, sometimes through public advocacy and organizing. One view of why we do this has us doing good; the reality is that we know little else. Living a life with purpose has its own rewards, of course, but beyond that is a simple truth: at the end of the day, I need to honor the struggles of my mother and father by working to ensure that some measure of fairness is afforded to all Americans.

Complicating the Quest for Equity:
Five Dimensions

Traditionally, the entry point to understanding the social dynamics associated with race, discrimination, and group advancement has been through the black experience. While there are numerous instances of racial or ethnic exclusion and oppression—the taking of Native American lands; the dispossession of Mexicans in the Southwest; the exclusion of Asians from legal immigration; prejudice and restrictions against the Irish, Jews, and other white ethnics; the internment of Japanese Americans during World War II—slavery, Jim Crow, and the struggle for black inclusion and empowerment have left the deepest mark on race relations.

Indeed, the dominance of the black-white paradigm is reflected even in census materials. Until the early 1970s, no data were collected separately on Latinos, only "white," "black," and "other." (This is the case, for example, with many of the long-term series on unemployment and poverty; for a brilliant dissection of the meaning of race in the census collection process, see Rodriguez, 2000.) It was even more recently that comprehensive data on Asians began to be collected, as the graphs in this book reflect. While the civil rights movement empowered a wide range of groups, it was clearly the conditions of African Americans that provoked moral outrage and mobilized people and campaigns around issues of social justice.

The Black-White Paradigm versus Multiculturalism

An analysis of the 1992 Los Angeles civil unrest—perhaps the most racially polarizing event of the past several decades—demonstrates how racial fault lines have shifted.

The riots triggered by the not-guilty verdict in the trial of white police officers charged with the beating of Rodney King were portrayed in the national media as a largely black-driven phenomenon (Smith, 1994). In fact, more Latinos were arrested than any other group, and most of the property damage occurred in heavily Latino neighborhoods (Pastor, 1995). Consequently, any analysis of the riots root causes in the context of black-white tensions focused on joblessness when in fact there is a subtle but critical distinction between black and Latino poverty. In Los Angeles and elsewhere, Latinos tend to have slightly higher rates of employment than blacks, but they tend to work low-wage jobs and can more accurately be classified as "working poor."

Similarly, a strictly black-white perspective overlooks the Asian American experience. Many Asian American groups are doing relatively well economically—the traditional marker of effects of discrimination—but there is a pattern of anti-Asian sentiments, and racial profiling that stereotypes Asians as being foreign and too different.

Diversity versus Racial and Social Equity

Equity requires quite a bit more than electing a black man president, or the celebrity of Jennifer Lopez or Tiger Woods, or the presence in corporate boardrooms of a few token men and women of color. While examples of individual advancement abound, diversity at the top (elected officials, judges, corporate leaders, university presidents) does not necessarily spell equity at the bottom. The extraordinarily high poverty rates of African Americans, Latinos, and Native Americans should be of concern to everyone. Even the "model minority" Asian community faces economic hardships, exceeding those of white Americans. Educational opportunities are uneven, police treatment is disparate, and concentrated poverty is especially severe among minority Americans.

Achieving racial equality will require more than changing the skin tones of America's business and upper middle classes, important as this may be. While diversity is to be supported, it must be effectively tied to improving the life chances for all Americans who have been left behind. To do this, it is essential to push beyond the obvious yet hard-won antidiscrimination laws in order to make the promises of equality real. Connecting the inner city to living-wage jobs through mass transit, creating mixed-income communities, building full-service grocery stores in minority communities, are the kinds of yardsticks used to measure the success of the equity movement.

Universal versus Particular Strategies

Those most engaged in the pursuit of racial equity have debated the merits of the utility of "universal" strategies as opposed to "particular" strategies. Education provides fertile ground for understanding the difference. Bilingual education and special English-language instruction is viewed by many Latino and Asian leaders as especially critical for immigrants to make the transition to American society. But it is exactly the exclusivity of efforts like these that have triggered a backlash against Latino immigrants on the grounds that it has a polarizing, rather than assimilating, effect.

The universal view holds that increasing spending on all students is a more politically viable and effective approach because it unites people and deflects criticism of one ethnic group. This formerly led some, like sociologist William Julius Wilson, to argue that a government commitment to full employment might be the most effective and politically expedient vehicle for black advancement in the labor force.

Universalism has its rightful place: many of the key issues of the civil rights movement have been anchored in a universal approach, with defenders of affirmative action often noting it has remained politically viable partly because its main beneficiaries have been white women. But if race isn't part of the conversation when you contemplate, for example, a new "green jobs" program, the people who most need the jobs might be overlooked. Moreover, the "imagined" universal cannot hide the reality that when advocates argue for more spending on education for all of our kids, they are essentially asking an older and whiter generation to see their own futures as intertwined with people they often regard as different. Partly because of this, Wilson, one of the best-known proponents of universal strategies, has rescinded his support of "race-neutral" policies, instead stressing the need for policy framings that facilitate a frank discussion of the problems and build broad political support to alleviate them. In his view, building coalitions to promote more targeted policies underscores the gravity of racial inequity and in doing so gains widespread political support for the best, not the easiest, solutions (Wilson, 2009: 141).

Certainly, some issues—like the composition of America's prison population or policies toward immigrant integration—cannot be confronted without acknowledging the role of race. A new universalism would work not by papering over the different experiences of Americans, but rather by pointing out how Americans are part of the same social fabric. Underinvestment in "someone else's children" can create problems for everyone. As with the country's flawed urban policies, subsidized, racially conscious sprawl can damage the environment, isolate people, and arrest economic growth.

National versus Regional versus Local Responsibility

Those concerned with racial equity have sometimes debated whether the federal government should take the lead in reducing racial inequality or whether that role is better left to local jurisdictions. Long-time civil rights activists can be a bit wary of localism—after all, the assertion of states' rights was the pretext for maintaining Jim Crow, and federal intervention transformed the South's political and social landscape. At the same time, neighborhood-based efforts, particularly those coming under the rubric of "equitable development" (Fox and Axel-Lute, 2008), hold great promise for reshaping areas plagued by weakened institutions and shattered economies. In this effort, many of the key actors are local leaders and grassroots organizers rather than bureaucrats from Washington or state capitals.

But the national sets the context for the local. The sprawl that facilitated the departure of many white Americans from our central cities was not only the result of local zoning laws. Just as important were federally funded highway construction that encouraged local commuting, large federal subsidies for expansion of sewer and water infrastructure to outlying areas, and federal lending programs, including the mortgage interest deduction on suburban home purchases. Likewise, regardless of local efforts to reduce crime, improve police protection, and curb police abuses and harassment of young people in the community, the federal sentencing laws mandating harsher sentences for crack cocaine than powder cocaine has essentially produced two American justice systems on the ground: one black, the other white.

By requiring banks to provide loans in their local service areas, the federal Community Reinvestment Act (CRA), as another example, provided local residents with the opportunity to secure loans to purchase homes and cars and to invest in small businesses, and helped community development groups expand affordable housing stocks. And while the CRA has been accused—wrongly—of encouraging banks to lend recklessly to unqualified borrowers, banks are among the legislation's biggest supporters for widening its customer base.

Conversely, the best approaches to bridging the equity divide aren't always initiated at the national level. President Clinton's "Conversation on Race" in the late 1990s, for example, stumbled from meeting to meeting around the country, tending to produce shrill debates and limited results. In contrast, a series of conversations on "regional equity" organized across the country by interfaith, labor, and other groups in the early 2000s have produced a remarkable convergence of business, labor, civic, and community leaders (Pastor, Benner, and Matsuoka, 2009).

These regionalist proponents, faced with a scale at which "the other" is a flesh-and-blood neighbor and not an abstract rival, have helped communities coalesce around shared interests. It all suggests that while the federal government remains extraordinarily important, the geography of social change is itself changing and so too must our approaches to achieving racial equity.

Structural Factors versus Individual Initiative

This issue of national versus local debate parallels the discussion of structural factors versus individual initiative. Activists and liberals tend to focus on impediments writ large: public policies that stack the decks against community advancement. Conservatives tend to stress the individual success stories: with enough of what Latinos call *ganas*, or individual desire, anyone can make it.

Uncommon Common Ground celebrates the individual and recognizes that negative outcomes can result from personal failings or lack of initiative. At the same time, it stresses how best to design policies that allow all Americans to realize their potential without exerting Herculean effort. Some Americans manage to beat the odds, but changing the odds will help even more.

A Call on Leadership

In a country with no dominant ethnic minority, "minoritarian" leadership will be needed to identify what unites different groups under a single tent. Many minority leaders have been forced to develop such skills through years of being the first, only, and lonely person of color in boardrooms, think tanks, and faculty and city council meetings. Significant investments, financial and personal, are required to build new leadership for new conversations in a new America.

Obama has modeled minoritarian leadership well, but he is also an example of two other leadership qualities. First, he speaks beyond his constituency. From the start Obama was *a* black candidate but not *the* black candidate. He was able to speak beyond his constituency—meaning the black one selected for him—and turn moral values into practical policy matters in all dimensions of American governance, including health care, climate change, and the very refashioning of our domestic economy. Speaking on issues other than race hardly denies racial equity but instead gives that leader greater relevance and reach.

Second, Obama positioned his campaign squarely in the center of a racially conscious social movement, and social movements can foment change by providing political support to elected officials when they make unpopular but prudent decisions, and applying political pressure when elected officials stray too far afield from the tenets of equity. Over the years, we three have come to value social movements as the vehicles for long-lasting change, even though they make change over the course of decades, not years.

We are reminded of the words of a community leader shortly after the Los Angeles civil unrest. Called to yet another urgent meeting of minority representatives and looking around the room at the people offering a frantic flurry of suggestions about new programs and policies, he began to worry that steps quickly taken might not lead to a road firmly constructed. As the discussion hit a lull, he leaned back and commented: "There is an immediate need to think long-term."

In America today, against the backdrop of a raging recession, populist anger, and deep uncertainty, there is an immediate need to think long-term. This book welcomes those of good will to engage in a conversation about the future of America.

Notes

[1] Adam Nagourney, "Obama Elected President as Racial Barrier Falls," *New York Times*, November 5, 2008.

[2] Jimmy McCarty, "Police Violence Undercuts Pundits' 'Post-racial' Rhetoric," Sojourners' Blog, January 16, 2009, http://blog.sojo .net/2009/01/16/police-violence-undercuts-pundits-post-racial-rhetoric.

[3] U.S. Census Bureau, U.S. Population Projections, Table 4: "Projec-

tions of the Population by Sex, Race, and Hispanic Origin for the United States: 2010 to 2050" (NP2008-T4), release date: August 14, 2008, http://www.census.gov/population/www/projections/summary tables.html.

[4] Teresa Watanabe and Francisco Vara-Orta, "Small Turnout, Big Questions," *Los Angeles Times*, May 2, 2007.

References

ACORN Fair Housing. 2007. "Foreclosure Exposure: A Study of Racial and Income Disparities in Home Mortgage Lending in 172 American Cities." ACORN Housing Corporation.

Applied Research Center. 2009. "Race and Recession: How Inequity Rigged the Economy and How to Change the Rules." http://www.arc .org/recession.

Blackwell, Angela Glover. 2007. "Fighting Poverty with Equitable Development." In John Edwards, Marion Crain, and Arne L. Kalleberg, eds., *Ending Poverty in America: How to Restore the American Dream*. New York: New Press.

Fox, Radhika, and Miriam Axel-Lute. 2008. *To Be Strong Again: Renewing the Promise in Smaller Industrial Cities*. Oakland, CA: PolicyLink.

Frey, William H. 2009. "How Did Race Impact the 2008 Presidential Election?" Brookings Institution. Available at http://www.aei.org/ docLib/FreyJune12A.pdf.

Hayes-Bautista, David, Werner O. Schink, Jorge Chapa, and Douglas X. Patino. 1988. *Burden of Support: Young Latinos in an Aging Society*. Stanford, CA: Stanford University Press.

Heckman, James J., and Paul A. LaFontaine. 2007. "The American High School Graduation Rate: Trends and Levels." Cambridge, MA: National Bureau of Economic Research Working Paper 13670. http:// www.nber.org/papers/w13670.

Horne, Jed. 2006. *Breach of Faith: Hurricane Katrina and the Near Death of a Great American City*. New York: Random House.

Mishel, Lawrence, and Joydeep Roy. 2006. *Rethinking High School Graduation Rates and Trends*. Washington, DC: Economic Policy Institute.

Myers, Dowell. 2007. *Immigrants and Boomers: Forging a New Social Contract for the Future of America*. New York: Russell Sage Foundation.

Pastor, Manuel. 1995. "Economic Inequality, Latino Poverty and the Civil Unrest in Los Angeles." *Economic Development Quarterly* 9 (3): 238–258.

———. 2008. "State of the Region: The New Demography, the New Economy, and the New Environment." Program for Environmental and Regional Equity and the Bay Area Social Equity Caucus (SEC).

Presented at the SEC 10th Anniversary State of the Region Conference, December 15, 2008.

Pastor, Manuel, Chris Benner, and Martha Matsuoka. 2009. *This Could Be the Start of Something Big: How Social Movements for Regional Equity Are Reshaping Metropolitan America*. Ithaca, NY: Cornell University Press.

Pastor, Manuel, and Rhonda Ortiz. 2009. "Immigrant Integration in Los Angeles: Strategic Directions for Funders." Program for Environmental and Regional Equity (PERE).

Pastor, Manuel, and Deborah Reed. 2005. *Understanding Equitable Infrastructure Investment for California*. San Francisco: Public Policy Institute of California.

powell, john. 2009. "Post-Racialism or Targeted Universalism?" *Denver University Law Review* (Special Issue: Obama Phenomenon) 86 (1): 785–806.

Rodríguez, Clara E. 2000. *Changing Race: Latinos, the Census, and the History of Ethnicity in the United States*. New York: New York University Press.

Smith, Erna. 1994. "Transmitting Race: The Los Angeles Riot in Television News." Research Paper R-11, Joan Shorenstein Barone Center, John F. Kennedy School of Government, Harvard University.

Tilove, Jonathan. 2008. "Obama Made Inroads with White Voters Except in Deep South." *Times-Picayune*, November 8.

Wilson, William Julius. 1999. *The Bridge over the Racial Divide: Rising Inequality and Coalition Politics*. Berkeley: University of California Press.

Wilson, William Julius. 2009. *More Than Just Race: Being Black and Poor in the Inner City*. New York: W. W. Norton.

2

Color Lines

Conversations about race in America are almost always unpleasant. To the ears of many white Americans, complaints of racism sound shrill, antiquated, and self-serving. Many black Americans are exasperated and angered by their quotidian encounters with discrimination and racism, feelings that are exacerbated when they hear others accuse them of seeing things that are not there. Latinos grow weary hearing the issue of race reduced solely to black and white relations. Asians sometimes feel invisible to the outside world, caricatured as a monolithic "model minority," their successes resented by others. To Native Americans, there is a sad irony, that the country's original people are today its most forgotten. Despite all the talk of a postracial America, and the very real climb up the socioeconomic ladder for some people of color, the story of race in America is neither old nor new, but one long, evolving narrative, rooted in a painful history of oppression and exploitation.

European settlers' genocidal campaign against indigenous populations left racism's indelible imprimatur on the New Land, but slavery and its aftermath is the template that has since framed all interactions across race and ethnicity. When immigrants arrive in this country, they enter into a cauldron of tensions, rivalries, and polarizing realities that were shaped and defined by the enslavement and brutalization of Africa's descendants. America's growing diversity raises a call for new thinking about diversity and the structures of inequity, but the trick is to avoid losing sight of historical truths while adjusting to new realities.

Growing Diversity

Recent Census Bureau data indicate that not only have Latinos eclipsed African Americans as the largest minority population in the United States,[1] but also that Latinos in twenty of the twenty-five most populous counties outnumber blacks (see Table 2-1; Table 2-2 reports on the demographics of America's largest metropolitan areas). In California, Hawaii, New Mexico, and Texas, nonwhites already outnumber whites; Nevada, Maryland, Georgia, Arizona, Mississippi, and New York State trail closely behind.[2]

California, the country's most populous state, became a pioneer in minority-majority politics in 1999 when its white population receded below the 50 percent mark for the first time; by 2007, their numbers had dipped to 43 percent of the state's 36.6 million residents.[3] That same year, Latinos comprised over 36 percent of California's total population, up from 26 percent in 1990; Asian and Pacific Islanders accounted for nearly 13 percent, up from 9 percent in 1990. African Americans accounted for 6 percent of the population, and Native Americans less than 1 percent.[4]

In Los Angeles, the state's largest and most diverse county, the Latino population increased by 40 percent between 1990 and 2007, and now stands at nearly 4.7 mil-

TABLE 2-1. Percent Race for the
25 Largest U.S. Counties, 2007

	White	Black	Latino	Asian
Los Angeles County, California	29	9	47	13
Cook County, Illinois	45	25	23	6
Harris County, Texas	36	18	39	6
Maricopa County, Arizona	59	4	30	3
Orange County, California	47	2	33	16
San Diego County, California	51	5	30	10
Kings County, New York	36	33	20	9
Miami-Dade County, Florida	18	18	62	1
Dallas County, Texas	36	20	38	4
Queens County, New York	31	18	26	21
Riverside County, California	43	6	43	5
San Bernardino County, California	36	8	47	6
Wayne County, Michigan	50	41	5	3
King County, Washington	69	6	7	14
Clark County, Nevada	52	9	28	8
Broward County, Florida	48	24	23	3
Santa Clara County, California	38	2	26	31
Tarrant County, Texas	55	14	25	4
New York County, New York	49	14	25	11
Bexar County, Texas	32	7	57	2
Middlesex County, Massachusetts	80	4	6	8
Alameda County, California	37	13	21	25
Suffolk County, New York	75	7	13	3
Philadelphia County, Pennsylvania	39	43	11	5
Sacramento County, California	52	10	20	14

Source: U.S. Census Bureau, 2007 ACS.
Note: Counties are sorted in descending order by 2007 population.

lion people, the nation's largest Latino population.[5] The county's API population increased by 43 percent over the same period to nearly 1.3 million, representing the largest Asian community in the U.S. In contrast, the county's black population fell 9 percent, while its white population decreased 21 percent (see Figure 2-1).[6]

At the national level, Asian American and Latino immigrants are no longer primarily gravitating to traditional "gateway" states. Mexican immigrants still live in traditional

TABLE 2-2. Percent Race for the 25
Largest U.S. Metropolitan Areas, 2007

	White	Black	Latino	Asian
New York-Northern New Jersey-Long Island, NY-NJ-PA	51	17	21	9
Los Angeles-Long Beach-Santa Ana, CA	33	7	44	14
Chicago-Naperville-Joliet, IL-IN-WI	56	18	20	5
Dallas-Fort Worth-Arlington, TX	53	14	27	5
Philadelphia-Camden-Wilmington, PA-NJ-DE-MD	68	20	6	4
Houston-Sugar Land-Baytown, TX	43	17	33	6
Miami-Fort Lauderdale-Pompano Beach, FL	38	19	39	2
Washington-Arlington-Alexandria, DC-VA-MD-WV	51	26	12	8
Atlanta-Sandy Springs-Marietta, GA	54	31	9	4
Boston-Cambridge-Quincy, MA-NH	78	6	8	6
Detroit-Warren-Livonia, MI	69	23	4	3
San Francisco-Oakland-Fremont, CA	46	8	20	22
Phoenix-Mesa-Scottsdale, AZ	59	4	30	3
Riverside-San Bernardino-Ontario, CA	40	7	45	6
Seattle-Tacoma-Bellevue, WA	72	5	7	11
Minneapolis-St. Paul-Bloomington, MN-WI	82	6	5	5
San Diego-Carlsbad-San Marcos, CA	51	5	30	10
St. Louis, MO-IL	76	18	2	2
Tampa-St. Petersburg-Clearwater, FL	70	11	14	3
Baltimore-Towson, MD	63	28	3	4
Denver-Aurora, CO	67	5	22	4
Pittsburgh, PA	88	8	1	2
Portland-Vancouver-Beaverton, OR-WA	78	3	10	6
Cincinnati-Middletown, OH-KY-IN	83	12	2	2
Cleveland-Elyria-Mentor, OH	73	19	4	2

Source: U.S. Census Bureau, 2007 ACS.

Note: Metropolitan areas are sorted in descending order by 2007 population.

states like California, Texas, Illinois, and Arizona. But in
their 2005 study, Víctor Zúñiga and Rubén Hernández-
León found that nontraditional states like Georgia, Florida,
North Carolina, New York, Nevada, and Colorado follow
in the top ten (2005: xiv). Drawn by job opportunities in
thriving industries, they are looking for slower-paced,
rural lifestyles similar to those in their native lands. Nevada
was the fastest-growing state between 1990 and 2008, seeing its population more than double.[7] Much of Nevada's
growth was driven by Asians and Latinos settling in Las

**FIGURE 2-1. Ethnic Population Changes
in Los Angeles County**

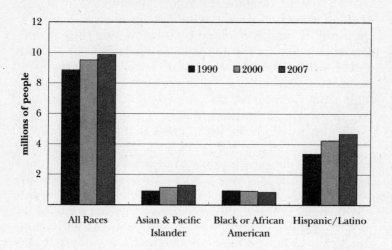

Vegas to fill new jobs in the construction and service sectors. Nevada's Asian and Pacific Islander population soared as much as 36 percent between 1990 and 2007 to 165,908 and the state's Latino population outpaced even that rate, rising 418 percent to 644,485.[8]

Atlanta, Georgia, and its surrounding suburbs also experienced significant increases in the Latino and Asian populations, as immigrants poured into the region for jobs in construction, food processing, and textiles. Between 1990 and 2007, the Latino population in both Gwinnett and Cobb counties increased dramatically, by 1,460 and 739 percent respectively; the Asian population increased by 624 percent in Gwinnett County and 265 percent in Cobb.[9]

Since Hurricane Katrina hit on August 29, 2005, many Latino immigrants have relocated to Louisiana, lured by the promise of higher wages and a large abundance of work related to cleanup efforts (McCarthy et al., 2006). In 2004, about 4.9 percent of the New Orleans metropolitan region was Latino. In 2006, that number had increased to 5.7 percent and in 2007 was 6.2 percent.[10] Elizabeth Fussell (2009) writes that the census underestimates the highly mobile Latino population, not to mention the difficulty in counting the undocumented population. She cites a 2006 report released by the Louisiana Department of Health and Hospitals that finds the Latino population in the five-parish area around New Orleans to be 8.2 percent, a count higher than official estimates (Fussell, 2009: 8; Louisiana Population Health Institute, 2006).

Also included on the list of areas that have seen rapid change is Massachusetts. While generally not known for its diversity, the state is home to nearly 1 million foreign-born residents, 30 percent of whom arrived in 2000 or later.[11] Lowell, a former garment-manufacturing community turned high-tech job center, has a thriving Asian community and the second-largest population of Cambodian Americans in the United States, behind Long Beach, California (Fletcher, 2000).

Latino immigrants, mostly Mexican, have been steadily pouring into central and western Iowa over the past decade to work in meatpacking plants, and when U.S. Secretary of Agriculture Tom Vilsack served as governor of Iowa, he openly invited immigrants to settle in the state to help solve Iowa's labor shortage.

In general, Latinos have a relatively high rate of labor force attachment, a fact that belies the welfare-dependent depictions of them in anti-immigrant campaigns. However, the jobs typically pay low wages, and Latino communities continue to be characterized by concentrations of low-income households. (See Box 2-1 for an example of Latino and Thai garment workers joining forces to improve workplace conditions.)

This growing diversity in the country is reinforced by the diversity that exists within racial and ethnic groups themselves. The Latino community, for example, is actually comprised of many different communities. As Figure 2-2 delineates, Mexicans comprise the bulk of U.S. Latinos,

Box 2-1. Accepting Diversity
and Building Coalitions

Julie Su (2009) writes of the 1995 federal and state police raid of an El Monte, California, suburban tract home where Thai garment workers were forced to work as virtual slaves—a case that received international media attention. Seventy-two garment workers had been imprisoned by their Thai captors in a barbed-wire-encircled apartment complex nearby. They worked for less than a dollar an hour sewing blouses, shorts, skirts, and dresses for local retailers, usually working from 7 a.m to midnight or 1 a.m. Over several years, because of fear and reprisals, few workers escaped.

Immediately following the raid, the workers were taken into custody by the U.S. Immigration and Naturalization Service (INS) and were virtual prisoners again, until a coalition of community activists headed by Julie Su of the Asian Pacific American Legal Center, along with the Thai Community Development Center, Koreatown Immigrant Workers Alliance, Coalition for Humane Immigrant Rights of Los Angeles, and UNITE (the garment workers union, now UNITE-HERE!) succeeded in securing the workers' freedom. Once out of INS detention, the workers needed to find housing, medical care, and retraining for new work or access to other garment shops. The workers were overwhelmingly women, did not speak English, and lacked formal education.

Despite this, the Thai garment workers through their volunteer lawyers filed the first federal lawsuit of its kind directly asserting the liability of retailers, manufacturers, and subcontractors. In addition, the California State Legislature passed Assembly Bill 633, making manufacturers and retailers responsible for garment workers' wages when their contractors fail to pay.

According to Su, the Thai workers joined forces with a group of Latino garment workers who toiled in the same deplorable conditions. The workers ultimately defied the odds and fought back against the sweatshop pyramid of retail stores on the top, followed by brand retailers, factory owners, and subcontractors, and on the very bottom, the garment workers themselves who sewed the garments. The victory of Thai immigrants and Latino workers in their common struggle against exploitation in garment sweatshops exemplifies the potential of working-class people to change their workplace conditions (Su, 2009: 13–21).

FIGURE 2-2. Composition of the U.S. Latino Population, 2007

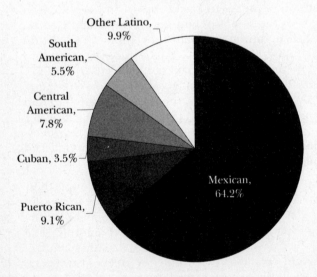

TABLE 2-3. Demographic Characteristics of U.S. Latino Population, 2007

CHARACTERISTIC	White	Black	Latino, total	Mexican	Puerto Rican	Cuban	Central, South	Other Latino
PERCENT DISTRIBUTION								
AGE DISTRIBUTION								
Under 5 years old	5.6	8.1	10.7	11.8	9.3	7.2	7.9	10.0
5 to 14 years old	11.6	15.8	18.2	19.4	19.4	11.8	15.1	17.6
15 to 44 years old	39.0	45.6	49.5	49.7	45.1	43.9	54.3	41.9
45 to 64 years old	28.4	22.1	16.3	14.8	19.1	22.4	17.7	20.9
65 years old and over	15.4	8.3	5.4	4.4	7.2	14.6	4.9	9.7
FAMILY TYPE								
Married couple	80.7	44.7	66.6	69.4	52.3	75.7	62.7	66.2
Female householder, no spouse present	13.6	45.7	24.1	20.7	40.1	18.3	28.0	25.4
Male householder, no spouse present	5.6	9.5	9.3	9.9	7.6	6.2	9.3	8.5
EDUCATIONAL ATTAINMENT								
Persons 25 years old and over								
High school graduate or higher	86.2	82.3	60.3	53.9	73.5	79.8	65.4	77.9
Bachelor's degree or higher	29.1	18.5	12.7	9.0	16.4	27.2	17.9	18.9

Source: Census Bureau 2009 Statistical Abstract of the United States, Tables No. 38, 9, 221 (http://www.census.gov/compendia/statab/cats/population.html) for data on Latinos and Latino subgroups and 2007 American Community Survey 1-Year Estimates for data on white and black populations.

Note: In this table, "Black" includes Latinos who identify as black.

TABLE 2-4. Economic Characteristics of U.S. Latino Population, 2005–2007

PERCENT DISTRIBUTION

CHARACTERISTIC	White	Black	Latino, total	Mexican	Puerto Rican	Cuban	Central, South	Other Latino
LABOR FORCE STATUS								
Civilian labor force	62.7	59.5	65.4	65.7	60.1	60.0	72.1	62.0
Employed	59.6	52.1	60.0	60.3	53.9	56.6	67.1	56.5
Unemployed	3.1	7.4	5.3	5.4	6.3	3.4	5.0	5.5
Not in labor force	37.3	40.5	34.6	34.3	39.9	40.0	27.9	38.0
FAMILY INCOME IN 2006								
Less than $10,000	3.1	11.7	7.5	7.4	11.6	5.1	5.1	8.7
$10,000 to $19,999	5.6	13.9	13.2	13.9	13.6	11.9	10.7	12.8
$20,000 to $29,999	7.9	13.1	14.6	15.7	12.3	11.8	13.6	12.7
$30,000 to $39,999	9.1	11.8	13.4	14.1	11.3	11.1	13.9	11.9
$40,000 to $49,999	9.4	9.8	11.2	11.5	9.3	9.1	12.2	10.5
$50,000 to $59,999	9.0	8.0	8.7	8.7	7.8	8.1	9.2	8.8
$60,000 or more	56.0	31.7	31.4	28.7	34.1	43.0	35.2	34.7
Median income (dol.)	$66,931	$39,316	$40,981	$39,034	$41,386	$50,697	$45,413	$43,455
Families below poverty level	6.0	21.3	19.0	20.6	21.4	11.0	13.2	18.1
Persons below poverty level	8.0	23.4	20.0	21.6	22.5	12.7	14.2	18.4
HOUSING TENURE								
Owner-occupied	73.8	46.5	49.2	50.7	39.7	61.1	44.4	51.3
Renter-occupied	26.2	53.5	50.8	49.3	60.3	38.9	55.6	48.7

Source: U.S. Census Bureau, Pooled 2005–2007 American Community Survey. Analysis by the Program for Environmental and Regional Equity (PERE).

with Puerto Ricans and Cubans the next-largest groups in terms of nationality.

Although these communities share a common language and similar heritage, their experiences in America are often markedly different. The Mexican-origin population, for instance, is generally younger and less educated than other Latinos (see Tables 2-3 and 2-4).

Puerto Rican populations are characterized by very high rates of female-headed households, high rates of detachment from the labor force, and the lowest income levels and homeownership rates of any Latino group. Cubans, on the other hand, are much older, generally have higher levels of educational attainment, and have the highest income levels and homeownership rates of any Latino national group. Within the two groups, there is also a racial divide, with black Cubans and black Puerto Ricans generally faring worse than their lighter-skinned brethren.

Asians are the fastest-growing population, their numbers increasing by 50 percent in the 1990s and another 30 percent from 2000 to 2008.[12] Census figures for 2008 indicate that median household income for Asians exceeds that of whites. This is partly because households often include multiple earners but it is also the case that many Asians—immigrants and nonimmigrants alike—have fared well in America's labor markets. College attendance rates for eighteen-to-twenty-one-year-olds are also well above those of any other racial group.

Figure 2-3 breaks down the Asian and Pacific Islander population from the 2007 American Community Survey. Chinese and Asian Indian are the most populous groups, followed by Filipino, and then Vietnamese. This represents a significant shift from 1990, when Japanese were the third-largest group. Table 2-5 offers selected data on the Asian subgroups for the years 2005 through 2007, the most recent period for which statistics are available.

Chinese and Filipinos are largely foreign-born, with

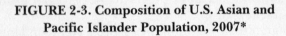

FIGURE 2-3. Composition of U.S. Asian and Pacific Islander Population, 2007*

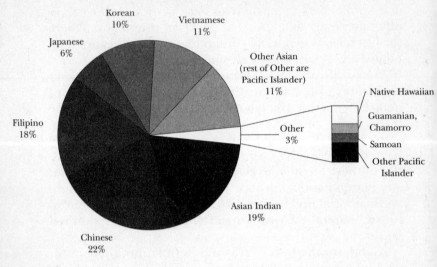

per capita income very close to the Asian American average; yet, some Chinese are quite poor, driving up the group's overall poverty rate to 10 percent, suggesting an extreme level of inequality within the Asian American and Pacific Islander community. Japanese Americans are now largely U.S.-born and boast the highest levels of income of all the Asian groups. On average, Asian Indians seem to be highly educated and high-earning recent immigrants. Koreans and Vietnamese are also more recent immigrants, but their education levels are lower, as is their per capita income.

---

*Figures include single race, single ethnicity individuals only, resulting in smaller population counts for groups that are disproportionately multiracial, including Filipinos, Japanese, and Pacific Islanders.

TABLE 2-5. Demographic Characteristics of U.S. Asian Populations, 2005–2007

CHARACTERISTIC	Chinese	Filipino	Japanese	Asian Indian	Korean	Vietnamese
MIGRATION						
Percent U.S.-born Nationals	29.8	32.5	59.5	26.0	23.9	32.7
Percent Foreign-born Nationals	70.2	67.5	40.5	74.0	76.1	67.3
AGE						
Median Age of Selected Population	37.0	37.0	45.0	32.0	35.0	34.0
INCOME						
Per Capita Income (as % of Asian and Pacific Island avg.)	105.5	96.1	128.3	122.9	91.0	75.4
Poverty Rates for Individuals	10.4	4.9	7.1	6.7	11.7	12.5
EDUCATION						
Male: College Grad or Higher	55.9	44.3	53.0	73.6	61.4	29.3
Female: College Grad or Higher	48.6	50.6	40.6	62.9	47.4	23.2

CHARACTERISTIC	Hawaiian	Laotian	Cambodian	Thai	Hmong	Samoan
MIGRATION						
Percent U.S.-born Nationals	98.8	37.2	37.8	24.1	54.4	84.2
Percent Foreign-born Nationals	1.2	62.8	62.2	75.9	45.6	15.8
AGE						
Median Age of Selected Population	37.0	30.0	27.0	36.0	19.0	26.0
INCOME						
Per Capita Income (as % of Asian and Pacific Island avg.)	83.3	56.4	52.6	84.3	35.5	52.2
Poverty Rates for Individuals	12.1	12.8	18.5	11.9	27.1	17.8
EDUCATION						
Male: College Grad or Higher	17.3	11.6	15.9	46.8	14.7	8.5
Female: College Grad or Higher	15.7	11.1	11.8	37.4	9.1	8.3

Source: U.S. Census Bureau, Pooled 2005–2007 American Community Survey. Analysis by the Program for Environmental and Regional Equity (PERE).

The Native American population is arguably the most challenged of all minority groups. If wealth formation is the key to intergenerational upward mobility, then the taking of land and other assets from America's first residents has surely been a structural barrier. Table 2-6 offers a brief look at this diverse population.

American Indians tend to be younger, less educated, and poorer. Over a quarter of American Indians lived in poverty in 2007, an improvement from 31 percent in 1990. In 1989, the poverty rate for Native Americans living on reservations was reported to be an appalling 51 percent; in 1999, the comparable figure was just under 40 percent, a figure that nonetheless reflected improvement, perhaps because of the rise of gaming and other revenue sources.[13]

In the year 2000, only about 21 percent of Native Americans lived on reservations and trust lands, another 16 percent lived in tribal jurisdiction or designated areas, and the vast remainder was spread across the rest of the United States.[14] The urbanization of Native Americans has been dramatic: while 13.4 percent of the Native American population lived in urban areas in 1950, that figure in 1990 was 56.2 percent (Thornton, 2001: 142) and reached 61 percent by 2000.[15] While part of the increase in the urban American Indian population was simply a rise in self-identification, federal programs were also launched to disperse people from reservations to capitalize on what were perceived to be wider job and educational opportunities in cities. With urbanization has come rising rates of intermarriage: today about 75 percent of all Native American marriages are with non-Indians.[16]

This drives at a larger point: America includes an increasing number of people who identify as belonging to several races or ethnicities. Starting with the 2000 Census, residents have been able to identify themselves as having more than one race. The 2007 American Community Survey estimates that more than 6.5 million people identified as belonging to at least two racial classifications.

TABLE 2-6. Demographic Characteristics of Selected American Indian Populations, 2005–2007

CHARACTERISTIC	American Indians, Aleuts, & Eskimos	Total Population
AGE DISTRIBUTION		
Under 10 years old	14.5	13.5
10 to 19 years old	17.5	14.1
20 to 29 years old	14.9	13.6
30 to 39 years old	14.0	13.7
40 to 49 years old	15.4	15.2
50 to 59 years old	12.1	12.9
60 to 69 years old	6.7	8.1
70 years and over	4.8	8.8
FAMILY TYPE		
Married couple	40.1	49.8
Female householder, no spouse present	37.4	30.2
Male householder, no spouse present	22.5	20.0
EDUCATIONAL ATTAINMENT		
Percent high school graduate or higher	78.6	84.3
Percent bachelor's degree or higher	13.5	27.2
Percent graduate or professional degree	4.6	10.0
FAMILY INCOME IN 1989		
All families	$31,673	$46,548
Married-couple families	$55,043	$70,833
Female householder, no husband	$18,923	$25,298
POVERTY RATES, 2005–2007 (BY FAMILY)		
Married-couple families	11.1	4.7
Male householder, no wife	26.9	14.6
Female householder, no husband	37.1	23.5
POVERTY RATES, 2005–2007 (PERSONS)	25.6	13.0

	Total Population in thousands
POPULATION, 1980–2007	
American Indian, Aleut & Eskimo Population	
1980	1,420
1990	1,794
2000	2,069
2005–2007	2,036
TEN LARGEST TRIBES	
Cherokee	284
Chippewa	107
Choctaw	82
Lumbee	63
Apache	52
Eskimo	49
Iroquois	42
Creek	38
Blackfoot	26
Chickasaw	18
TEN STATES WITH LARGEST POPULATION OF AMERICAN INDIANS, ALEUTS, AND ESKIMOS	
Arizona	258
Oklahoma	238
New Mexico	172
California	167
North Carolina	101
Alaska	88
Washington	79
Texas	72
South Dakota	65
Montana	53

Source: U.S. Census Bureau, Pooled 2005–2007 American Community Survey, analysis by the Program for Environmental and Regional Equity (PERE); Data on 1980 total American Indian, Aleut, and Eskimo population from U.S. Dept. of Commerce, *We the...First Americans,* Bureau of the Census, issued Sept. 1993; Data on 1990 and 2000 total American Indian, Al... ¡ Eskimo population from U.S. Census Bureau, 1990 Census (STF1) and 2000 Census (SF1), respectively.

Accepting Diversity

Real progress has been made in achieving cross-racial understanding and acceptance. Many, many people point to the historic election of President Obama as solid evidence of American transformation. Against many predictions to the contrary, Obama won victories in states with some of the largest white populations in the country. The symbols and signs, both substantive and superficial, are everywhere.

Oprah Winfrey, an African American, remains an icon for American women of all races. Linda Alvarado not only broke the gender rules by becoming the president and CEO of Alvarado Construction, but she is also the first Hispanic to own a major-league baseball franchise—the Colorado Rockies.

Judge Sonia Sotomayor, a New Yorker of Puerto Rican descent, has blazed new judicial trails as Barack Obama's choice to replace retiring Justice David Souter on the Supreme Court. A black woman, Ursula Burns, is the CEO at Xerox Corporation. Tiger Woods forever changed the face of golf by being the first Masters champion of Asian or African American descent—and is, in fact, both. Yao Ming proved that Asians can make it big in the NBA, and Matthew Mitcham, an openly gay male competitor in the 2008 Olympics, captured the gold in diving. South Asian, American-born actor Kal Penn recently became associate director of the White House Office of Public Engagement—breaking more than one paradigm in American and South Asian culture in so doing.

Popular culture has never been more racially integrated.Hip-hop culture has created the kind of multiracial scene that rock 'n' roll never did. Artists like the Black Eyed Peas regularly rap in Tagalog, Pitbull's lyrics are in Spanish and are all over the radio, and even white rapper Eminem is in on this scene. Latino music is emerging as a strong force, not only in traditional formats such as salsa but also as crossover genres like reggaetón. Hollywood's racial barriers have been significantly relaxed. Asian-influenced cinema has broken out of the art house with movies like *Crouching Tiger, Hidden Dragon*.

Intermarriages continue to become more common: between 1980 and 2007, while the total number of married couples increased by only 22 percent, the total number of interracial married couples increased by 350 percent, and the number of married couples including someone of Hispanic origin and someone not of Hispanic origin increased by 252 percent.[17] Considering pooled data from the 2005–2007 American Community Survey from which we can provide a more detailed characterization of intermarriages by both race and Hispanic origin, we find that among the nearly 4.3 million intermarried households in the U.S. (about 7.6 percent of all married-couple households) 43 percent of these unions are between whites and Latinos, 17 percent are between whites and Asian Americans, 12 percent are between whites and "others," 9 percent are between whites and African Americans, and 7 percent are between whites and Native Americans.[18]

Politics has also become more diverse. In 2009, the Washington-based Joint Center for Political and Economic Studies reported that there were over 10,000 black elected officials throughout the nation.[19] In 1970, there were only 1,469. Further, in a sign of cross-racial acceptance, of 622 black state legislators in 2007, 30 percent represented predominantly white districts, and black mayors have been elected with significant white support in cities such as Cincinnati, Buffalo, and Iowa City (Ifill, 2009). As for Latinos, the National Association of Latino Elected and Appointed Officials (NALEO) reports that there were 3,128 Latino elected officials in 1984; as of June 1999, there were 4,966—a nearly 60 percent increase over fifteen years; and now in 2009, there are more than 6,000 Latino elected and appointed officials.[20]

Research and data pertaining to Asian American elected officials remain scarce; however, Asian American office-holders are not. According to the *National Asian Pacific American Political Almanac*, hundreds of Asian Americans hold elected offices in local, state, and national governments and also serve as judges and appointed officials (Lai and Nakanishi, 2001). The Obama Cabinet includes the following minority members: Attorney General Eric Holder (Justice) is the first African American to hold this position;[21] Secretary Hilda Solis (Labor) is the first Hispanic woman to serve as a secretary in the Cabinet;[22] Secretary Steven Chu (Energy) and Secretary Eric Shinseki (Veterans Affairs) are the first Asian Americans to hold their positions.[23]

Among the groups discussed in minority politics, the most recent addition of openly lesbian, gay, bisexual, and transgendered (LGBT) appointed and elected officials appears to be growing rapidly as well. Pioneers of the LGBT civil rights movement, such as Harvey Milk, about whom the 2009 movie *Milk* was written, paved the way for the 635 LGBT officials to serve openly all across the United States today.[24] In 2008, Jared Polis of Colorado was the first openly gay male candidate and nonincumbent to be elected to the U.S. House of Representatives. Congresswoman Tammy Baldwin of Wisconsin and Congressman Barney Frank of Massachusetts, both openly gay, ran for reelection for the House in 2008 and won. A nationwide survey and poll conducted by *Zogby America* in 2008 indicates that Americans appear increasingly open to gay or lesbian candidates (Gay & Lesbian Leadership Institute, 2009). See Table 2-7 for more information.

While the victories of minority leaders in unprecedented positions are a testament to their political ability to craft coalitions, growing acceptance by Americans is also part of the story. As Figure 2-4 illustrates, the percentage of Americans indicating that they would be willing to vote for

TABLE 2-7. Voter Support of an Openly Gay or Lesbian Candidate

American voter responses to this question: If an openly gay or lesbian candidate were to run for state legislature in your district and they were the candidate that most shared your views on political issues, would you vote for them?

	Definitely/ Probably	Definitely	Probably	Probably Not	Definitely Not	Not Sure
All	70.8%	45.2	25.6	11.5	14.9	2.9
Men	69.6	44.9	24.7	12.6	16.3	1.5
Women	71.8	45.4	26.4	10.4	13.5	4.2
Democrat	77.6	52.8	24.8	8.6	10.7	3.1
Republican	58.6	34.3	24.3	17.0	22.1	2.3
Independent	78.7	50.4	28.3	7.1	10.6	3.6
Progressive	84.5	70.7	13.8	0.5	11.1	4.0
Liberal	84.6	68.8	15.8	4.2	8.7	2.5
Moderate	81.2	48.5	32.7	7.6	9.3	1.9
Conservative	59.0	30.4	28.6	19.3	18.8	3.0

Source : Gay & Lesbian Leadership Institute, 2009 Zogby America Survey of Likely Voters, www.glli.org/professional_development/research.

a black president rose from less than 40 percent in the late 1950s to more than 90 percent in the late 1990s—and the number who actually voted in 2008 was enough to secure the Obama victory, with the vast majority of black and white Americans replying to pollsters that race would have no impact, positive or negative, in their decision-making process (see Figure 2-5).

The 2008 election marked the decline of a little-discussed "Southern Strategy." This political tool appealed to racist sentiment, solidifying the southern vote into a strongly white, Republican powerhouse. Starting with Nixon and reaching an apogee with Clinton, southern politicians held fairly unified power. But in 2008, coastal states like Virginia and North Carolina voted for Obama, marginalizing the efficacy of the southern strategy.[25] It seems that even the South might be softening to diversity, although as Box 2-2 shows, old attitudes are hard to shake.

FIGURE 2-4. Social Acceptance of a Black President

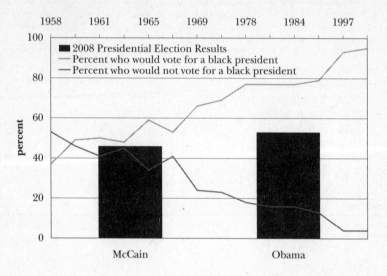

FIGURE 2-5. Social Acceptance of a Black President

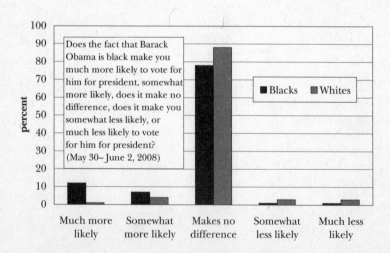

**Box 2-2. An Analysis of Voting Patterns in the 2008
Presidential Election**

Although Barack Obama did better with white voters
overall than the past two Democratic nominees, Massachusetts Senator John Kerry and Vice President Al
Gore, exit polls also found that he did worse among that
group in certain Deep South states, especially Alabama,
Mississippi, and Louisiana. The people in those states
proved impervious to his appeal, with support dropping
by ten percentage points among white Louisianians, for
instance, the sharpest decline in white support for the
Democratic ticket from 2004 to 2008 recorded in any
state (Tilove, 2008).

Many point to these statistics as an indication that the
South is marching to a different rhythm than the rest
of the country. However, there's a second, related trend
that is worth noting. A map published by the *New York
Times* after the election showed voting patterns by counties. The *Times* found that 22 percent of the nation's
counties voted more Republican than four years ago.
By this measure, the relatively greater support for
McCain—and the negative response to Obama—was not
primarily in the Deep South, but rather a swath north
of there, running from West Virginia, mainly through
Kentucky, Tennessee, Arkansas, Missouri, and Oklahoma, states where the Democratic Party had maintained a high level of influence over white voters. One
conclusion is that racist attitudes are still prevalent in
parts of the South, and beyond.

FIGURE for Box 2-2. Republican Voting Patterns by County*

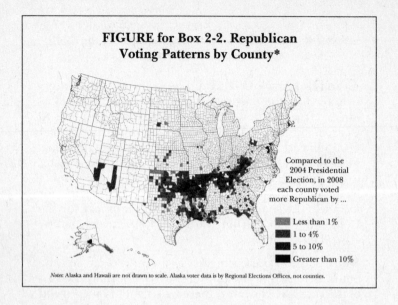

Compared to the 2004 Presidential Election, in 2008 each county voted more Republican by ...

■ Less than 1%
■ 1 to 4%
■ 5 to 10%
■ Greater than 10%

Notes: Alaska and Hawaii are not drawn to scale. Alaska voter data is by Regional Elections Offices, not counties.

Partly as a result of these attitudinal shifts, both of the major political parties seem to have given up explicitly racist signals and statements and have resorted to "coding," as exemplified in the harsh anti-immigrant positions of the Republican Party. Many minorities see this for what it is. Still, explicit racial messages are out—in early 2009, when a Republican member of the Texas House of Representatives, Betty Brown, suggested in a public hearing that Asian American voters should adopt surnames that are "easier for Americans to deal with" at voting poll sites, the public outcry was so real that the other members of the Texas House immediately called on Brown to apologize for her "shameful" comment.[26] Diversity is also becoming an accepted fact of business culture. Business magazines and leaders routinely discuss the value of a multiethnic workforce as a way

*Design inspired by exit poll maps from the *New York Times*. Recreated by USC's Program for Environmental and Regional Equity using actual voting data from Dave Leip's Atlas of U.S. Presidential Elections.

to reach new domestic and international audiences. A 2004 listing by *Fortune* of the "50 Best Companies for Minorities" includes more than just the percentage of minority workers in the ranks. The best companies, they say, promote minorities at the top in order to change the culture of the entire corporation. "People of color made up almost 21 percent of boardrooms in 2003, compared with 19 percent the year before and 11 percent in 2001." For them, it's not just about diversity; it's also about opportunity for employees.[27] And sometimes diversity opens opportunity for the company itself, enabling it to actually outperform its competitors in terms of reaching new markets and tapping new skills.[28] Diversity, it appears, might even have become part of the bottom line.

Mixed Attitudes

In the spring of 2003, as the Iraq War was beginning, researchers pretended to search for apartments in Los Angeles County. Responding to Internet ads with identical messages, the researchers used names that "sounded" either white (Patrick McDougall), black (Tyrell Jackson) or Arabic (Said Al-Rahman). Landlords responded most positively to the names associated with whites, inviting nearly 90 percent of the McDougalls to view their apartments; nearly two-thirds of the landlords responded positively to e-mails with the Arabic name, and only about 56 percent responded favorably to e-mails from Tyrell Jackson (Carpusor and Loges, 2006).

Our nation's darkening complexion has clearly changed the way Americans *talk* about race, compared to, say, our parents, or grandparents. But as the experiences of Said Al-Rahman and Tyrell Jackson illustrate, it is much less clear how much Americans have changed what they *think* about race. Critical race scholar john powell (2009) explains that Americans have virtually erased explicit racism, but explicit racism is only 2 percent of our cognitive process. When measured by questions like "Do you discriminate?"

for most, the answer is "No."[29] But the other 98 percent of our thinking includes unconscious bias that is fairly high among Americans and is triggered by pictures, buzzwords, etc. This type of prejudice—sometimes unknowingly and not always just confined to whites—helps keep race-based decisions and structures alive.

Individual perceptions are mixed. According to a July 2008 *New York Times*/CBS News poll on the state of race relations,[30] almost 60 percent of black respondents said race relations were generally bad, compared with 34 percent of whites. Four out of ten blacks surveyed said that there has been no progress in recent years in eliminating racial discrimination; however, fewer than two in ten whites said the same thing. And about one out of four white respondents said they thought that too much had been made of racial barriers facing black people, while half of black respondents said not enough had been made of racial impediments faced by blacks. The 2008 poll also indicated almost 70 percent of blacks said they had encountered a specific instance of discrimination based on their race—compared with 62 percent in 2000; over 50 percent of Latinos said they had been the victim of racial discrimination; while only 26 percent of whites polled said they had faced an instance of racial discrimination.[31]

Obama's election has seemingly left Americans more sanguine about race relations. A poll published by the *New York Times*/CBS News on April 22, 2009, marking Obama's first hundred days in office,[32] found that the majority of Americans agree that race relations have generally improved. In particular, the percentage of African Americans agreeing with this statement doubled from the earlier poll conducted in July 2008. Furthermore, the poll showed a staggering increase of African Americans agreeing that the United States is heading in the right direction; 70 percent of black respondents agreed compared with only 34 percent of white respondents. Many attribute this progress to Obama.[33]

Still, whites continue to hold some deep-seated preju-

dices about African Americans and Latinos. Using 2000
General Social Survey (GSS) data, Ronald Weitzer and Steven Tuch found that 48 percent of whites view blacks as
"violence–prone" (2004: 306). Sociologist Jeffrey Dixon's
analysis of the same raw data shows that 35 percent of
whites surveyed believe blacks to be lazy, 25 percent view
blacks as unintelligent, and 34 percent view blacks as lacking a commitment to strong families (2006: 2181, 2203).
Latinos are similarly viewed, but Asians and Pacific Islanders are not; they are saddled with a unique set of stigmas
discussed later in this chapter. And although whites have
come a long way in accepting interracial marriage, nearly
one-fifth—19 percent—continue to oppose such marriages,
as reflected in 2004–2005 data (Bobo and Charles, 2009:
253).

Although data pertaining to Asian Americans remain
scarce, racial discrimination and harassment are both
still very prevalent within this community. When a 2007
national survey of LGBT Asian and Pacific Islander Americans asked their subjects if they had experienced discrimination or harassment in their lives, an alarming 85 percent
say they had experienced at least one form of discrimination as a result of their race or ethnicity. Nearly four out of
five (78 percent) respondents agreed that Asian and Pacific
Islanders in the lesbian, gay, bisexual, and transgender
community experience racism within the white LGBT community, with more than a third of the respondents saying
they "strongly agree" with this statement (Dang and Vianney, 2007: 44).

With an increasing number of people of color calling
America home, racial and ethnic conflicts are no longer
limited to clashes between a white majority and ethnic
minorities. According to studies conducted by the Public Policy Institute of California (Cain, Citrin, and Wong,
2000) blacks, Latinos, and Asian Americans may share
an interest in advocating for antidiscrimination policies,
but competition for political offices and jobs, especially at
the local level, creates tensions. For example, while many

immigrant groups want bilingual education, such programs are often not a priority for other minorities born in
the United States.[34] While a majority of Californians think
positively about the contributions of immigrants, 45 percent of African Americans believe immigrants are a burden
to the economy, compared to 22 percent of Latinos. At the
same time, 53 percent of the white population and 29 percent of Asians thought immigrants were a burden (Hajnal
and Baldassare, 2001). Indeed, whites often seem to be
more anti-immigrant than blacks—49 versus 44 percent
want less immigration—which is striking given that people
with higher incomes tend to be more pro-immigrant (Gallup poll, June 2003, cited in Pastor and Marcelli, 2004:
119). Manuel Pastor and Enrico Marcelli (2004) acknowledge the tensions that exist between blacks and Latinos
but also point to research suggesting that blacks see Latinos as potential allies in broader coalitions for economic
advancement.

Defining the Black-White Paradigm

America is a young country; it was less than fifty years
ago that lawmakers fully tackled the legacy of Jim Crow
through the Civil Rights Acts of 1965. The first wave of
students involved in forced busing to integrate schools in
the early 1970s is just now reaching middle age. No one
should expect America to recover from 350 years of racism so quickly. Anyone familiar with the histories of ancient
civilizations understands the historical insignificance of a
few decades. Remember, ". . . by the middle of the twentieth century, the color line was as well defined and as firmly
entrenched as any institution in the land. After all, it was
older than most institutions, including the federal government" (Franklin, 1993: 36).

With the nation changing fast, and immigrants often
casting their struggles in the tropes of the civil rights movement, it is tempting to look beyond the black-white framework and insist that other structures now govern race

relations and social and economic opportunity. While there is some truth to that insight, this book argues to the contrary: as the populations of other racial minorities grow, it becomes increasingly important to address the fundamental question of fairness for African Americans, which affects the fortunes of the other groups. The black-white economic and social divide—created by slavery and cemented through years of servitude and subjugation—has shaped the modern American state and social policy.

This is not to diminish the violence directed at Native Americans, but, analysts argue that "race in America took on a deeper and more disturbing meaning with the importation of Africans as slaves" (Hacker, 1992: 3). Slavery demanded that black and white Americans coexist, forge intimate relationships, and collaborate in the most shameful acts of degradation that both forged and damaged the psyche of the nation. Slavery set the rules, so to speak, for the etiquette of oppression and injustice. "If race figures so centrally in the life of the United States, it has much to do with the kind of country America is and has been from its start" (Hacker, 1992: 217).

The fact is that the inferiority attributed to blacks has defined policy discussions and the way other racial minorities are viewed. W. E. B. Du Bois foretold the American predicament virtually a century ago: "The problem of the twentieth century is the problem of the color line" (Du Bois, 1903: 3). Not even Du Bois could have appreciated the full impact of his prediction today, according to the historian John Hope Franklin (1993). Gunnar Myrdal, a Swedish economist and social reformer, called attention to the unique plight of African Americans in his groundbreaking 1944 report, *An American Dilemma: The Negro Problem and American Democracy*. Not only did Myrdal find the unequal status and treatment of African Americans a stain on the fabric of a country that proclaimed the values of freedom, equality, and justice, but he also noted a uniqueness that applied only to African Americans (Myrdal, 1944). Of all ethnic and racial groups, only African Americans were thought to be "unassimilable" to the point that "amalgamation" with white Americans was intensely and staunchly prohibited. While the Japanese and Chinese were also considered "unassimilable" groups, this intensity of feeling around "amalgamation" applied only to African Americans.

Twenty-four years later, the Kerner Commission wrote that "[w]hat white Americans have never fully understood—but what the Negro can never forget—is that white society is deeply implicated in the ghetto. White institutions created it, white institutions maintain it, and white society condones it" (Kerner Commission, 1968: 2). Maggie Potapchuk (2005) takes this a step further, saying that since whites created this system and the strategies that maintain it, white people have the greatest burden to end it.

Attitudes part and parcel to white privilege and the second-class status of African Americans remain deeply ingrained. In *Rage of a Privileged Class*, Ellis Cose relates a conversation he had with Ed Koch, former mayor of New York, about the problems of Brooklyn's Crown Heights neighborhood, a predominantly black community with a large Jewish presence. During the conversation, the former mayor remarked that the Jews think "the city ought to give them a little credit" for staying in the community when so many other white groups moved out. "Why, I wondered as he talked, should any group get special credit for not maniacally shunning blacks? What kind of a society have we created in which it is considered acceptable to flee entire communities merely because members of another race move in?" (Cose, 1993: 189).

Racial prejudice against African Americans continues to shape the public policy agenda in subtle, and not so subtle, ways. Myths about black people and black images stir debate about public policies, and when those policies are misguided, all Americans are hurt. For example, the stereotype of the single black mother as a long-term welfare recipient who would rather have another child than work her way off public assistance has driven welfare reform, even though young single mothers have lower welfare dependency and are as likely to be white as black. The loss of the safety net for poor children hurts families of all races, but the stereotype of black schoolchildren as rowdy and uninterested in learning may have, subconsciously or not, resulted in the abandonment of the nation's public schools. This has turned public high schools across the country into dropout factories, hurting all children who cannot completely isolate themselves from the system and raising the national costs associated with less skilled and less competitive workers.

Because this country's understanding of race is polarized along the black-white axis, other groups are forced to make equally sharp distinctions. They are forced to define themselves in ways that are unnatural and perhaps uncomfortable to them, lumping Koreans and Chinese together as "Asians" when their language, histories, and experience in the country are quite different. Moreover, as journalist Juan González writes, "[t]his country's stark black-white dichotomy is alien to Latinos. Rather, to varying degrees, based on the country of origin and even the region within the home country, ethnic identification, or nationality, remains more at the core of Latino identity" (González, 2000: 184). Even though the 2000 Census offered Americans sixty-three racial categories from which to choose for self-identification, 42 percent of people nationwide who identified themselves as Latino on the Census picked "other," as their racial category (48 percent chose "white"). In fact, 97 percent of the 15.4 million Americans who chose "other" were Latino (Martínez, 2001: 1A).

Both black and white Americans long ago lost the opportunity to embrace the diversity within their communities. As slaves, blacks were stripped of all connection with their homelands so that today they are largely reduced to identifying with a continent rather than a country. Caribbean Americans of African origin do not necessarily consider themselves "African Americans." Neither do recent African immigrants. In denying African Americans their identity by treating them as a monolith, Anglo Americans, French Americans, Italian Americans, and Irish Americans were rendered simply "white." Often overlooked during discussions about the importance of diversity and preserving minority cultures is the fact that we have always been a nation of minorities. The heretofore white "majority" has never been a monolith either. When Americans reduce each other to a skin color, everyone gets diminished in each other's eyes. And as a matter of practicality, in a globalizing world, the more we as a nation can relate to the diverse cultures of the world, the better.

To emphasize the significance and singularity of black inequality is not to argue that the black struggle for justice is more important than the struggle of others. Instead, it is a way to acknowledge that resolving the structural inequities that perpetuate the black-white divide is the key to unlocking the value of our increasingly diverse society. Over the past 150 years, the battles for justice for African Americans, including the movement for civil rights, have continued to inspire those who seek justice, fairness, and inclusion—notably women, members of other racial minorities, and gays. The African American struggle demonstrated that, as blacks gain ground, so do all others in this mosaic that is America.

The Lingering Black-White Paradigm

The embedded nature of inequality growing out of the black-white paradigm can be demonstrated by looking at two aspects of racial discrimination. First is the pattern of racial violence against blacks, which further stresses the entrenchment and widespread nature of antiblack sentiment. The other example—the persistent segregation of African Americans—even more vividly demonstrates the continuing discrimination that African Americans face.

In spite of its growing diversity and blurring of color lines, the United States remains racially segregated. John Iceland (2009) finds that as immigration from around the world continues, distinct patterns of racially distinct integration proceed. In order of ease of integration, Europeans, then Asians and Latinos, and then blacks become (or don't) part of America's fabric. Iceland believes that Asians and Latinos are blurring the distinct nature of the color line, but his conclusions also point to the continuing harm of that line: over time, black immigrants become less, not more, integrated with mainstream America. Meanwhile, Sunday morning remains the most segregated time in America—reflected in part in the deep surprise many had when discovering the language and phrasings of Barack Obama's minister, Jeremiah Wright. And despite all of the progress with school integration, the vast majority of white students do not go to school with many Asians, blacks, Latinos, or Native Americans.

Racial violence against African Americans also remains widespread. While the number of hate crimes has waned (see Figure 2-6), the proportion of hate crimes against blacks has remained disproportionately large and steady, as indicated in Figure 2-7, indicating little progress, since their share of the population has also remained steady (remember Figure 1-1). This is important because it demonstrates that, despite growing diversity, racist attitudes toward blacks are what continue to sculpt the emotional landscape.

The black-white paradigm is so embedded that in the midst of dealing with their first widely publicized violent tragedy, Asian Americans had to find their place on that racially polarized axis. In 1982, Vincent Chin was killed in Detroit by autoworkers who were making anti-Japanese comments. In meetings, Asian American activists wrestled with the question "Should Asian Americans downplay race to stay in the 'safe' shadows of the white establishment? Or should they step out of the shadows and cast their lot with the more vulnerable position of minorities seeking civil rights?" (Zia, 2000: 70). They probably did not have much of a choice. "In the end, we reached a consensus: to fight for what we believe in, we would have to enter the

FIGURE 2-6. Hate Crime Incidents as Reported to the FBI, 2000–2007

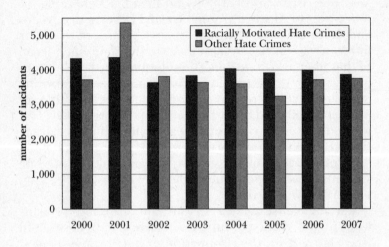

FIGURE 2-7. Racial Hate Crimes by Racial Group

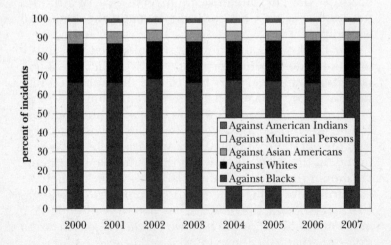

Box 2-3. Overcoming Hate and Breaking Silence

On August 10, 1999, Joseph Santos Ileto, a Filipino American postal worker, was gunned down while delivering mail in Chatsworth, Los Angeles, by a self-professed white supremacist named Buford O. Furrow. Just hours before, Furrow had fired shots into a playground full of children at the North Valley Jewish Community Center in Granada Hills, California.

Around the time of Ileto's death, the national media had prominently focused on the brutal hate crimes perpetuated against James Byrd, an African American man in Texas, and Matthew Shepard, a gay man in Wyoming. However, in August 1999, the national media focused on the Jewish children, not Joseph Ileto. Even in Los Angeles, his death received minimal coverage.

In response, the Ileto family, led by his brother Ismael Ileto, became national spokespersons for victims of hate crimes regardless of the victims' racial, religious, or sexual orientation, and have participated in events sponsored by the National Rainbow Coalition, the National AFL-CIO Union Convention, and the Million Moms March against gun violence. The case of the Ileto family, as reported in *Untold Civil Rights Stories*, movingly illustrates the untapped political power that lies in localized individual and family activism, despite fears of retaliation, death threats, and neglect by the mass media (Kwoh, 2009: 43–51).

---

arena of civil rights and racial politics. Welcome or not, Asian Americans would put ourselves into the white/black race paradigm" (Zia, 2000: 71). These unspeakable acts have continued to galvanize the community, as shown in Box 2-3.

Racially motivated violence has taken new forms as well. In the post-9/11 era, a pernicious anti-immigrant, radicalized ideology has formed that works against all persons of darker skin or non-Christian religion. The American-Arab Anti-Discrimination Committee reported a significant increase in violent hate crimes following the aftermath of the 9/11 attacks—documenting over seven hundred violent cases directed against Middle Easterns, South Asians, and Arab Americans within the first weeks following the attacks.[35] The incidents included: in Stockton, California, a Sikh being shouted at and called an "Iraqi" by white teens in a van; in Tulsa, Oklahoma, a Pakistani native being beaten; in Chicago, a firebomb being tossed at an Arab community center; and in Denton, Texas, a "Molotov cocktail" (i.e., a gasoline bomb) thrown against the side of an Islamic society's building. These many reported cases of racially motivated hate crimes indicate two noteworthy patterns. First, the incidents did not always occur with a clear motivation of bias; rather, they developed in that direction as the altercation intensified. Second, hate crimes and vigilante violence seem to be directly related to a sense of collective guilt and spirit of vengeance, as shown in the wake of the 9/11 attacks (American-Arab Anti-Discrimination Committee Research Institute, 2008).

This violence against Muslims and those perceived as Muslims reflects the impact of popular culture, but it also reflects the role of the state. This intertwining of attitudes and state action is also seen in how Mexicans and Latinos, some nonimmigrant, many legal, bear the brunt of raids carried out by U.S. Immigration and Customs Enforcement (ICE) teams across the nation. Some of the tragic results, including the separation of families, are discounted because of notions of legality and illegality but also because there is a particular set of racial perceptions that fail to lift up the humanity—and the suffering—of those who are affected.

The separation of peoples in our cultural imagination is also reflected in our urban geography. Segregation, a phenomenon harking back to the middle of the last century, has actually carried over into the new century. Black-white segregation persists, although it has declined when measured by a so-called dissimilarity index—a term that roughly means the percentage of a group, say blacks, that would need to move so that they were evenly spread among another ethnic group, say white, in a particular area (see Figure 2-8).

Figure 2-9 shows the pattern for the thirty most populous metropolitan areas in the United States: while black-white segregation has dropped, it is still much greater than Latino-white segregation. It is also striking that blacks and Latinos are more likely than blacks and whites to live together, reflecting the new mix in many of our urban communities.

Although progress is evidenced, blacks remain more

FIGURE 2-8. Black-White Segregation in the Thirty Metropolitan Areas with the Greatest Black Population

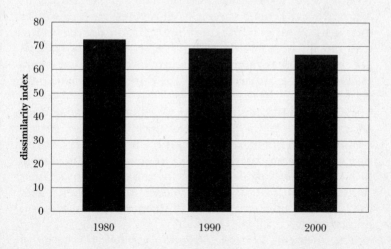

FIGURE 2-9. Segregation in the Thirty Largest Metropolitan Areas for Whites, Blacks, and Latinos

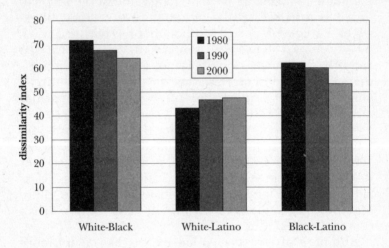

segregated than any other racial group (Iceland, 2009). In addition, their segregation is not alleviated by wealth, as has been the case for every other ethnic and racial group. Iceland's analysis shows that of blacks, Hispanics, and Asians, blacks remain the most segregated even at higher incomes. Of all groups, their segregation decreases the least quickly with wealth, and the most affluent individuals are segregated at rates only slightly lower than the poorest Hispanics and Asians (2009: 47). Douglas Massey and Nancy Denton, in coining the phrase "residential apartheid," argued that residential segregation is at the heart of African American inequality: it undermines the social and economic well-being of blacks in the United States because it breeds concentrated poverty; joblessness; educational failure; crime; social, geographic, and economic isolation; and a host of other ills (Massey and Denton, 1993: 2). Their analysis remains one of the most convincing and quoted analyses of black isolation.

The enduring racial segregation is partly the result of

longer-term historical patterns. The suburbanization of
America in the 1950s and '60s solidified segregation as white
Americans left the cities in droves. Just as African Americans
gained access to metropolitan areas long denied them, the
value of those properties plummeted. As white people continued to leave cities, and as more well-off African Americans
spread out within cities, isolated neighborhoods of concentrated poverty and urban disinvestment proliferated. It is
perhaps no coincidence that this movement for exclusion
(the suburbanization of America)—supported by racially
biased housing policies that kept African Americans out of
the suburbs—came at the same time that civil rights leaders
were mobilizing a movement of inclusion.

The phenomenon of "white flight" to the suburbs has
been a staple of the American landscape, and, even though
the most recent Census data show that more minorities
are moving to the suburbs, integration is not necessarily increasing. Iceland attributes this to tipping points:
"Whites tend to exhibit a stronger preference than [non-
whites] for same-race neighbors and would be less comfort-
able as a numerical minority. Since each minority group
has a preference for a greater number of coethnic neighbors than most whites could tolerate in their own neighborhood, this likely often leads to "tipping" toward a
majority-race makeup rather than a stable neighborhood
mix" (2009: 28). As a new generation of whites move back
to the central city, minorities are being displaced by sheer
economics; whites can typically afford higher housing costs
as developers buy up rental property and rebuild. Gentrification is the latest incarnation of white residential exclusion. Chapter 4 further examines the key issues of sprawl
and gentrification. Often overlooked by the framework
of the white-black color line, Latinos and Asians are segregated too. Although there is disagreement on whether
their situations parallel the experience of African Americans, Wei Li (1998) and Ayse Pumak (2004) have found
Asian Americans to form separate, and sometimes wealthy,
suburban ethnic communities. The pattern of segrega-

tion, even when seemingly voluntary, can be a troubling trend that points to the embeddedness of racial divisions in American society.

Limits of the Black-White Paradigm

The black-white lens fails to bring sharp focus to all aspects of the current racial order. Until recently, immigration was an issue that had not veered far off the black-white axis. After the Civil War, the South needed rebuilding, and nonslave states had a continued need for cheap labor. The fact that no one wanted to hire blacks precipitated a large wave of European immigration. Hundreds of thousands came from Germany, Ireland, and Italy and, after periods of initial discrimination and struggle, these individuals and communities were eventually assimilated into the white mainstream.

Chinese and Japanese workers were among the first Asians to arrive in the country in the nineteenth century. At the time, there was much discussion about where Asians fit in relation to African Americans. San Francisco's *Daily Alta California*, the most influential paper at the time, ran an editorial arguing that the Chinese are "morally a far worse class to have among us than the Negro" (Cose, 1992: 32). Around the same time, a state appellate court invalidated the conviction of a white man who had killed a Chinese man because blacks, mulattoes, and American Indians were not allowed to provide evidence in court—and by extension, neither were the Chinese, as in this case.

A change in immigration policy in 1965—precipitated by the civil rights focus on inclusion—unexpectedly shifted the flow of immigrants to people coming from Asia and Latin America rather than from Europe. President Johnson insisted on a bill that treated soon-to-be citizens with the same degree of evenhandedness mandated by the new Civil Rights Act of 1965; the logical result was, thus, curtailing efforts to keep people out based on country of origin. This historic legislation set the stage for the increase in diversity America is experiencing today (Cose, 1992: 109).

As more foreign-language speakers have joined the U.S. population, questions have arisen about the appropriate language of instruction in schools. The question of language goes to the heart of identity, particularly for Latinos. Language issues prove that what constitutes a "racial issue" cannot be confined to skin color. Similarly, speaking a language with Middle Eastern origins—Arabic or Farsi, for example—immediately awakens a new xenophobia. This new fear extends to South Asians and can also be triggered by skin hue, dress, or religious affiliation without regard to the facts. These issues fall outside the black-white paradigm but are equally searing and important.

There are also nuances of Latino poverty that a black-white framework doesn't reach. Where black poverty tends to be characterized by the high incidence of joblessness, this is not so for Latinos. Mexicans are often disproportionately represented in the working poor, experiencing high employment rates but generally earning below official poverty levels. Puerto Ricans, who are urban and tend to mirror the black community in their exclusion from the job market, have high welfare rates as well as high rates of female-headed households. Cuban Americans often come from more privileged backgrounds and have strong support from refugee-supporting networks.

While Asian Americans share certain common minority experiences, such as poverty and social discrimination, they have unique issues as the model minority and breaking through the glass ceiling. The black experience in America is not a perfect paradigm for understanding the experiences of Asian Americans. For the Asian American population, "minority" is not synonymous with "disadvantaged." Clearly, high levels of poverty mark many Asian communities, including the Vietnamese, Laotians, Hmong, and Tongans, but many Asian groups are doing well economically. Their experience and reality is complex (Ong, 2000).

The migration of Asians and Pacific Islanders to the

FIGURE 2-10. Poverty Rates by Racial/Ethnic Group, Los Angeles, 1999

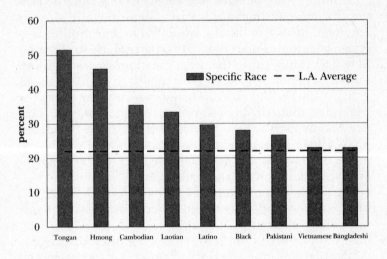

United States covers two separate periods[36]: earlier immigration (1850s–1970) consisted mainly of people from China, Japan, Korea, the Philippines, and India arriving to labor on railroads and in fisheries, mines, and other industries in America. Later immigration (1970–1990s) included many Asians from Cambodia, Vietnam, Thailand, Laos, and also the Hmong. This particular group of Southeast Asians were categorized as *refugees*, as opposed to *immigrants*, because they were escaping war and violence in their home countries, hence conceiving resettlement in the United States.[37] Many researchers believe this distinction between circumstances of migration correlates to the inequality within the Asian American and Pacific Islander community that includes disparity in income, education, English proficiency, and other socioeconomic indicators (Hien, 1995). According to Laureen Chew, associate dean and professor of Asian American studies at San Francisco State University, ". . . neither they [the refugees] nor the

American society were adequately prepared for resettlement . . . the refugees did not understand American culture and were unprepared for the hostility they met in
their resettlement communities."[38]

Even for those who are better prepared or even U.S.-
born, there are challenges in the area of social discrimination. Recent research suggests that even though the
Asian population may be highly educated, the "rate of
return" on education is lower for this group than it is for
Anglos. While some of this may reflect the difficulty
of gauging education's value when immigrants have
received their degrees in another country, one study
found that the returns are even lower for U.S.-born and
less recent immigrants (Pastor and Marcelli, 2001). The
pattern suggests that Asian Americans may be experiencing problems with upward mobility—breaking through
what has been termed the "glass ceiling" to the top of corporate and political leadership.

Asian Americans are often perceived as being more
"foreign" than anyone else. During World War II, Japanese Americans were interned in far greater numbers
than both German and Italian Americans. Asian Americans have been viewed through many negative and limited
lenses, but perhaps the most insidious stereotype—insidious because it is meant to be a compliment—is the increasingly common view of Asian Americans as the "model
minority." Though seemingly positive in connotation, the
term obscures a more accurate and complex depiction of
Asian Americans, who, as mentioned earlier in Table 2-5,
also suffer high poverty rates. Pop culture is even beginning to address a more nuanced understanding of Asian
Americans. Although the 2008 film *Gran Torino* with Clint
Eastwood was criticized as being "too generic and pre-
programmed,"* the movie gave a realistic portrayal of a

---

*See the full critique of *Gran Torino* by *Chicago Sun Times* writer
Roger Ebert at http://rogerebert.suntimes.com/apps/pbcs.dll/article?
AID=/20081217/REVIEWS/812179989.

Hmong community and their struggles with poverty, education, and gangs within the American suburbs. The term "model minority" masks the struggles and needs of Asian Americans, not all of which are shared by their black and Latino counterparts.

Further, the term "model minority," expressed as if a compliment, shifts blame onto other minority groups, who become rhetorically leveraged as less than "model" in character, while downplaying the importance of a more thorough examination of the real discrimination and oppression experienced by Asian Americans.

So why does it matter? The experiences of nonblack racial minorities are unique and unacknowledged by most Americans because our mind-set does not make room for them. If the United States is to make progress in racial equity, then a full and diverse picture needs to be painted. Without understanding the reality of the struggle, how can Americans join together to put forward useful solutions?

Notes

[1] U.S. Census Bureau, 2007 American Community Survey (ACS).

[2] Ibid.

[3] U.S. Census Bureau, Population Estimates for States by Race and Hispanic Origin: July 1, 1999 (ST-99–32).

[4] All data from 1990 and 2007 discussed here are from U.S. Census Bureau, 1990 Census (STF1), and 2007 ACS, respectively.

[5] Ibid.

[6] U.S. Census Bureau, 1990 Census and 2007 ACS.

[7] U.S. Census Bureau, 1990 Census (STF1) and 2008 Population Estimates.

[8] U.S. Census Bureau, 1990 Census (STF1) and 2007 ACS.

[9] Ibid.

[10] Calculated by the Program for Environmental and Regional Equity using data downloaded from American FactFinder. Beginning in 2005, the metropolitan area also included Metairie and Kenner, Louisiana.

[11] U.S. Census Bureau, 2007 ACS.

[12] U.S. Census Bureau, 1990 Census (STF1), 2000 Census (SF1), and 2008 Population Estimates.

[13] Poverty figures for 1989 are from the U.S. Dept. of Commerce, Bureau of the Census, *We the . . . First Americans*, issued September 1993. The 1999 figures were calculated by the Program for Environmental and Regional Equity using data downloaded from American FactFinder.

[14] U.S. Dept. of Commerce, Bureau of the Census, *We the People: American Indians and Alaskan Natives in the United States*, issued February 2006.

[15] Calculated by the Program for Environmental and Regional Equity using data downloaded from American FactFinder.

[16] Tabulations by the Program for Environmental and Regional Equity (PERE) of IPUMS 2005–2007 Pooled ACS data. The reported figure is the percentage of all married-couple families with at least one American Indian spouse that are interracial (i.e., in which one spouse is not American Indian).

[17] U.S. Census Bureau, *The 2009 Statistical Abstract, The National Data Book*, http://www.census.gov/compendia/statab/tables/09s0059.pdf. In the reported figure for "interracial married couples," the term refers to marriages between two people from different racial categories when all races and ethnicities are divided into three groups: whites, blacks, and other race (including all other races and ethnicities combined). Hispanics can be included in any of the three categories.

[18] Tabulations (here and in the following paragraph) by the Program for Environmental and Regional Equity (PERE) of IPUMS 2005–2007 Pooled ACS data. Intermarried households are defined as those in which the householder is married to someone of another race or ethnicity using the following six categories: white, African American, Latino, Asian American (Asians and Pacific Islanders), Native American, and Other (all other groups). This categorization places all Latinos in the "Latino" group, thus leaving all other groups "non-Latino." Note that the universe is restricted to couples in which one person per couple is the householder, so the reported totals understate the actual number of couples.

[19] *2008 Annual Report*, Joint Center for Political and Economic Studies, p. 6.

[20] *NALEO 2008 General Election Profile: Latinos in Congress and State Legislatures After Election 2008: A State-by-State Summary*, p. 24.

[21] For the official U. S. Dept. of Justice biography of Attorney General Holder, see http://www.usdoj.gov/ag/aghistory/holder_e.html.

[22] League of United Latin American Citizens, press release, "The National Hispanic Leadership Agenda Congratulates Secretary Hilda Solis Upon her Swearing-In," March 13, 2009, http://www.lulac.org/advocacy/press/2009/solis4.html.

[23] U. S. House of Representatives, Fifteenth District of California, press release, "Congressional Asian Pacific American Caucus (CAPAC) applauds President-elect Obama's Selection of Two Asian Americans

to Cabinet Positions," December 15, 2008, http://www.house.gov/list/speech/ca15_honda/cabinet.html. For a listing of White House Cabinet officials, see http://www.whitehouse.gov/administration/cabinet.

24 2009 Report, Gay & Lesbian Leadership Institute. See http://www.glli.org/out_officials.

25 Adam Nossiter, "For South, a Waning Hold on National Politics," *New York Times*, November 11, 2008.

26 Joshua Rhett Miller, "Asian-Americans Blast Texas Congressman's Call for 'Easier to Deal With' Names," *Fox News*, April 9, 2009, http://www.foxnews.com/politics/2009/04/09/asian-americans-blast-offensive-comment-texas-lawmaker.

27 Cora Daniels, "50 Best Companies for Minorities," Fortune/CNNMoney.com, June 28, 2004.

28 Ibid.

29 See john powell's interview with Campaign for America's Future, "What the Right, and the Left, Doesn't Get About Race," http://www.ourfuture.org/audio-media/2009041829/what-right-and-left-doesnt-get-about-race.

30 *New York Times*/CBS Poll, "On Race in America, and the Candidates," July 16, 2008, http://www.nytimes.com/imagepages/2008/07/16/us/20080716_POLL_GRAPHIC.html.

31 Adam Nagourney and Megan Thee, "Poll Finds Obama Isn't Closing Divide on Race," *New York Times*, July 16, 2008, http://www.nytimes.com/2008/07/16/us/politics/16poll.html.

32 *New York Times*/CBS News poll, "Obama's 100th Day in Office," http://documents.nytimes.com/new-york-times-cbs-news-poll-obama-s-100th-day-in-office#p=1.

33 Sheryl Gay Stolberg and Marjorie Connelly, "Obama Is Nudging Views on Race, a Survey Finds," *New York Times*, April 28, 2009, http://www.nytimes.com/2009/04/28/us/politics/28poll.html.

34 Report, 2000, Summary of Findings. "Ethnic Context, Race Relations, and California Politics," Public Policy Institute of California.

35 American-Arab Anti-Discrimination Committee Research Institute, *2003–2007 Report on Hate Crimes and Discrimination Against Arab Americans*, p. 11, http://www.adc.org/PDF/hcr07.pdf.

36 For more in-depth information on these two periods of Asian migration, see http://www.ericdigests.org/1994/asian.htm.

37 For further definition of immigrant and refugee categorization, see http://www.encyclopedia.com/doc/1G2-3401803957.html.

38 See study guide by Laureen Chew, Ed.D., Irene Dea Collier, and the Center for Asian American Media, p. 4, at http://distribution.asianamericanmedia.org/wp-content/uploads/pdfs/study_guides/akaDonBonus_StudyGuide.pdf.

References

American-Arab Anti-Discrimination Committee Research Institute. 2008. *2003–2007 Report on Hate Crimes and Discrimination Against Arab Americans*. Washington, DC: American-Arab Anti-Discrimination Committee.

Asian Pacific American Legal Center and the Asian American Justice Center. 2004. *A Community of Contrasts: Asian Americans and Pacific Islanders in the United States*. Los Angeles: Asian Pacific American Legal Center.

Bobo, Lawrence, and Camille Charles. 2009. "Race in the American Mind: From the Moynihan Report to the Obama Candidacy." *ANNALS of the American Academy of Political and Social Science* 621 (243): 243–259.

Cain, Bruce, Jack Citrin, and Cara Wong. 2000. *Ethnic Context, Race Relations, and California Politics*. San Francisco: Public Policy Institute of California.

Carpusor, Adrian, and William Loges. 2006. "Rental Discrimination and Ethnicity in Names (Top Interactive Paper)." Paper presented at the annual meeting of the International Communication Association, Dresden International Congress Centre, Dresden, Germany, June 16. http://www.allacademic.com/meta/p90145_index.html.

Cho, Wendy K. 2000. "Tapping Motives and Dynamics Behind Campaign Contributions: Insights from the Asian American Case." University of Illinois at Urbana-Champaign. Typescript.

Cohen, Sarah, and D'Vera Cohn. 2001. "Racial Integration's Shifting Patterns." *Washington Post*, April 2.

Cose, Ellis. 1992. *A Nation of Strangers: Prejudice, Politics, and the Populating of America*. New York: William Morrow.

———. 1993. *Rage of a Privileged Class*. New York: HarperCollins.

Dang, Alain, and Cabrini Vianney. 2007. *Living in the Margins: A National Survey of Lesbian, Gay, Bisexual, and Transgender Asian and Pacific Islander Americans*. New York: National Gay and Lesbian Task Force Policy Institute.

Dixon, Jeffrey. 2006. "The Ties That Bind and Those That Don't: Toward Reconciling Group Threat and Contact Theories of Prejudice." *Social Forces* 84 (4), 2179–2204.

Du Bois, W. E. B. 1903. *The Souls of Black Folk*. Chicago: A. C. McClurg & Co.; Cambridge, MA: University Press John Wilson and Son.

Fletcher, Michael A. 2000."Growing Population Confronts Bias." *Washington Post*, October 2.

Franklin, John Hope. 1993. *The Color Line: Legacy for the Twenty-First Century*. Columbia: University of Missouri Press.

Fussell, Elizabeth. 2009."Hurricane Chasers in New Orleans: Latino Immigrants as a Source of a Rapid Response Labor Force." *Hispanic Journal of Behavioral Sciences* 31 (3): 375–394.

Gay and Lesbian Leadership Institute. 2009. "Out Officials in the United States." Accessible at http://www.glli.org/out_officials.

González, Juan. 2000. *History of Empire: A History of Latinos in America*. New York: Penguin.

Hacker, Andrew. 1992. *Two Nations: Black and White, Separate, Hostile, Unequal*. New York: Scribners.

Hajnal, Zoltan, and Mark Baldassare. 2001. *Finding Common Ground: Racial and Ethnic Attitudes in California*. San Francisco: Public Policy Institute of California.

Hien, Jeremy. 1995. *From Vietnam, Laos, and Cambodia: A Refugee Experience in the United States*. New York: Twayne Publishers.

Iceland, John. 2009. *Where We Live Today: Immigration and Race in the United States*. Berkeley: University of California Press.

Ifill, Gwen. 2009. *The Breakthrough: Politics and Race in the Age of Obama*. New York: Doubleday.

Katznelson, Ira. 2005. *When Affirmative Action Was White*. New York: W. W. Norton.

Kerner Commission. 1968. *Report of the National Advisory Commission on Civil Disorders*. New York: Bantam.

Kwoh, Stewart. 2009. "An Ordinary Family Educates to Prevent Hate Crimes: The Case of Joseph Ileto." In Stewart Kwoh and Russell Leong, eds., *Untold Civil Rights Stories: Asian Americans Speak Out for Justice*. Los Angeles: Asian Pacific American Legal Center and UCLA Asian American Studies Center.

Kwoh, Stewart, and Russell Leong, eds. 2009. *Untold Civil Rights Stories: Asian Americans Speak Out for Justice*. Los Angeles: Asian Pacific American Legal Center and UCLA Asian American Studies Center.

Lai, James, and Don T. Nakanishi, eds. 2001. *National Asian Pacific American Political Almanac, Special Edition*. Los Angeles: UCLA Asian American Studies Center.

Li, Wei. 1998. "Anatomy of a New Ethnic Settlement: The Chinese Ethnoburb in Los Angeles." *Urban Studies* 35 (3): 479–501.

Louisiana Population Health Institute. 2006. *Louisiana Health and Population Survey Report, November 27. For Orleans, Jefferson, Placquemines, St. Bernard, and St. Tammany parishes*. Accessible at http://popest.org/popes tla2006/files/MigrationReport_FINv4.pdf.

Martínez, Anne. 2001. "New Choices on 2000 Census Fail to Offer Right Racial Fit for Many Latinos." *San Jose Mercury News*, May 25.

Massey, Douglas S. 2001. "Residential Segregation and Neighborhood Conditions in U.S. Metropolitan Areas." In Neil J. Smelser, William Julius Wilson, and Faith Mitchell, eds., *America Becoming: Racial Trends and Their Consequences*. Washington, DC: National Academy Press.

Massey, Douglas S., and Nancy A. Denton. 1993. *American Apartheid: Segregation and the Making of the Underclass*. Cambridge, MA: Harvard University Press.

McCarthy, Kevin F., D. J. Peterson, Narayan Sastry, and Michael Pollard. 2006. "The Repopulation of New Orleans After Hurricane Katrina." *RAND Gulf States Policy Institute, Technical Report*. Santa Monica, CA: RAND Corporation.

Morin, Richard. 2001. "Misperceptions Cloud Whites' View of Blacks." *Washington Post*, July 11.

Myrdal, Gunnar. 1944. *An American Dilemma: The Negro Problem and American Democracy*. New York: Harper & Brothers.

Ong, Paul M. 2000. "The Asian Pacific American Challenge to Race Relations." In Paul M. Ong, ed., *The State of Asian Pacific America: Transforming Race Relations*. Los Angeles: Leadership Education for Asian Pacifics (LEAP), Asian Pacific American Public Policy Institute, and UCLA Asian American Studies Center.

Ong, Paul M., and Suzanne J. Hee. 1994. "Economic Diversity." In Paul Ong, ed., *The State of Asian Pacific America: Economic Diversity, Issues, and Policies*. Los Angeles: Leadership Education for Asian Pacifics, (LEAP), Asian Pacific American Public Policy Institute, and UCLA Asian American Studies Center.

Pastor, Manuel Jr., and Enrico Marcelli. 2001. "Men N the Hood: Spatial, Skill, and Social Mismatch for Male Workers in Los Angeles." *Urban Geography*, 21 (6): 474–496.

————. 2004. "Somewhere over the Rainbow? African Americans, Unauthorized Mexican Immigration, and Coalition Building." In Steve Shulman, ed., *The Impact of Immigration on African Americans*. Piscataway, NJ: Transaction Publishers.

Potapchuk, Maggie. 2005. "Doing the Work: Unearthing Our Own White Privilege." In Maggie Potapchuk, Sally Leiderman, Donna Bivens, and Barabara Major, eds., *Flipping the Script: White Privilege and Community Building*. MP Associates and the Center for Assesment and Policy Development (CAPD).

powell, john. 2009. "Post-Racialism or Targeted Universalism?" *Denver University Law Review* (Special Issue: Obama Phenomenon) 86 (1): 785–806.

Pumak, Ayse. 2004. "Geography of Immigrant Clusters in Global Cities: A Case Study of San Francisco." *International Journal of Urban and Regional Research* 28 (2): 287–307.

Su, Julie. 2009. "Freeing Ourselves from Prison Sweatshops: Thai Garment Workers Speak Out." In Stewart Kwoh and Russell Leong, eds., *Untold Civil Rights Stories: Asian Americans Speak Out for Justice*. Los Angeles: Asian Pacific American Legal Center and UCLA Asian American Studies Center.

Thornton, Russell. 2001. "Trends Among American Indians in the United States." In Neil Smelser, William Julius Wilson, and Faith Mitchell, eds., *America Becoming: Racial Trends and Their Consequences*. Washington, DC: National Academy Press.

Tilove, Jonathan. 2008. "Obama Made Inroads with White Voters Except in Deep South." *Times-Picayune*, November 8.

Weitzer, Ronald, and Steven Tuch. 2004. "Race and Perceptions of Police Misconduct." *Social Problems* 51 (3): 305–325.

Zia, Helen. 2000. *Asian American Dreams: The Emergence of an American People*. New York: Farrar, Straus & Giroux.

Zúñiga, Víctor, and Rubén Hernández-León, eds. 2005. *New Destinations: Mexican Immigration in the United States*. New York: Russell Sage Foundation.

3

American Progress
and Disconnection

Some years ago, David Ayón, a Latino political scientist then based at Loyola Marymount University, participated in a classroom seminar one of us organized on race and racism. As the mostly white students in the audience, earnest in their curiosity about how to bridge racial differences, listened, he made a remark that recalled *Guess Who's Coming to Dinner*, the famous 1960s movie with Sidney Poitier: "I don't really care whether you invite me over to your house for dinner. I want to *own* a house."

The audience was stunned.

What Ayón spoke to, bluntly, was the difference between diversity and equity. The two are by no means mutually exclusive, as researchers have found that intergroup contact tends to diminish prejudice and deepen empathy for "the other," which is often a stepping-stone for achieving equitable policies. However, as Ayón pointed out, few people want to arrive at the table as a junior partner, particularly since junior partners are often ignored. So, revamping America means setting our sights, clearly, on equity.

As Chapter 2 noted, there are signs that race relations in the United States are improving, but relative economic conditions have stagnated. Figure 3-1 charts median family income from 1947 to 2007, adjusted to reflect 2007 dollars.* Gains from the civil rights movement did increase the median income of African American households, but the gap between black and white incomes widened as the nation moved into the eighties. This was at about the same time that demographers were beginning to take note of the Latino and Asian immigrants pouring into cities and statistics began to sort Americans by categories more descriptive than "black," "white," and "other." Since many Latinos classify themselves as white in racial if not ethnic terms, the phrase non-Hispanic white or "Anglo" came into common use. Thus, while the data shown in the chart for whites after 1972 includes Hispanics who identify themselves as white, the more relevant data by way of comparison is that for non-Hispanic whites.†

The newly identified Latino families have fared poorly in recent years, with overall incomes falling to levels only marginally higher than that of African Americans. As noted

---

*Figures 3-1 and 3-2 hide a decoupling of Asian and Pacific Islander communities in 2002. From 1987 to 2001, data from the two groups are blended, but from 2002 onward, the graph only reflects those identifying as Asian—dropping Pacific Islanders, many of whom have more economic difficulties. This disaggregation adds to a persistent concern when looking at data for Asians: sample sizes are very small, which leads to lower reliability.

†Throughout this book, racial and ethnic categories group all people who identify as Hispanic into the Hispanic or Latino category. While the question used to identify "Hispanic" people may have changed over the past four decades, the contemporary American Community Survey question asks the surveyees to respond "yes" or "no" as to whether or not they identify as Spanish/Hispanic/Latino. This question supplements one identifying race, so is reflective of heritage, nationality group, lineage, or country of birth. For a more detailed explanation, see the American Community Survey's definitions page or http://www.census.gov/acs/www/UseData/Def.htm.

FIGURE 3-1. U.S. Resident Median Family Income, 1947–2007 in 2007 Dollars

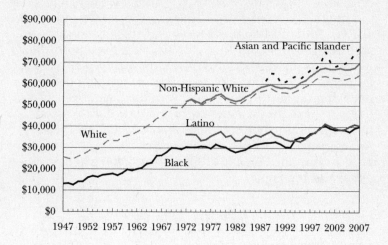

FIGURE 3-2. U.S. Median Household Income in 2007 Dollars

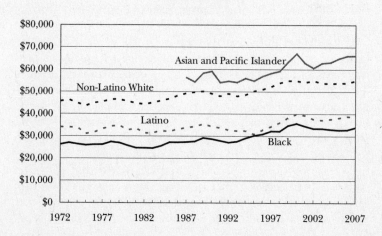

in Chapter 2, median Asian American family income has actually tracked slightly above that of the median for white Americans.

Figure 3-2 focuses on the more recent period from 1972 to 2007, and on median *household* income, once again adjusted for inflation. In this chart, all groups post lower incomes, primarily because this count includes nonfamily households consisting of one individual or unrelated people living under the same roof, with the former especially likely to have lower incomes. At the dawn of the twenty-first century, the bottom line is that, with the exception of Asians, America has not narrowed the racial economic gap, and, at best, since the mid-1990s onward, the gap has actually stayed the same.

The Color of Work

Why the divergence in income? One factor is simply the relatively high levels of unemployment experienced by the largest U.S. minority groups. As illustrated in Figure 3-3, black and Latino unemployment is consistently higher than that for whites.

Two trends, however, are worth noting. First, through the 1990s, the African American and Latino unemployment rates converged, partly reflecting a strong economy and likely reflecting government policy; in the 2000s, however, the gap reopened, with African Americans faring badly in the recession at the beginning of the millennium and doing even worse since. Solutions for high black unemployment have involved increased education, but recent work by sociologist Algernon Austin (2009) shows that, at all levels of education, blacks have higher joblessness rates than other groups. Second, the gap between the joblessness of these groups and that of white Americans typically grows in a recession (such as the mid-1970s, early 1980s, and early 1990s). This is true of the latest recession for college-educated workers, as Austin accounts for in Figure 3-4. It is such a deep downturn

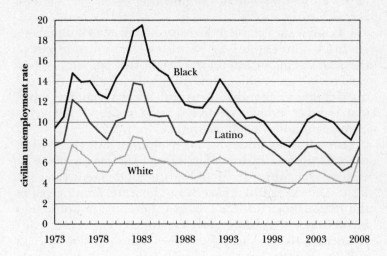

FIGURE 3-3. Unemployment Rates
by Race/Ethnicity, 1973–2008

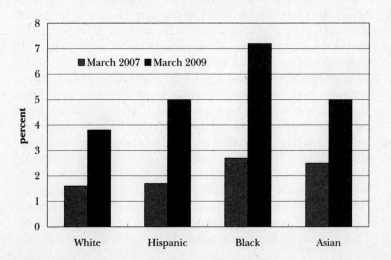

FIGURE 3-4. Unemployment Rates for the
College-Educated, by Race

that, when looking at the entire labor force for 2008 (Figure 3-3), whites had come within four percentage points of black unemployment—an unprecedented event in our recent history.

Of course, a sustained recovery would significantly benefit blacks and Latinos, as was the case in the latter part of the 1990s. This signals an important issue raised by Harvard sociologist William Julius Wilson and others: despite the fact that it seems like a neutral or even technical topic, sustaining economic growth is a key part of any civil rights agenda and, now, national agenda.

Growth does not solve all problems; but the nation can't begin to address many of its problems without it. Despite the convergence of low unemployment rates for whites, blacks, and Latinos throughout the boom years of the 1990s, there was still a large differential in household income, one that has slightly expanded. The reason: differences in the incomes of those who do work. Figures 3-5 and 3-6 show the usual weekly earnings of male and female full-time workers, respectively.

Several points are clear. First, the gap between the earnings of white and African American males has been remarkably persistent; the only moments when it has really narrowed have been at the end of a long boom of growth, as in the late 1990s. The gap actually widened in the last presidential administration, and research demonstrates that it's not just a matter of labor market placement: even in the low-wage market and taking into account individual, job, and employer characteristics, the wage difference persists (Acs and Loprest, 2009a). Second, the much-ballyhooed closing of the economic gap between white and African American women was true through the 1970s, but the difference widened during the 1980s and 1990s and has tracked along the same path into the twenty-first century. Finally, Latino incomes for full-time workers have been steadily lower for both men and women than the earnings of other groups. Given that Latino *household* income actually exceeds that of African

**FIGURE 3-5. Median Usual Weekly Earnings of Male
Full-Time Workers, 1979–2007, in 2007 Dollars**

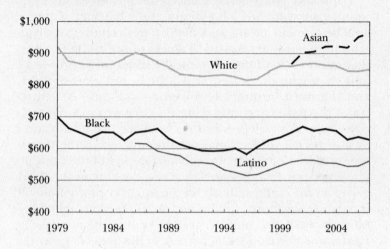

**FIGURE 3-6. Median Usual Weekly Earnings of Female
Full-Time Workers, 1979–2007, in 2007 Dollars**

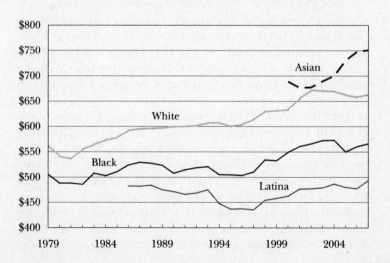

Americans, this suggests that Latino homes have many wage earners.

While any job is better than none, it does make a difference what sort of job you get and what sort of pay is attached. Focusing on jobs that do not require a college education, Gregory Acs and Pamela Loprest (2009b) find that minority workers are typically hired into entry-level jobs requiring the fewest skills, the lowest expectations, and the most minimal requirements. Figure 3-7 illustrates the pattern, considering for each group what percent of the noncollege jobs they hold require certification or not. By way of explanation, the first bar in the graph indicates that of all the noncollege jobs held by whites, 60 percent require high school degrees. Looking at the third bar from the right, only about one-quarter of the noncollege white workforce holds entry-level positions requiring no credentials. In contrast, 44.1 percent of the noncollege Latino workforce and 42.8 percent of the noncollege workforce have entry-level jobs; this likely reflects lower levels of degree holding but it may also reflect the perceptions of employers and thus the sorting of employment.

Figure 3-8 shows that in this same strata of jobs Latinos are less likely to hold positions requiring daily reading, writing, speaking, calculations, computer use, or filling out forms. The skill sets used by white and black workers are about the same, except that blacks hold positions requiring less arithmetic and less computer use. Without on-the-job training, this trend only deepens a racially distinct skills gap.

Robert Cherry (2010) connects this disadvantage in the low-skill labor market with higher layoff rates, arguing that racial minorities are the first to go. Such job volatility is an increasingly relevant measure in the twenty-first century. This contributes to labor market instability for people of color, according to *The State of Working America*, an annual report produced by the labor-affiliated Economic Policy Institute. Because workers in this century are more likely to work many jobs instead of one over the course of

FIGURE 3-7. Percent of Noncollege Jobs for Which a Specific Factor Is Extremely Important or Required for the Job, by Race/Ethnicity of Recently Hired Worker, 2007

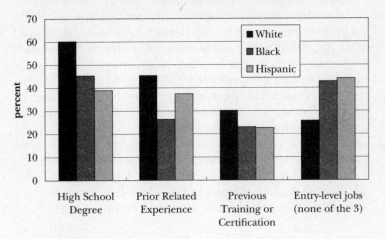

FIGURE 3-8. Percent of Noncollege Jobs in Which a Given Task Must Be Performed Daily, by Race/Ethnicity of Recently Hired Worker, 2007

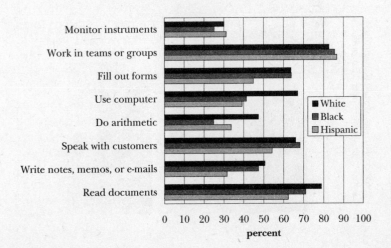

a career (Mishel, Bernstein, and Boushey, 2003), layoffs leave employees less likely to qualify for insurance, pensions, increases in salary, length of job tenure, and vacation times that accrue from promotions.

Labor turnover yields income volatility. In Figure 3-9, we look at this issue over two periods—the early 1990s and the early 2000s. We confine our attention to households earning less than 300 percent of the poverty rate since higher-income households tend to have ups and downs due to swings in the stock market or dividend income; by limiting our attention to this group, we are focusing on the typical household that relies primarily on wages. As can be seen, volatility has risen for all Americans—but the gaps have widened between whites and people of color.

Calculations by Mishel et al. (2003) show that blacks, Latinos, and even Asians are less likely to remain in their jobs than whites. And while data can certainly help tell this

FIGURE 3-9. Income Volatility by Race, 1991–1992 and 2001, for Households Earning Below 300 Percent of the Federal Poverty Level

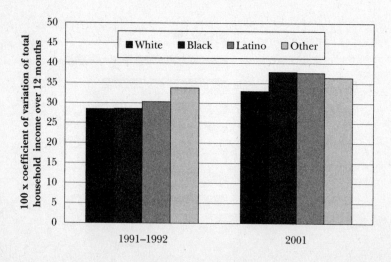

story, Barbara Ehrenreich (2001) and Katherine Newman (1999) do a great job using anecdotes to convey the gravity of losing a job. Newman's accounts of minority workers in Harlem show how difficult it is for some workers to get—and keep—even a low-skilled, low-paying job. And Ehrenreich shows that the conditions and low pay of low-wage jobs often result in high turnover. For example, low-income workers are less likely to hold stable daytime hours (Acs et al., 2001), making child-care arrangements a challenge for workers assigned evening shifts or unpredictable hours. As Figure 3-10 illustrates, job retention drops precipitously when an employee moves from the one-year to the two-year mark across all racial categories, but once again this change is greater for people of color.

Figure 3-11 illustrates the long-term trends for poverty. Despite the relative lack of movement in median household income noted earlier, there was in fact progress in reducing the black-white poverty differential through the 1960s. The reasons were straightforward: the new oppor-

FIGURE 3-10. Job Retention by Race, 1996–1999

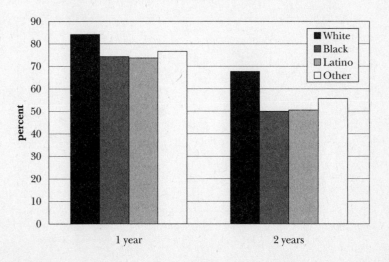

tunities wrought by the struggle against discrimination and the long economic boom of the 1960s.

The gap between blacks and whites, however, was quite persistent through the 1970s and 1980s; not until the long recovery of the 1990s do we see African Americans once again making relative gains. The Clinton years (between 1992 and 2000) were a time of strong economic improvement for blacks, as evidenced by the dramatic decline in black poverty (with persistent poverty thereafter).

The 1990s also brought another phenomenon: for the first time, Latino poverty actually exceeded (and then almost equaled) African American poverty. This is partly due to the influx of foreign-born Latinos, many of whom work for lower wages and often directly compete with U.S.-born Latinos in working-class occupations that occupy the lower tiers of the American economy. Asian Americans have a poverty rate that is slightly higher than that of Anglos, although that gap has narrowed in recent

FIGURE 3-11. Percentage of Individuals in the U.S. Living Below the Poverty Line, 1959–2007

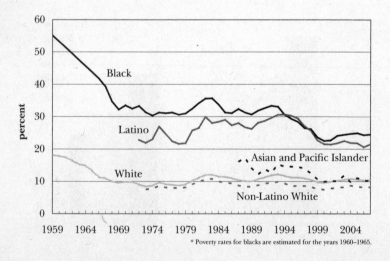

* Poverty rates for blacks are estimated for the years 1960–1965.

years. This pattern suggests that higher household and family incomes are partly driven by the sheer size of Asian households.

Race and Well-Being: Will These Differences Persist?

Against a backdrop of rising gaps in labor market volatility and income levels, we now face the need to restart an economy that has been mired in crisis. The future isn't necessarily bright. Figure 3-12, for example, indicates that nearly a third of all African American and Latino children live in poverty. Even with a steep decline in poverty among Asian children, nearly one in ten lives in poverty, which is a rate slightly higher than that for white children.

Part of the reason for the high rates of childhood poverty among African Americans and Latinos is the extraordinarily high rates of female-headed households. As can

FIGURE 3-12. Child Poverty Rate by Race/Ethnicity

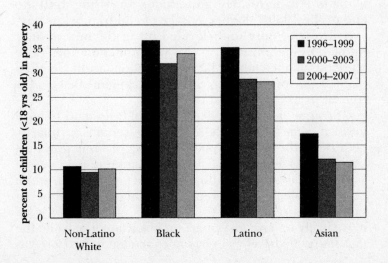

FIGURE 3-13. Percentage of Total Related Children in Female-Headed Households, by Poverty Status, 1960 to 2007

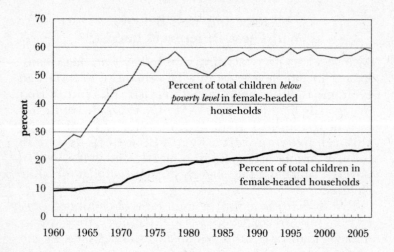

be seen in Figure 3-13, the total percentage of children living in female-headed households was rising until the end of the 1980s; the percentage of children below poverty in such households leveled off in the new millennium. The stabilization in this phenomenon does raise questions about whether family formation factors, so often blamed for low incomes, can really explain the current trends.

Of course, female-headed households do tend to have lower incomes than male-headed households, primarily because of the occupational clustering of women in low-wage sectors and lingering discrimination in pay, as well as the difficulties of holding full-time employment while being the sole provider of income, child care, and supervision. As Figure 3-14 illustrates, this set of challenges is far more likely to have an impact on black families: while the past few years have brought some increase in the percent-

FIGURE 3-14. Children in Black Families, 1968–2007

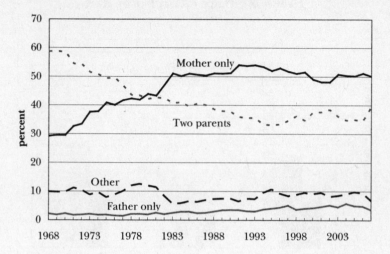

age of black children living in two-parent households and some decline in those living in female-headed households, just about half of all black children are growing up without their father at home.

Figure 3-15 also illustrates how minority children have significantly less access to health insurance, with one-fifth of Latino children uninsured. The numbers would be significantly worse—on the order of at least five percentage points more per group—if not for federal and state government efforts in recent years to expand the number of poor children covered by government programs, providing a hint of the power of equitable policies if fully realized.

While access to health care is important, it is only part of the story. In spite of high rates of poverty and limited access to health care, Latino infant mortality rates are quite similar to those of whites (see Figure 3-16), suggesting that Latino mothers' overall level of good health is able to largely offset deficits that are more commonly associated with higher rates of infant deaths. This "Latino paradox"

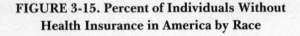

FIGURE 3-15. Percent of Individuals Without Health Insurance in America by Race

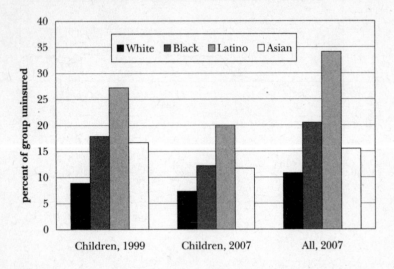

has been identified by David Hayes-Bautista, a professor of medicine at UCLA.

However, the black-white gap in infant mortality rates is significant—and other risks along the way, including higher rates for blacks of death by homicide, lead to very large racial gaps in life expectancy (see Figure 3-17).

As Melvin Oliver and Tom Shapiro (1995) argued in their pathbreaking book, *Black Wealth, White Wealth*, one's broader chances in life—not just for survival but for success—are really determined not by income but by wealth or assets, particularly since wealth can be passed on from generation to generation. As Figure 3-18 shows, there are tremendous racial gaps in rates of homeownership, a traditional indicator of wealth. Latinos' homeownership rates have risen steadily, eclipsing in 2005 African Americans' homeownership rates, and seem to have reached a plateau just under 50 percent. White Americans, meanwhile, made steady

FIGURE 3-16. Infant Mortality Rates by Race, 1990–2004

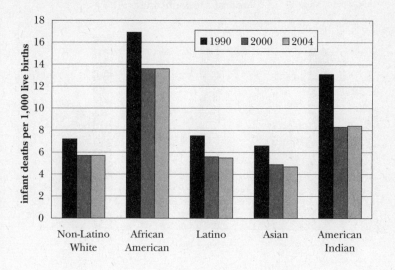

FIGURE 3-17. Life Expectancy at Birth for Whites and Blacks, 1970–2005

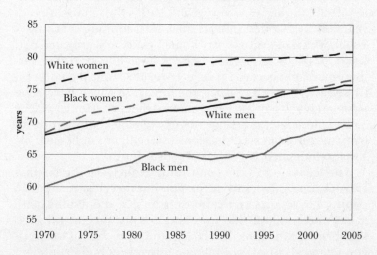

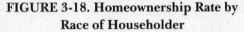

**FIGURE 3-18. Homeownership Rate by
Race of Householder**

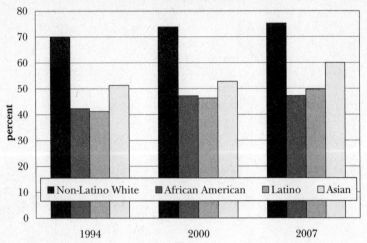

gains on their already high figures, and Asian Americans
are close to meeting them.

In his book *Being Black, Living in the Red*, Dalton Conley (1999) argues that this wealth gap is the culmination of
years of color-coded policies such as "redlining" (ACORN,
2000), which steers minority home buyers to segregated and
less desirable neighborhoods. Such a wealth gap "is not easily remediable because it largely results from the cumula-
tive effects of racial policies, the impact of which have been
passed down from one generation to the next (Conley, 1999:
134)." These inequities are not irreversible, but their dura-
bility means that racial divisions in wealth are unlikely to be
wholly eliminated anytime in the near future.

The legacy—and the continuing reality—of discrimina-
tory lending is evident in the current foreclosure crisis. A
plethora of reports on the housing bubble and its aftermath
all seem to suggest that race and not just income affected
the structure of loans. While it would seem logical for lenders to charge risky, low-income borrowers higher interest

rates on mortgages, Figure 3-19 illustrates that the racial character of high-priced loans doesn't diminish in higher-income brackets. In fact, wealthy blacks are significantly more likely to have a high-cost loan than the poorest whites (Institute on Race and Poverty, 2009). Banks covered by the Community Reinvestment Act (CRA) do help provide lower-cost loans in areas plagued by high-cost loans, but the CRA would help close racial gaps if lending institutions also took into consideration race and ethnicity overall (California Reinvestment Coalition et al., 2009).

Figure 3-20 explores the impact of foreclosures on the San Francisco Bay Area between October 2005 and October 2008. People of color made up more than two-thirds of the residents in the areas with the highest rates of foreclosures; whites made up two-thirds of the residents in the areas with the lowest rates of foreclosures. By wiping away assets, the tide of foreclosures is widening the wealth gap between whites and minorities.

Wealth, unlike income, keeps on giving through interest, dividends, and accumulation. Figure 3-21 indicates that financial wealth is even more unequally distributed than is homeownership. The Applied Research Center's report "Race and Recession" (2009) uses Federal Reserve data to show that while people of color have had modest wealth increases, whites have significantly more wealth and greater gains over time (see Figure 3-22).

Wealth accumulation is also affected by a lack of banks in low-income communities. Instead, residents in these communities rely on check cashers, payday lenders, high-cost remittance services, and high-interest home and car loan lenders. The Brookings Institution (Fellowes and Mabanta, 2008) estimates that a full-time worker forced to rely on check cashers over the span of a work life will lose about $40,000 to unnecessary fees. That's bad enough, but it's even worse because if a bank had not only deposited the check but then provided access to a savings bond, the total kitty at retirement would be nearly $90,000; if the deposits were made into a mutual fund designed for small-scale

FIGURE 3-19. High Cost Home Purchase Loans,
Across 172 Cities

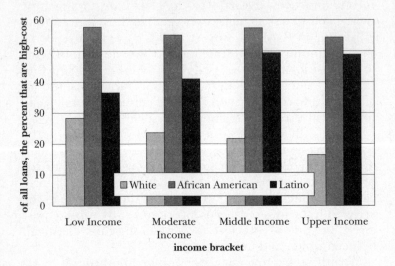

FIGURE 3-20. Bay Area Foreclosure Rates
by Race/Ethnicity

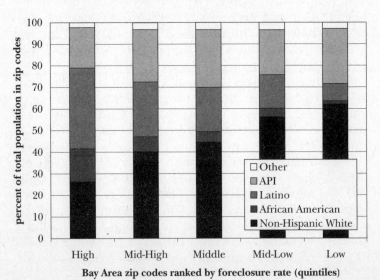

FIGURE 3-21. Mean Household Wealth, in 2009 Dollars

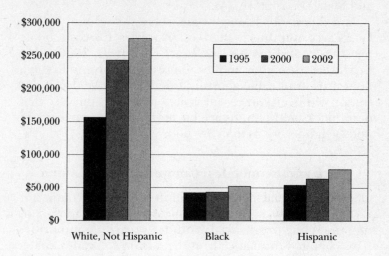

FIGURE 3-22. Median Net Worth for Families, 1992–2007

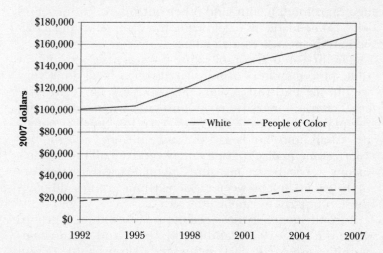

investors, the total would have hit over $360,000 (Fellowes and Mabanta, 2008: 1, 14).

And this is only the tip of the iceberg. Poorer areas also face scarce and thus higher-cost groceries, car costs, home insurance, and health care costs (Fellowes, 2006). It is expensive to be poor and even more expensive to live in a poor area. And while gentrification has led to a deconcentration of poverty in recent years, it remains the case that poor blacks and Latinos are far more likely to be living in poor neighborhoods than are poor whites.

Race and Economics: Complicating the Story

Of the many challenges that comprise the new frontier for racial issues, closing the economic and wealth gap is paramount. While overt social attitudes regarding minorities have changed dramatically in the past few decades, material progress has been far more paltry, and in some cases, the situation has worsened in the first years of the twenty-first century. To avoid having the future bring more of the same, we need to make it easier for minorities to improve neighborhood, health, and other outcomes. But progress will also be made by recognizing the complexity of factors behind the persistent inequalities.

The first step in complicating the story is a recognition that some members of minority groups have done very well in the past thirty years. Figure 3-23 charts the Gini coefficient—a measure economists use when considering inequality that ranges between zero for "perfect equality" (if all households had the same income) and one for "perfect inequality" (if one family received all the nation's income). This figure measures inequality within members of the group, not between racial or ethnic groups, although those comparisons can be inferred.

Income inequality has been on the rise within all groups since the early 1970s, and black, Asian, and Latino communities are particularly bifurcated, with wealthy African American celebrities and athletes, and the chronically unem-

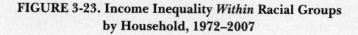

FIGURE 3-23. Income Inequality *Within* Racial Groups by Household, 1972–2007

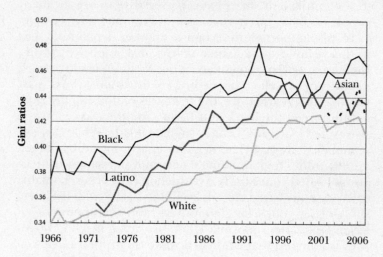

ployed; a growing wave of successful Chinese business-people and Southeast Asian refugees; accomplished Latino entrepreneurs and struggling day laborers. All these combinations make for increased income inequality among members within each group, but one group stands out: inequality among blacks is higher than that of any other group.

This also makes for some confusion in the public's vision of progress. You can clearly point to some individuals "making it," particularly in highly visible fields—and it becomes easy to suggest that discrimination has faded and that the remaining disparities may, in fact, be due to differences in talent, ambition, and skills. This view imagines away the effects of structural discrimination in terms of uneven educational opportunities, unstable family incomes, undesirable spatial locations, and other factors that make it difficult for children and parents to realize their dreams.

But rather than assuming that the exception proves the

rule—rather than letting a combination of complacency and blame take root—policymakers and civic leaders need to contemplate the average or typical experience for many people of color. And here there is quite a long way yet to go.

It's also important to recognize another dynamic implicit in this rising economic inequality *within* minority groups. Increasing polarization of economic fortunes could weaken democracy as well by deepening the isolation of very poor people. In an earlier era, the strictures of housing discrimination forced the black and Latino middle class to live in segregated black and Latino neighborhoods. While this lack of mobility obviously had negative effects, including limited opportunities to gain home equity and personal wealth, it also lessened community dysfunction. Physician, bankers, teachers, and elected officials lived side-by side with mailmen, short-order cooks, single mothers, and the unemployed, leaving social networks intact, and providing neighborhoods with leadership that could articulate their point of view at City Hall, on the shop floor, and at the school. Inner-city communities of today have been left without those stabilizing influences as middle-class blacks and Latinos have moved to housing opportunities in the suburbs.

Meanwhile, those who just moved away now find themselves at risk of losing their assets as a wave of foreclosures has hit many suburban communities in what the Federal Reserve Bank of Atlanta calls "hot-market regions," including all California metros, Las Vegas, Phoenix, and Miami (Immergluck, 2009: 26). The challenge for urban reformers is to restore a sense of stability and hope to those isolated inner-city—and, increasingly, poor suburban—neighborhoods (see Berube and Kneebone, 2006), and connect their residents to the economic mainstream. Some of the strategies for combating inner-city decay and re-creating stable mixed-income communities are noted in Chapter 4 under our policy discussion of healthy metropolitan communities. So race matters, but place matters as well—and new strategies to promote racial equity will need to consider spatial or regional issues, too.

Minority Small Business: A Bright Spot

Despite the stagnation of income and wages, there has been one bright spot on the economic horizon: the increase in minority businesses. The number of black-owned firms grew 93 percent from 1992 to 2002, well above the national rate of 33 percent. The number of Hispanic-owned firms increased at nearly the same pace (82 percent), while the number of Asian-owned firms rose by 88 percent. The tendency to form enterprises can be seen through the prism of another statistic: Figure 3-24 shows that although black self-employment rates are still generally the lowest—and by quite a bit—of any ethnic group for every level of income, in the middle-to-higher income ranges (above $40,000) Latinos are already nearly as likely to be self-employed as whites.

Similarly, immigrants are 30 percent more likely to start a business than native-born residents, representing 16.7

FIGURE 3-24. Self-Employment Among Minorities, 2005–2007

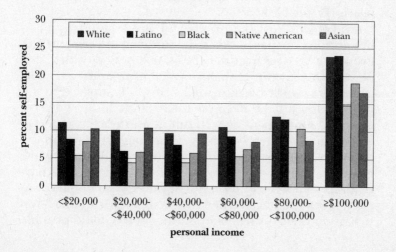

percent of *new* business owners and 12.5 percent of *all* business owners. Their enterprises span high- and low-skilled sectors and are geographically concentrated in California, New York, Florida, and New Jersey. In California, their businesses total about one-quarter of the state's business income. In the nation, immigrant business income is 11.6 percent of the total, about $67 billion. Despite the popular notion that immigrants drain our economy, these immigrants boost it (Fairlie, 2008).

Small businesses have continued their dramatic growth: from 1982 to 2002, the number of African American–owned firms nearly quadrupled, while the number of Hispanic-owned firms rose by 554 percent and the number of Asian-owned firms rose by 458 percent, all much greater than the 191 percent increase in all firms over the same period of time. Growth has generally been slower in the more recent period, 1997–2002, partly because growth rates for the earlier period were based on such a small baseline. Still, the number of black, Latino, and Asian firms grew faster than that of white firms between 1997 and 2002: 45.4 percent for blacks, 31.1 percent for Latinos, and 26.7 percent for Asians versus 7.5 percent for whites (the growth in the number of publicly held companies was nearly 30 percent).

And it isn't just the number of firms: minority businesses also outpaced white businesses in terms of the growth of receipts over the 1997–2002 period, with a 19.1 percent increase for Hispanic-owned firms and a 24.5 percent increase for black-owned firms as compared to 4.3 percent for whites. Receipts for Asian firms grew faster than for white firms as well but at a lower 9.3 percent. The overall pattern—both over the long haul and in the recent period—suggests that minority businesses have been establishing themselves, exploring new niches, particularly exports based on immigrant ties to home countries, and with black-owned firms, also servicing the "new urban markets" (such as in ethnic foods) made possible by the significant presence of people of color in America's densely populated central cities.*

Despite growth, minority firms are still underrepresented: African Americans, for example, were 11.8 percent of the population in 2002, but black-owned firms were only 5 percent of all firms; Latinos accounted for 13.5 percent of the population and 6.6 percent of all firms.[1] Although still low, these shares are higher than in the past—from 1982 to 2002, minority businesses grew from 7 percent to 18 percent of the national share.

The majority of minority firms are very small. In 2002, for example, nearly 40 percent of Latino-owned firms had receipts of less than $10,000; average annual receipts for Latino-owned businesses were slightly over $140,000, well below the nearly $1 million average for all firms. Indeed, many minority firms are essentially arrangements of self-employment: while 24 percent of all firms have employees, only 13 percent of the Hispanic firms and 8 percent of the black-owned firms hired outside workers. On the other hand, 29 percent of API-owned firms have employees, meaning they generate jobs.[2]

Even at this modest scale, however, minority companies can be good for equity and community development. A 1995 survey of the black-owned businesses in the Atlanta metropolitan area, for example, found that 24.6 percent of the employees in black-owned firms in the city of Atlanta came from low-income, inner-city neighborhoods; even black-owned businesses in suburban areas of Atlanta drew nearly 20 percent of their employees from low-income neighborhoods (Boston, 2001: 192). Harvard Business School professor Michael Porter, famous for exploring the competitive advantage of nations, touts the growth opportunities for minority-owned, inner-city firms and has

---

*While 1.8 percent of all businesses exported in 1992, 2.3 percent of Asian firms, and 2.5 percent of Latino firms were involved in exports.

argued that they and other small businesses are a key part of neighborhood revitalization (Porter, 1995).

Small businesses are, indeed, the greatest source of new employment in the inner city, but connecting local residents to these jobs is still an issue—the Initiative for a Competitive Inner City reports that only 22 percent of inner-city jobs are held by inner-city residents (Initiative for a Competitive Inner City, 2005). Thus, efforts that focus on encouraging the establishment of minority-owned businesses may help to promote workforce and community development for people of color, but to be truly successful, such strategies need to be linked with making local residents job-ready and job-connected.

Efforts to promote minority small-business and inner-city development may also help the nation's overall economic scenario, partly given the key role of small business in driving America's "new economy." The Milken Institute, usually concerned with broad economic trends, released a report focusing on minority business. The authors noted that "absent broad-based institutional investor participation in minority and immigrant business communities . . . continued growth in the American economy is impossible, affecting not just minority businesses but [also] putting the nation's macroeconomy at risk" (Yago and Pankrantz, 2000: iii).

To realize the potential, certain key issues will need to be addressed. For example, while the small scale of minority enterprise partly reflects a tendency to concentrate in the service sector, another limit on business growth is the "redlining" described earlier: nearly 37 percent of all businesses use bank credit, but the figure for minority businesses is 27 percent, with an especially low 15 percent for black-owned businesses. One study found that, controlling for the usual factors used to judge creditworthiness, Latino firms were 12 percent more likely to be denied credit, while black firms were twice as likely to be turned down (Cavalluzo and Cavalluzo, 1998). A later report found that differences in endowments—the characteristics of firms and their owners—explain about one-third of the difference in denial rates across minority groups, and for the difference between whites and blacks, that is related to credit history. While personal wealth is not a large factor in loan denials for blacks, it is slightly more so for Latinos and Asians (Cavalluzo and Wolken, 2005).

The Milken Institute report also suggested that there is a significant gap on the venture capital (VC) side, linking this in part to the separate social networks of minority owners and the larger venture investors. This has improved somewhat, thanks in part to newly available public pension funds for funding the minority VC industry, but these VCs usually target businesses that have highly educated owners with considerable management experience and which have sales revenues over $1 million—clearly the exception, not the rule, for minority businesses (Bates, Bradford, and Sass Rubin, 2006). Analyses of the longest-running firms owned by blacks suggest that minority procurement programs have been critical to gaining the experience needed to compete in the open market.

However, the legal environment for such specific programs has become problematic, despite the fact that such programs do seem to be effective at generating faster growth in minority enterprises (Boston, 2001: 214–217). With credit still denied and key tools for advancement taken off the table, one has to be doubly impressed by the entrepreneurial spirit now sweeping ethnic America—and wonder how much more could be accomplished in building individual and community wealth should policy leaders and financial lenders become more supportive.

The Driving Factors of Inequality

In considering the persistent patterns of inequality, the obvious question is "Why does it exist?" One factor is discrimination. While the popular notion is that most egregious abuses of racial preferences were eliminated by civil rights legislation, clear evidence of discrimination remains at the workplace and elsewhere. There are, of course, the dramatic statistics on credit denial and wealth accumulation presented earlier in the chapter—a trend that constrains the full potential of minority entrepreneurship. But discrimination persists in labor and housing markets as well, as indicated, for example, by the story of apartment searching in Los Angeles told in Chapter 2.

One telling study of employers' preferences, for example, suggests that black males continue to face an often unspoken skepticism in the hiring process, partly because of employer presumptions that younger African Americans lack the "soft skills"—workplace habits of promptness, courtesy, teamwork, and willingness to learn—that have become increasingly important in the contemporary workplace (Moss and Tilly, 2001). As can be seen in Figure 3-25, employers have extraordinarily negative views of black youth, particularly in terms of motivation.

A 1998 study by recruitment firm Korn/Ferry International suggests that the problem is not limited to the lower echelons of the workplace hierarchy. Nearly 60 percent of

FIGURE 3-25. Employer's Perception of Skills, by Race

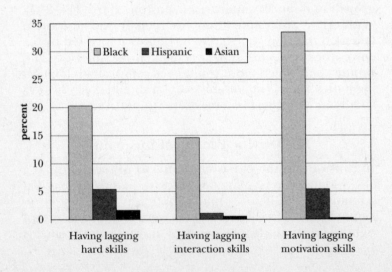

minority senior-level executives reported observing a double standard in assignments or harsh and unfair treatment of minorities, with the problems most severe for blacks and less so for Asians. The consequences of this disparity in treatment are quite real: the U.S. Department of Labor's Glass Ceiling Commission reported that fewer than 3 percent of the top-level managers in the nation's largest firms are minorities.[3] Even boards are not reflective of national demography. In 2004, only 6 percent of Fortune 1000 board seats were held by minorities.[4] While the nonprofit sector seems a likely candidate for greater inclusion, a 2006 study of nonprofit managers found that only 18 percent of executives under forty-five years old were nonwhite (Bell et al., 2006). Recall from Figure 1-3 that no less than 35 percent of this age group are minorities. There is also a lack of diversity on foundation boards. In 2000, 34.4 percent of foundation board members were women, and 10.9 percent were persons of color. Board members help shape the foundation's vision and policies, so it is imperative that the boards have skilled and resourceful members who are knowledgeable about diverse populations (Kwoh and Tang, 2003).

Discrimination in housing also remains a serious issue. Various "matched pair" tests—in which white and minority testers adopt similar background profiles to search for houses and observe for instances of discrimination—still yield evidence of steering by realtors.[5] The continuing patterns of residential segregation, albeit lessened from earlier decades, attest to this process. Meanwhile, social discrimination, including racial profiling by the police, continues to be a disturbing presence on the American scene. (See our discussion of john powell's analysis of conscious and unconscious racial decisions in Chapter 2 for underlying motivations.)

But discrimination by whites in employment and housing cannot fully explain the patterns, particularly given the evidence of attitudinal shifts and the long-term change in the legal climate regarding civil rights. While individual decisions to discriminate are important, key structural barriers to equality also remain, from the geographical mismatch that lands many minorities far away from employment to the disparities in drug sentencing that result as much from income as from race. Tackling the continuing disparities in social and economic opportunities requires new policies and strategies that are focused on achieving equity. Chapter 4 examines in more detail some of the emerging solutions to these persistent problems.

In addition to discrimination, another key factor in continuing inequality is that there are large educational differences among groups, accounting for some but not all of the differences in economic outcomes. To the extent that the educational gap is created by uneven access to quality education, aggressive policies should be developed. Part of the uneven quality of education in inner cities results in higher dropout rates among black and Latino students, as shown in Figure 3-26; dropout rates here refer to individuals between the ages of sixteen and twenty-four who are not enrolled in school or have not completed a high school program, including a GED. The national data actually masks the crisis of inner-city schools, which are a smaller percentage of the population but have high concentrations of drop-outs. For example, in Cleveland, one-third of black men above the age of twenty-five lack a high school diploma; in Cincinnati, only 19 percent of black male students graduate on time.[6] Latinos have nearly quadruple the rate of white dropouts, pulled so high mainly because of male dropouts. The difference between genders is much lower across other ethnicities.*

The mood in the country with regard to education

---

*The observant reader will note that the black failure to complete high school in Figure 3–26 is only about 11 percent, far short of the one-quarter figure with which we opened the book. That is because, following standard practice, we are reporting here the so-called "status dropout rate" for youths aged sixteen to twenty-four. Aside from allowing more time to complete high school and counting those still in school, this figure also includes those who obtain their GED. Interestingly, this dropout rate is higher for black females than for black males; the gender difference switches for Latinos, with males much higher than females.

FIGURE 3-26. High School Dropout Rates by Race, 1972–2006

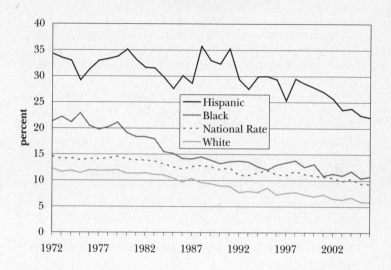

reform has generally been positive, with both Republicans and Democrats seeming to agree that targeting low-income minority schools is necessary. There is significant disagreement, however, on the mix of funding, testing, and parental choice that will help these schools improve their performance and the life chances of children in them. And some policies, designed to help all students, can be detrimental to some, as seen in Box 3-1. Still, a renewed focus on education has the potential to reduce inequalities later in life, and the consensus on targeting is heartening.

President Obama has picked up on this problem and reframed it. In his February 2009 speech to the joint houses of Congress, he said: "It is our responsibility as lawmakers and as educators to make this [education] system work. But it is the responsibility of every citizen to participate in it. So tonight, I ask every American to commit to at least one year or more of higher education or career training. This

Box 3-1. High School Exit Exams Leave Female and Minority Students Failing

High school exit exams, intended to increase student performance, actually decrease equity. In California,as a result of this new policy, minority and female students are graduating at even lower rates than white male counterparts. Graduation rates dropped between 15 and 19 percent for low-achieving black, Hispanic, and Asian students due to the implementation of the graduation exit exam, while the figure for white students was a statistically insignificant 1 percent. The corresponding decrease in graduation rates for female students as a whole was nearly twice as high as it was for male students. In sum, the exit exams in California have a large negative impact on graduation rates, with up to 22,500 students (4.5 percent) failing to receive their high school diplomas yearly due to the reinstatement of high school exit exams.

Especially unsettling, these students who fail are doing so at rates higher than makes sense, given their scores on other standardized tests. "Stereotype threat," where minority and female students perceive that they are expected to fail, adds pressure to an already high-stakes test. The authors of the study who discovered this argue that the combined pressures, rather than an implicit bias built into the exam, reduce performance and graduation rates.

Mandated public high school exit exams are growing in use throughout the nation, with twenty-two states requiring their use as of 2007, and four more intending to implement this policy by 2015. This will affect at least 70 percent of all students nationwide with the goal of achieving greater accountability and standardization of the graduation process. The authors of the study suggest stereotype threat intervention techniques or compensatory efforts to raise the performance capabilities of target student groups if exit exam policies are to be continued by state governments in the future (Reardon et al., 2009).

can be community college or a four-year school; vocational training or an apprenticeship. But whatever the training may be, every American will need to get more than a high school diploma."[7]

So it's a matter of personal responsibility, to be sure—but also a matter of social responsibility. Working for racial equity—trying to address the educational achievement and opportunity gaps—is part of working for a better America. And it's more important now than it ever was: the evidence suggests that while education has always mattered to economic outcomes, the returns to a degree, an extra year of school, or time in a good training program yield an even higher-percent increase than they did in an earlier time.

The reason is that the better jobs in our new economy are heavily skill-oriented—full of specialized knowledge and skills to enable working with technology and teams (Osterman, 2001: 75). In Chapter 4 (see Table 4-1), we detail growth in the high- and low-skilled occupations—but economic progress will only go to the former. For the low-skilled, there is a certain threat of getting stuck in dead-end jobs where few skills are required, few are learned, and little is earned.

Of course, the emphasis on education and skills for a new economy could lead some to think that the only standard for measuring progress is how many folks go on to a four-year university. In fact, community colleges are actually a linchpin for the future of our nation—they offer reasonably priced courses that offer highly useful skill upgrades—but they are typically undervalued and, as a result, underdeveloped. For adults and many minorities, they are a primary source of education after high school—35 percent of community college students are minorities and nearly 40 percent are the first in their generation to attend college. Even though most attention is focused on universities, nearly half of all undergrads attend community colleges.[8] In the next chapter, this book identifies community colleges as a key solution for creating the twenty-first century workforce.

Geography is also crucially important. In his seminal book *Poverty and Place*, Paul Jargowsky (1997) documented the increase in the concentration of poverty over the 1980s, particularly among people of color, in U.S. metropolitan areas. While African Americans and Latinos comprised less than 24 percent of the total U.S. population living in metropolitan areas, they were over 80 percent of those living in high-poverty conditions in urban America. This geographic isolation or concentration was not accidental. As Massey and Denton (1993) argue, racial discrimination in housing markets allowed whites an easier exodus from the city, and since blacks are more likely to be poor, boxing in communities through segregation will necessarily generate an increase in the concentration of poverty. This was, Massey and Denton stress, not simply a matter of private choice. As powell (2000) documents, a series of federal and local policies helped structure those choices, including early restrictions in Federal Housing Administration (FHA) loans, the insistence on large public housing projects, and local zoning laws and restrictive covenants.

This geographic concentration declined dramatically over the 1990s as the fruits of that economic boom, evidenced in some of our earlier data, began to reach minority populations (Jargowky, 2003). This was coupled with another phenomenon explored below—the suburbanization of the poor, particularly minorities who began to move to other parts of the metropolitan region (Swanstrom et al., 2004). The result was a deconcentration of the desperately poor but a spreading of the poverty problem in ways that suggested a need to have a more metropolitan approach.

The ongoing increase in the suburbanization of blacks and Latinos is shown in Figure 3-27. As the figure indicates, the suburbanization rates for whites and Asians still exceed the suburbanization rates for blacks and Latinos. Still, the gap is slowly closing as the image of the lily-white suburb gives way to the reality of a more multihued environment.[9] The challenge, of course, is that some of the outward movement has been to the older and often run-down "inner ring" suburbs immediately surrounding central cities, and these communities are frequently as fiscally and socially stressed as their central-city neighbors (Orfield, 1997).

However, those left behind in even high-poverty urban areas find their problems exacerbated in several different ways. Figure 3-28, for example, illustrates that employment has been moving rapidly to the outlying reaches of America's metropolitan regions where formerly few jobs were, but now the share of jobs is nearing the share of people.

FIGURE 3-27. Suburbanization of the Population in the 100 Largest Metro Areas, 1980–2000

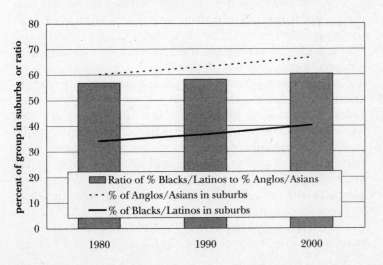

Partly as a result, the ratio of poverty in a region's principal (or larger) cities to poverty in its suburban areas has been rising consistently over the past several decades (see Figure 3-29). With the reurbanization of our cities, we might actually see this trend reverse—but given the vagaries of gentrification, the result might be an improvement in place but not racial equity.

Segregation and concentration also contribute to limited social networks. Despite the proliferation of job placement agencies and temporary employment firms, most job seekers still obtain employment through friends, neighbors, and acquaintances. In areas of concentrated poverty, social networks are often restricted to those in the immediate vicinity—and their connections with the job markets are not the best. As a result, finding good jobs is difficult for many inner-city residents (see Johnson et al., 2000, and Pastor and Marcelli, 2000). Glenn Loury (1998: 119) notes how neighborhood networks may also play a role in the formation of norms and expectations about employment, although he too stresses the straightforward way in which job connections matter. In his words, "Opportunity travels along the synapses of these social networks." Indeed, the lack of networks in inner-city communities is one way that inequality is reproduced over time, even when conscious discrimination may not be occurring. Efforts to build out of the deep recession must then make deliberate efforts to connect low-income people to jobs.

Concentrated poverty has a sharp impact on networks and contributes to other problems, such as higher crime rates, substandard housing, a lack of role models, and inadequate schools. It even affects the air we breathe: while wealthy communities can fight off "locally unwanted land uses" (LULUs) and wealthy individuals can choose to live elsewhere, LULUs like petroleum refineries and industrial plants are disproportionately concentrated near minority and low-income neighborhoods.

One measure of this reality is the likelihood of living near a facility listed in the U.S. Environmental Protec-

FIGURE 3-28. Suburbanization of Employment and Population in Top 100 Metro Areas, 1980–2000

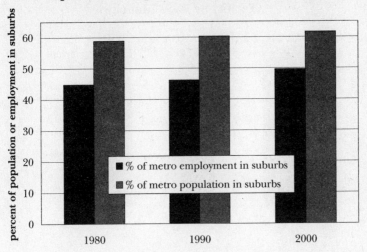

FIGURE 3-29. Ratio of Principal City to Metro Poverty in Top 100 Metro Areas, 1980–2000

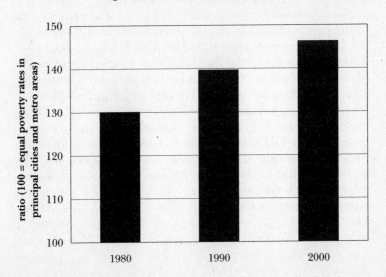

FIGURE 3-30. San Francisco Bay Area, 2000: Proximity to an Active Toxic Release Inventory (TRI) Facility by Race/Ethnicity

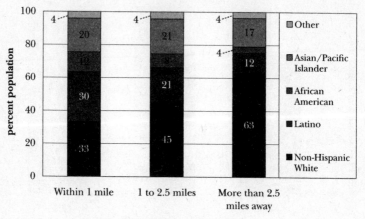

tion Agency's Toxics Release Inventory (TRI). Even in the pristine San Francisco Bay Area—a place that prides itself on its commitment to multicultural values and an egalitarian and open spirit—those living within one mile of a TRI facility with active air releases are two-thirds people of color, while those living more than two and a half miles away are just under two-thirds white (see Figure 3-30).

And this is not just an unfortunate correlation with income: Figure 3–31 indicates that while the likelihood of living near a TRI facility declines with household income, African Americans, Latinos, and Asians are more likely to be near such a facility at every level of income. Indeed, white households making less than $25,000 a year have a lower chance of facing exposure than do black, Asian, and Latino households making more than $100,000 a year (Pastor, Morello-Frosch, and Sadd, 2007). Concerns

FIGURE 3-31. Percentage Households Within 1 Mile of an Active TRI Facility (2003) by Income and Race/Ethnicity in the San Francisco Bay Area

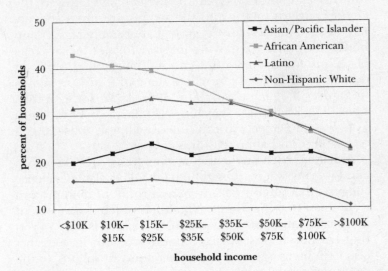

around climate change may offer opportunities to remedy some of these environmental injustices, an issue discussed in Chapter 4.

Another issue that is often viewed as worsening inequality but, if done right, can work toward the common good is immigration. Immigrants have a positive effect on the economy, shoring up labor supply, helping industries that might otherwise relocate offshore stay in place, and paying federal taxes and Social Security, while typically demanding little in return since many are often reluctant to make use of federal programs. They tend to settle in over time, buying houses, and contributing to their communities' vitality.

The problem is that all politics is local and every place has its own unique history, so that immigrants become characters in an already muddled drama that has likely been playing out for decades before their arrival. Immigrants may boost federal government revenue, but they can strain local services, including schools and hospitals. And in neighborhoods that are already a bit tattered, the changes are dramatic and the strains are often sharply felt. In Los Angeles, for example, Latinos, immigrants and nonimmigrants, are moving into the former heart of the black community in South Central. The resulting shift can be seen most strongly in school demographics, as shown in Figures 3-32a and 3-32b: in 1981–1982, for example, Locke High School, a flagship secondary school in South L.A., was 98 percent African American but in 2004–2005 it was 63 percent Latino (Pastor and Ortiz, 2009).

Much has been made of how immigrants are taking jobs and lowering wages, though in truth, all available evidence suggests that job displacement as a result of immigration is minimal to nonexistent. Nonetheless, job displacement is typically emphasized by the media, which is fond of pitting Latinos against African Americans. But immigrants also help invigorate the overall economy by adding to the labor and capital mix. This boosting of revenues and salaries can also help bump African Americans into managerial positions as the lower ranks get filled by immigrants. Where displacement and wage-dampening effects have been shown, the impact is on U.S.-born Latinos who are the closest substitutes in the labor market to immigrants.

Still, it is at the local level that people have seen the janitorial and hotel industries in some regions shift from primarily black to overwhelmingly immigrant. To defray these tensions, in Los Angeles, the Service Employees International Union (SEIU) has stepped in to organize workers, both black and Latino, for better economic outcomes. After victories in the hotel and janitorial industries, the largely Latino SEIU launched its Five Days for Freedom campaign in the summer of 2006 to sign up thousands of licensed security guards, a sector that is 70 percent African American in the region. Explicit in their campaign was the desire

FIGURE 3-32a. South Central Los Angeles High School Demography, 1981–1982 School Year

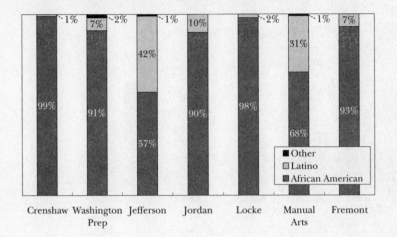

FIGURE 3-32b. South Central Los Angeles High School Demography, 2004–2005 School Year

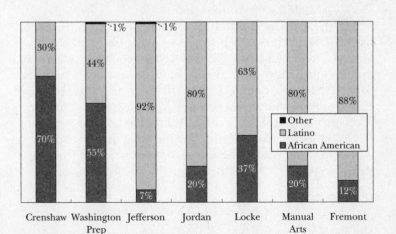

FIGURE 3-33. College-Educated Foreign-Born Workers in Unskilled Occupations, 2005–2006.

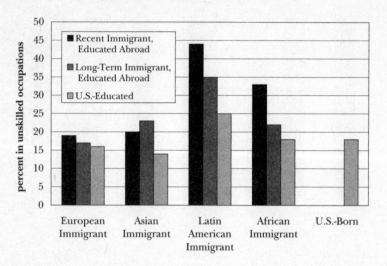

to bring economic benefits to black Angelenos, and in November of 2006, more than 5,000 guards won the right to unionize.[10] Actions like these calm real or perceived tensions associated with immigration.

Further, if the United States accepted more international credentials, it would lessen competition for low-wage jobs (see Figure 3-33). Unable to work in their fields, college-educated immigrants from Asia, Latin America, and Africa are working in unskilled professions. Permitting trained immigrants to work in their fields would be a "win-win" solution for everyone involved, freeing up jobs in the labor market for the people who most need them while opening up opportunities for newcomers who have valuable skills to contribute to the American economy.

A New World, A New Agenda

We have focused in this chapter on the economic side of our racial equity equation, stressing how continuing discrimination, differences in educational opportunity, and changes in our metropolitan geography have all played a role in the persistent racial inequalities we seek to explain—and address.

Of course, such a focus on the economy, education, and neighborhood can be a limited—and limiting—view. It is not enough to struggle for material equality. Working on improving human relations is essential for diminishing the stereotyping that reduces Asians to foreign "others," renders black and Latino teens special targets of police harassment, and transforms derogatory terms for Native Americans into accepted names for sports teams. Challenging these perspectives is a worthy battle—and it is one that will have real consequences, particularly to the extent that negative images in the media and elsewhere influence teachers' perceptions of students, employers' perceptions of workers, and Americans' perception of our common destiny.

Yet simply reducing prejudice is not enough. A more diverse America is a positive outcome; a more just America would be even better. Achieving equity will require material as well as psychological progress. To do so, America needs both an honest examination of the legacy we inherit, the present-day structures we need to transform, and the challenges the future will bring.

Thus, the economy is paramount—and now in a very new and urgent way. Moreover, calling for racial equity can no longer be considered a plea for special interests. Rather, it is a cry to right a ship that has gone desperately astray for virtually all Americans, and must be corrected for the least of us to make it work well for most of us.

Since the early 1970s, manufacturing centers have bled unionized jobs—once the stepping-stones to individual minority economic improvement—and the middle class has thinned. The dismantling of production to places in the developing world has been worrisome; but it has been greeted with the admonition that at least *we* would be keeping the knowledge jobs and thus would be able to survive and consume to our hearts' content.

But who are *we*? It turns out that *we've* thinned the middle. Engineers, scientists, and researchers huddle together, cranking out new ideas at the speed of light while service workers ease the way, making copies, fixing computer problems, networking phone lines, cleaning carpets. The new ideas that are created in this uneven synergy are turned material in the factories of other countries and returned here for sale. The occupational and income divide has become sharp—while there are professionals of all ethnicities, the bottom of the jobs ladder often seems delegated to blacks and Latinos.

But what happens when the whole game is up, when the artifice of consumption is ripped away by the reality of debt, when the proliferation of jobs without benefits spreads the worry about inadequate health insurance beyond Latinos and blacks, when the career ladders confronting all Americans miss rungs that many minorities have experienced for decades? In this sense, America is not simply in a postindustrial world—it is in a post-Katrina world, where the bitter fruit of our collective disconnection, in which we have left the most vulnerable the least protected, has spilled over into an entire city in the case of a hurricane and an entire nation in the case of the economy.

It all implies that achieving racial equity is central to our common American future. It implies that the civil rights agenda of the twenty-first century must go beyond traditional concerns to tackle the broad issues of economic opportunity and urban and metropolitan reform. And it implies that leadership must begin to build a world in which the concerns of what will soon not be the minority become the concerns of all.

Notes

[1] The percent of black and Latino business owners is based on Table 3 in Lowrey, 2007, where the number of firms by ethnicity was divided by "all firms," which includes publicly held firms.

[2] Unless otherwise cited, the data in this section are from Lowrey (2007).

[3] Todd Datz, "Equity," *CIO Magazine*, January 15, 2000.

[4] Torres, Blanca, "Women, Minorities Still Have Small Presence in Boardrooms," *Seattle Times*, October 3, 2004.

[5] For more on paired tests, see Fix and Turner, 1999. A study by the Urban Institute using paired tests found that minorities received less information about loan products and were more likely to be offered higher rates (Turner and Skidmore, 1999).

[6] *Untapped Potential: African-American Males in Northeast Ohio*, Policy-Bridge, December 2005; *The Rap on Culture: How Anti-Education Messages in Media, at Home, and on the Street Hold Back African American Youth*, PolicyBridge, May 2007.

[7] President Barack Obama, speech to a joint session of Congress, February 24, 2009.

[8] American Association of Community Colleges. January 2008 data, http://www2.aacc.nche.edu/research/index.htm.

[9] All data aggregated to the June 2003 Census definitions of Core-Based Statistical Areas (CBSAs) and Principal Cities from the 2000 Census tract level. Data for 1980 and 1990 from Geolytics Census CD 1980 and Census CD 1990—long-form summary data in 2000 census tract geography; 2000 data from the 2000 U. S. Decennial Census, SF1. Part of the changing demographics is due to immigration. University of Albany (GA) sociologist John Logan, who analyzed suburbs in 330 metropolitan areas, suggests that immigrants are moving to the suburbs "as their first step when they arrive in the country. It used to be you go to the city and then the suburbs" (Nasser, 2001).

[10] For more, see the Stand for Security Coalition's article at http://www.standforsecuritycoalition.com/news/061122ourweekly.html.

References

Acs, Gregory, and Pamela Loprest. 2009a. "Working for Cents on the Dollar: Race and Ethnic Wage Gaps in the Noncollege Labor Market." Low-Income Working Families, Paper 13. Urban Institute. March.

———. 2009b. "Job Differences by Race and Ethnicity in the Low-Skill Job Market." Urban Institute Brief No. 4. February.

Acs, Gregory, Katherine Ross Phillips, and Daniel McKenzie. 2001. "Playing by the Rules but Losing the Game: Americans in Low-Income Working Families." In Richard Kazis and Marc Miller, eds., *Low Wage Workers in the New Economy*. Washington DC: Urban Institute Press.

Applied Research Center. 2009. "Race and Recession: How Inequity Rigged the Economy and How to Change the Rules." http://www.arc.org/recession.

Association of Community Organizations for Reform Now (ACORN). 2000. *Home Equity and Inequity: An Analysis of Racial and Economic Dis-*

parities in Home Purchase Mortgage Lending in Fifty Metropolitan Areas. Washington, DC: ACORN.

Austin, Algernon. 2009. "Among College-Educated, African Americans Hardest Hit by Unemployment." Economic Policy Institute. Available at http://www.epi.org/economic_snapshots/entry/snapshots_20090422.

Bates, Timothy, William Bradford, and Julia Sass Rubin. 2006. "The Viability of the Minority-Oriented Venture-Capital Industry Under Alternative Financing Arrangements." *Economic Development Quarterly.* 20 (2): 178–191.

Bell, Jeanne, Richard Moyers, Timothy Wolfred, and Natasha D'Silva. 2006. *Daring to Lead 2006: A National Study of Nonprofit Executive Leadership.* CompassPoint Nonprofit Services and the Meyer Foundation.

Bertrand, Marianne, and Sendhil Mullainathan. 2003. "Are Emily and Greg More Employable than Lakisha and Jamal? A Field Experiment on Labor Market Discrimination." Cambridge, MA: National Bureau of Economic Research, Working Paper 9873.

Berube, Alan, and Elizabeth Kneebone. 2006. *Two Steps Back: City and Suburban Poverty Trends: 1999–2005.* Brookings Institution Metropolitan Policy Program, Living Cities Census Series.

Boston, Thomas D. 2001. "Trends in Minority-Owned Businesses." In Neil J. Smelser, William Julius Wilson, and Faith Mitchell, eds., *Becoming America: Racial Trends and Their Consequences.* Vol. 2. Washington, DC: National Academy Press.

California Reinvestment Coalition, Community Reinvestment Association of North Carolina, Empire Justice Center, Massachusetts Affordable Housing Alliance, Neighborhood Economic Development Advocacy Project, Ohio Fair Lending Coalition, and the Woodstock Institute. 2009. *Paying More for the American Dream III: Promoting Responsible Lending to Lower-Income Communities and Communities of Color.* Available at http://www.empirejustice.org/assets/pdf/publications/reports/american-dream-III.pdf.

Cavalluzo, Ken, and Linda Cavalluzo. 1998. "Market Structure and Discrimination: The Case of Small Businesses." *Journal of Money, Credit, and Banking* 30 (4): 771–792.

Cavalluzo, Ken, and John Wolken. 2005. "Small Business Loan Turndowns, Personal Wealth, and Discrimination." *Journal of Business* 78 (6): 2153–2177.

Cherry, Robert. 2010. *Third Way Policies: How They Can Help Working Families.* New York: NYU Press, forthcoming.

Conley, Dalton. 1999. *Being Black, Living in the Red: Race, Wealth, and Social Policy in America.* Berkeley, CA: University of California Press.

Ehrenreich, Barbara. 2001. *Nickel and Dimed: On (Not) Getting by in America.* New York: Henry Holt.

Fairlie, Robert. 2008. *Estimating the Contribution of Immigrant Business Own-*

ers to the U.S. Economy. Prepared for the Small Business Administration Office of Advocacy. Santa Cruz, CA, and Washington, DC.

Fellowes, Matt. 2006. *From Poverty, Opportunity: Putting the Market to Work for Lower Income Families*. Brookings Institution Metropolitan Policy Program. Washington, DC: Brookings Institution.

Fellowes, Matt, and Mia Mabanta. 2008. "Banking on Wealth: America's New Retail Banking Infrastructure and Its Wealth-Building Potential." Brookings Institution Metropolitan Policy Program. Washington, DC: Brookings Institution.

Fix, Michael, and Margery Austin Turner, eds. 1999. *A National Report Card on Discrimination in America: The Role of Testing*. Washington, DC: Urban Institute.

Hayes-Bautista, David E. 1993. "Mexicans in Southern California: Societal Enrichment or Wasted Opportunity?" In Abraham F. Lowenthal and Katrina Burgess, eds., *The California-Mexico Connection*. Stanford, CA: Stanford University Press.

Immergluck, Dan. 2009. "Intrametropolitan Patterns of Foreclosed Homes: ZIP-Code-Level Distributions of Real-Estate-Owned (REO) Properties During the U.S. Mortgage Crisis." Community Affairs Discussion Paper. Federal Reserve Bank of Atlanta.

Initiative for a Competitive Inner City (ICIC). 2005. *State of the Inner City Economies: Small Businesses in the Inner City*. Boston, MA, and Washington, DC: U.S. Small Business Administration.

Institute on Race and Poverty. 2009. "Communities in Crisis: Race and Mortgage Lending in the Twin Cities." University of Minnesota Law School.

Jargowsky, Paul. 1997. *Poverty and Place: Ghettos, Barrios, and the American City*. New York: Russell Sage Foundation.

———. 2003. *Stunning Progress, Hidden Problems: The Dramatic Decline of Concentrated Poverty in the 1990s*. Brookings Institution Center on Urban and Metropolitan Policy. Washington, DC: Brookings Institution.

Johnson, James H., Jr., Elisa Jayne Bienenstock, Walter C. Farrell, Jr., and Jennifer L. Glanville. 2000. "Bridging Social Networks and Female Labor Force Participation in a Multiethnic Metropolis." In Lawrence D. Bobo, Melvin L. Oliver, James H. Johnson, Jr., and Abel Valenzuela, Jr., eds., *Prismatic Metropolis: Inequality in Los Angeles*. New York: Russell Sage Foundation.

Kom/Ferry International. 1998. "Diversity in the Executive Suite: Creating Successful Career Paths and Strategies." http://www.komferry.com/.

Kwoh, Stewart, and Bonnie Tang. 2003. "The Foundation Board for the Twenty-First Century." In Frank L. Ellsworth and Joseph Lumarda, eds., *From Grantmaker to Leader*. Hoboken, NJ: John Wiley.

Loury, Glenn C. 1998. "Discrimination in the Post-Civil Rights Era: Beyond Market Interactions." *Journal of Economic Perspectives* 12 (2): 117–126.

Lowrey, Ying. 2007. *Minorities in Business: A Demographic Review of Minority Business Ownership*. Office of Economic Research, Office of Advocacy. Washington, DC: U.S. Small Business Administration.

Massey, Douglas S., and Nancy A. Denton. 1993. *American Apartheid: Segregation and the Making of the Underclass*. Cambridge, MA: Harvard University Press.

Mishel, Lawrence, Jared Bernstein, and Heather Boushey. 2003. *The State of Working America 2002/2003*. Economic Policy Institute and Cornell University Press. Ithaca, NY: Cornell University Press.

Moss, Philip, and Chris Tilly. 2001. *Stories Employers Tell: Race, Skill, and Hiring in America*. New York: Russell Sage Foundation.

Nasser, Haya El. 2001. "Minorities Reshape Suburbs." *USA Today*, July 9.

Newman, Katherine. 1999. *No Shame in My Game: The Working Poor in the Inner City*. New York: Knopf and the Russell Sage Foundation.

Oliver, Melvin, and Tom Shapiro. 1995. *Black Wealth, White Wealth: A New Perspective on Racial Inequality*. New York: Routledge.

Orfield, Myron. 1997. *Metropolitics: A Regional Agenda for Community and Stability*. Washington, DC: Brookings Institution Press.

Osterman, Paul. 2001. "Employers in the Low-Wage/Low-Skill Labor Market." In Richard Kazis and Marc Miller, eds., *Low Wage Workers in the New Economy*. Washington, DC: Urban Institute Press.

Pastor, Manuel Jr., and Enrico Marcelli. 2000. "Men N the Hood: Spatial, Skill, and Social Mismatch for Male Workers in Los Angeles." *Urban Geography* 21(6): 474–496.

Pastor, Manuel, Rachel Morello-Frosch, and James Sadd. 2007. *Still Toxic After All These Years: Air Quality and Environmental Justice in the San Francisco Bay Area*. Santa Cruz, CA: Center for Justice, Tolerance, and Community.

Pastor, Manuel, and Rhonda Ortiz. 2009. *Immigrant Integration in Los Angeles: Strategic Directions for Funders*. Los Angeles: Program for Environmental and Regional Equity and the Center for the Study of Immigrant Integration at the University of Southern California.

Porter, Michael E. 1995. "The Competitive Advantage of the Inner City." *Harvard Business Review*, May/June.

powell, john a. 2000. "Addressing Regional Dilemmas for Minority Communities." In Bruce Katz, ed., *Reflections on Regionalism*. Washington, DC: Brookings Institution Press.

Reardon, Sean F., Allison Attebury, Nicole Arshan, and Michal Kurlaender. 2009. "Effects of the California High School Exit Exam on Student Persistence, Achievement, and Graduation." Institute for Research on Education Policy and Practice at Stanford University.

Swanstrom, Todd, Colleen Casey, Robert Flack, and Peter Dreier. 2004. "Pulling Apart: Economic Segregation Among Suburbs and Central Cities in Major Metropolitan Areas." Brookings Institution Metropolitan Policy Program. Washington, DC: Brookings Institution.

Turner, Margery Austin, and Felicity Skidmore, eds. 1999. *Mortgage Lending Discrimination: A Review of Existing Evidence*. Washington, DC: Urban Institute.

Yago, Glenn, and Aaron Pankrantz. 2000. *The Minority Business Challenge: Democratizing Capital for Emerging Domestic Markets*. Santa Monica, CA: Milken Institute.

4

Urgent Challenges

In the previous incarnation of *Uncommon Common Ground*, six issues were identified as the central challenges shaping the quest for equity in the new millennium. Seven years later, this new book revisits several of these because, unfortunately, some of them have become even more pressing, as indicated in Chapter 3.

One of these issues is education. With an aging baby boomer workforce, preparing the next generation of workers is critical. In this regard, school reform is necessary, but reliance on schools alone to educate the next generation seems shortsighted. Entire communities are needed to provide the full assortment of supports that will help today's young children of color reach their full intellectual potential. So we revisit education with a discussion grounded in the comprehensive strategies that are needed to have every child succeed.

We also make an explicit connection between education and the employment pipeline, examining how to connect young people of color to twenty-first century jobs. Recognizing that the economy is always changing, we have

---

Box 4-1. Immigrants Transform Lewiston, Maine

In Maine, one of the whitest states in the country, refugees from Somalia have brought the economically depressed former mill town of Lewiston back to life (Ellison, 2009). Settling into the decaying town center, the first Somali immigrants moved to Lewiston in 2001, and quickly spread word to their friends and relatives back home that they had found a place to build a new life. Soon more Somalis were arriving, followed by Sudanese, Congolese, and other Africans. Today, per capita income in Lewiston is up, crime is down, and in 2004, *Inc.* magazine named Lewiston one of the best places in the U.S. to do business. Enrollment in local universities has actually increased as young people flock to Lewiston to experience the diverse and energized community.

---

moved from a focus on the digital economy in our earlier volume to today's emerging "green" sector, with its potential to create millions of new jobs in infrastructure and the building trades.

Just as critical to our nation's future are immigrants and their integration, the next issue that is revisited. Over the past decade, the debate around immigration has mostly revolved around immigration controls—that is, border security and removing illegal immigrants through workplace raids. While any good (and politically viable) immigration policy will include more secure borders with more consistent enforcement, it will also include strong measures to integrate the immigrants that are here. Consider, for example, how Somalian, Congolese, and other African immigrants have brought the former mill town of Lewiston, Maine, back to life (see Box 4-1), and this is just one example of the revitalization new entrants can bring. More profoundly, immigrants are a crucial part of the replacement workforce for baby boomer retirees. Current Americans have a vested interest in the successful integration of immigrants; at the same time, immigrants count on Americans to make the investments that will help their families and communities thrive.

The fourth issue—incarceration and prisoner reintegration—requires strategies to help ex-offenders build new lives. One in fifteen black adult men are serving time in prison or jail, as are one in thirty-six adult Hispanic men.[1] Eight years ago, our earlier volume identified high rates of incarceration among men of color as a pressing issue. In the intervening period, not much has changed. Failure to reintegrate ex-convicts into their communities is a drag on the economy, driving up unemployment, drying up tax revenues, and reducing spending power.

A fifth issue involves recognizing our new economic and social geography. The Brookings Institution calls America a "MetroNation." Eight in ten Americans live in urban areas, and jobs are found there at the same ratio. In the past, urban America was seen as a menacing place, a hub for crime, decay, and the free-riders produced by the welfare state. But, as cities and suburbs have become more diverse (95 percent of immigrants and 90 percent of minorities lived in metros in 2000)[2], metropolitan areas have become rich with possibilities.[3] Harnessing this potential, however, requires a renewed emphasis on equity and policies that promote long-term economic growth. At a time when sprawled-out living may be less appealing because of high gas prices and declining home values, now is the time to reshape our metropolitan regions into communities of opportunity for everyone.

Part of that effort involves a sixth issue: our national need to address climate change policy. Communities of color have long been disproportionately impacted by airborne toxics emitted from diesel trucks, refineries, and power plants. These emissions have contributed to poor air quality in their neighborhoods and asthma in their children. Such communities may also be most at risk from climate change (Lin, 2008). The harms of climate change will affect everyone, but not equally. Underresourced communities that are least equipped to respond to large-scale climate events will be the ones bearing the brunt of the impact.

The Road Ahead: Key Issues for the Twenty-First Century

Comprehensive Education

In his first speech to a joint session of Congress, President Obama described America's high dropout rate as a "prescription for economic decline," and said that a goal of his administration is "to ensure that every child has access to a complete and competitive education, from the day they are born to the day they begin a career." He will do his part, he said, and students must do theirs. "Dropping out of school is no longer an option. It's not just quitting on yourself, it's quitting on your country—and this country needs and values the talents of every American."[4]

President Obama is not the only leader taking a strong stance on education. Former Houston Mayor Bill White also saw the writing on the wall. "In a global economy, the single most important issue facing our country is an educated workforce." The mayor instituted a program called Reach Out to Dropouts in which volunteers, including the mayor himself and his school superintendent Abelardo Saavedra, go door to door encouraging high school students to return to school. Reach Out has recaptured more than 5,500 dropouts in Houston since it started in 2004 (Fields, 2008).

As a nation, we cannot afford to leave a single student behind. For one, there are costs to society: a high proportion of dropouts end up in prison and others wind up falling short in their ability to contribute to the economy. A nonpartisan youth advocacy group, America's Promise Alliance, has estimated that cutting the number of dropouts in half would generate $45 billion annually in new tax revenue, assuming enough jobs are generated to accommodate the graduates (Fields, 2008). For another, all children are deserving of sound educations and an opportunity to fulfill their potential.

For many students stuck in poor neighborhoods and attending poorly equipped, failing schools, dropping out might seem like a reasonable option.* Yet this has lifelong negative repercussions. In 1964, students who dropped out "earned 64 cents for every dollar earned by an individual with at least a high school degree." In 2004, they "earned only 37 cents for each dollar earned by an individual with more education"—including high school, college, and post-graduate degrees (Rouse, 2005:1).

It is encouraging to see a growing number of state and national policies reflect the view that all children deserve to be well educated. A number of lawsuits around the country have petitioned courts to order state governments to more equitably distribute school funds, invoking the constitutional rights of all children to receive a quality education.[5] The federal government, under George Bush, also seemed to share this belief, creating performance targets for the poorest and lowest-performing schools—otherwise known as "dropout factories"—through the No Child Left Behind program. The program was faulted, however, for not providing sufficient resources to achieve these targets.

The sad reality is that many children of color are stuck in poor schools because they are trapped in the vicious cycle of poverty. In 2007, when Barack Obama was running for

---

*Many children of color attend income- and race-segregated schools that commonly receive less funding, have fewer qualified teachers, less challenging curricula, larger classes, and poorer facilities. As cited in "Comprehensive Educational Equity: The Path to Meaningful Opportunity for Excellence," notes prepared by Edmund Gordon for the 2008 Teachers' College Educational Equity Conference. Used with the permission of the author.

president, he summed up the challenge this way: "What's most overwhelming about urban poverty is that it's so difficult to escape—it's isolating and it's everywhere. If you are an African American child unlucky enough to be born into one of these neighborhoods, you are most likely to start life hungry or malnourished. You are less likely to start with a father in your household, and if he is there, there's a fifty-fifty chance that he never finished high school and the same chance he doesn't have a job. Your school isn't likely to have the right books or the best teachers. You're more likely to encounter gang-activities than after-school activities. And if you can't find a job because the most successful businessman in your neighborhood is a drug dealer, you're more likely to join that gang yourself. Opportunity is scarce, role models are few, and there is little contact with the normalcy of life outside those streets."[6]

Low-income children account for 46 percent of public school enrollment in the United States and 54 percent of enrollment in the South. A similar pattern is emerging in the West and Southwest in states like California, New Mexico, and Oregon (Viadero, 2007). A growing body of research suggests that these low-income children lack the comprehensive supports that are needed to succeed in school (Gordon, Bridglall, and Meroe, 2005). Not all of a child's life takes place in school. A successful education comes down to more than reading and arithmetic. Many children in well-off communities participate in after-school programs, library trips, museum trips, tutoring, and summer camp, and benefit from parents who have the time and initiative to supervise homework assignments and otherwise get involved with education. Factors such as not having access to health care, healthy foods, safe parks, and playgrounds can also affect a child's learning.

These gaps suggest the need for a comprehensive approach to education. A funding initiative recently launched by the Atlantic Philanthropies seeks exactly these amenities for disadvantaged middle school students and their families. A partnership of schools, local nonprofits, and community groups, it is called Elev8 and operates in New Mexico, Chicago, San Francisco, and Oakland, California.[7]

A program in New York's Harlem neighborhood, the Harlem Children's Zone (HCZ), focuses on the healthy development of more than 10,000 children in a hundred-block area. Founded by Geoffrey Canada, HCZ seeks to fill the gaps that are typically lacking in the lives of low-income children, providing programs to strengthen families, improve social and economic well-being, and foster learning and growth. As a presidential candidate, Obama said this: "The philosophy behind the project is simple—if poverty is a disease that infects an entire community in the form of unemployment and violence, failing schools and broken homes, then we can't just treat those symptoms in isolation. We have to heal that entire community. And we have to focus on what actually works."[8]

The Harlem Children's Zone deploys a "conveyor belt" strategy offering a successive array of services. Before birth, Baby College prepares prospective parents with courses on childhood nutrition, constructive disciplinary methods, and effective methods for educating toddlers. At the age of four, prekindergarten children attend Harlem Gems, where they are taught international languages. As they get older, the Promise Academy awaits, two charter schools that supplement long days of learning with youth development programs. For instance, the TRUCE Fitness and Nutrition Center (TRUCE is an acronym for The Renaissance University for Community Education) has trained middle school students to analyze the factors that lead to obesity and diabetes in Harlem. TRUCE has also provided opportunities to focus on academic growth and career readiness through the use of the arts, media literacy, and multimedia technology. Youth publish a quarterly newspaper and produce an award-winning cable TV program.

Results are beginning to show. Will Dobbie and Ronald Fryer (2009) find that the effects of the HCZ in middle school reverse the black-white achievement gap in math and close it in English skills. For elementary students, both racial achievement gaps are closed. It appears, however, that children in the lower grades are initially doing better than children in the higher grades, having benefited from HCZ's early childhood programs. They conclude that while community investments may be responsible for some of the results, they are not enough to close the achievement gaps; high-quality schools must be part of the mix.

HCZ represents where the nation needs to go. Many cities around the country could benefit from such an approach and, in fact, President Obama agrees. As a candidate for president, he said, "There's no reason this program should stop at the end of those blocks in Harlem. It's time to change the odds for neighborhoods all across America." As president, he is following through on his idea to "replicate the Harlem Children's Zone in 20 cities across the country"[9] to help improve educational and other social and economic outcomes (Aarons, 2009).

Other emerging approaches, such as Multiple Pathways (see Box 4-2) and multisectoral councils on education, appear promising. Thirty-eight states have at least one "P–16" or "P–20" council (from pre-school to college and beyond) comprised of representatives from education, and business and community leaders for the purpose of educational reform, up from twenty-five in 2000 (Cech, 2008). The hope is that new policies will emerge to create a more seamless continuum along the educational pathway and lead to a greater percentage of traditionally underrepresented students at the higher levels of education. Early indications are that the committees work best when they are chaired by governors (Cech, 2008) and when goals are targeted and specific (Dounay, 2008). Arizona, for instance, is working toward the goal of reducing its high school dropout rate by 12 percent by 2012. Hawaii is aiming to increase the number of working adults who hold a two-year or a four-year degree to a rate of 55 percent. And Kentucky has begun to make headway in achieving its goal of doubling the number of

Box 4-2. "Multiple Pathways" to College and Careers

One promising approach to educational reform is known as "Multiple Pathways." This framework suggests that all children should be prepared for college *and* careers, not one or the other as done through tracking. Multiple Pathways does away with the "ubiquitous comprehensive high school" in favor of smaller schools and programs within high schools—"pathways" that "provide both the academic and real-world foundations students need for advanced learning, training, and preparation for responsible civic participation" (Oakes and Saunders, 2008: 6). This approach bridges high school and college by blending career and technical training with college preparatory classes. Vocational training was greeted with a backlash as it tracked many minority students into careers with less mobility or prestige. But pure college prep classes can lack the application that helps students connect what they're learning now with their future career. Multiple Pathways attempts to do both by teaching geometry through an architecture course, chemistry through a culinary arts class, and Spanish through an international business class. Students choose their general interest, say arts and entertainment, and learn both practical and theoretical skills that enable them to continue straight to higher education or defer it for a few years while working in a trade to save up money.

In 2004, a high school in a low-income Latino community in San Diego, California, made the transition from a large high school to four small magnets called Kearny High Educational Complex. One of the magnets, Stanley E. Foster Construction Tech Academy (CTA), has a student body of 475 ninth- through twelfth-graders, more than half of whom are Latino. Graduates who study architecture, engineering, and construction are given priority enrollment into San Diego State University's College of Engineering with a full scholarship guaranteed. Eighty-one percent of CTA's 2007 graduating class were accepted to college, 36 percent to four-year universities. Moreover, the 2007 graduating class retained 99 percent of ninth-graders from four years earlier (Oakes and Saunders, 2008).

As an approach, Multiple Pathways faces challenges and barriers to widespread implementation yet appears promising as a way to increase high school graduation rates among low-income youth.

people who hold bachelor's degrees, from a 1997 baseline, to 580,000 by 2020 (Dounay, 2008).

A Look at the Data. The trade publication *Education Week* estimates that nearly 1.23 million high school students in the class of 2008 failed to graduate on time.[10] Latinos and African Americans make up a disproportionate share of this population, with high school completion rates by this measure hovering below 60 percent. Figure 4-1 illustrates part of this disparity while complicating the picture, partly because we examine, as is standard in the labor market literature, whether high school is ever completed, including with a GED. Among adults older than twenty-five, all groups have made gains in the level of high school completion.. However, in terms of college completion rates, black Americans over twenty-five have inched forward while the rate of Latino improvement remains very limited. Asian educational achievement is extraordinarily high, far surpassing that of even white Americans; while this partly reflects the arrival of highly educated Asian immigrants, many U.S.-born Asians have also achieved great success in education. At the same time, the high-achieving Asian Americans overshadow significant educational challenges, primarily among Southeast Asians and Pacific Islanders.

**FIGURE 4-1. Changing Educational Levels of the U.S.
Noninstutional Poulation of Adults Older than
Twenty-Five, 1990–2007**

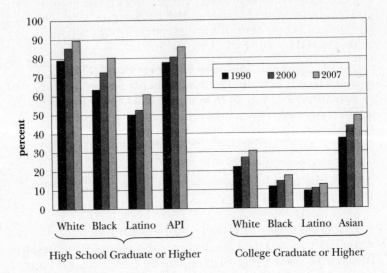

These differences in education make a big difference in economic outcomes, although they do not tell the whole story. Figure 4-2 shows earnings by educational category for white Americans, African Americans, Asians, and Latinos. As can be seen, earnings rise with education for all groups. Note, however, that sharp black-white earnings disparities persist at almost every educational level, suggesting that education alone will not erase the effects of discrimination, the lack of access to employment networks, and other factors. In fact, the black-white earnings disparity is reversed only at the doctorate level; the rub is that while African Americans are gaining ground at the doctorate level they are still underrepresented in that group, making up about 5 percent of doctorates but representing 11 percent of the population among people twenty-five years and older.[11]

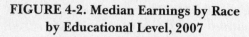

FIGURE 4-2. Median Earnings by Race by Educational Level, 2007

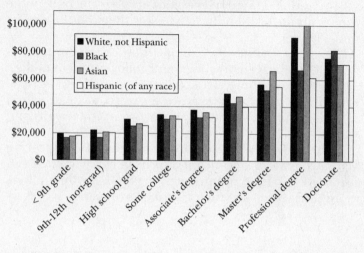

There are also persistent gaps between whites and Latinos at every educational level.* As for Asians, they trail whites at every level below a master's degree. This suggests that the economic success of Asians is due to high levels of education; while their return on education is generally lower (once we control for levels or degrees), they compensate with more years of school. Finally, note that it is only among the most educated (with master's degrees and beyond) that whites may earn less than Asians (and even black Ph.D.s). While some of this may be a statistical fluke due to a lower sample size (fewer Ph.D.s of color, hence less reliability in the numbers), it does suggest one reason why the well-educated pundits

---

*The data on Latinos with doctorates come from 2005 data, adjusted for inflation, because no median earnings data for Latino doctorates was reported for 2007 due to small sample size. An alternative method of adjustment, using the 2005 ratio of white-to-Latino Ph.D. median earnings to estimate the 2007 Latino Ph.D. earnings, yields virtually the same result.

who write the national narrative sometimes seem to think discrimination and disparity have disappeared: it is less salient in their class, but it is persistent for the bulk of the American population directly below them on the educational ladder.

Figure 4-3 shows the composition of the contemporary elementary, high school, and college student bodies; as can be seen, there is a noticeable drop-off for African Americans and Latinos as we move from high school to college, and a sizeable gain for Asian Americans and whites.

Education is also not just a matter of completing years; there is a significant gap in performance at different steps along the process. Figure 4-4 offers a look at one measure—average reading proficiency scores by

FIGURE 4-3. Composition of Elementary, High School, and College Enrollment in the United States by Race and Hispanic Origin, 2007

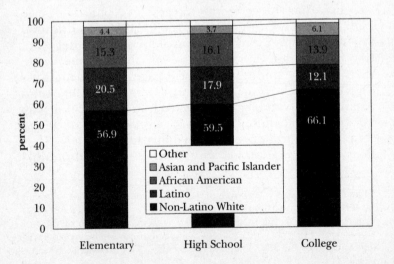

age and ethnicity for the period 1990–2004. The gaps in scores between white children and black and Hispanic children are large at all age levels but particularly among younger children; one sign of hope involves the significant improvement for black and Latino nine-year-olds, but what is worrisome is the decline in scores for seventeen-year-olds of all ethnicities between 1990 and 2004, particularly Latinos.* Asians in the younger age groups have made substantial gains in reading scores, surpassing white scores by 2004.

Christopher Jencks and Meredith Phillips (1998: 45) have written that "if racial equality is America's goal, reducing the black-white test score gap would probably do more to promote this goal than any other strategy that could command broad political support." Earlier research suggested that some of the difference in performance on standardized tests may have to do with "stereotype anxiety"—students believing that by virtue of their membership in a particular group they are not expected to do well. In the 1990s, social psychologist Claude Steele of Stanford University, for example, found that minority students who were asked to list their race before taking an exam did worse than those who did not—and he suggested that the request for self-identification led to a buy-in of societal doubts about their performance.[12]

At a time when a black man occupies the highest office in the nation, perhaps black students will start thinking of themselves differently. Researchers are starting to document what they have called "an Obama effect,"

---

*The data for math scores follow a similar pattern, although the gap is generally less severe between whites and their Latino counterparts for all ages and between whites and their black counterparts in the youngest age category; the gap is more severe between whites and blacks for the middle age category. Asians outpoint whites in math scores across the three age groups, but particularly in the younger two.

FIGURE 4-4. U.S. Average Reading Proficiency Scale Scores, 1990 through 2004 Long-Term Trend Summary, Chart for Ages 9, 13, and 17

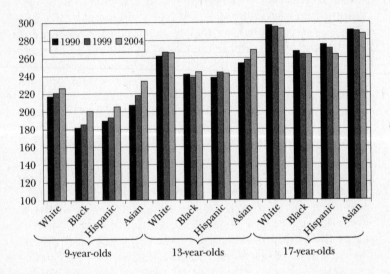

showing that a performance gap that existed before he won the Democratic Party's presidential nomination—in the form of a twenty-question test administered to white and black students—all but disappeared after his acceptance speech and again after the presidential election (Dillon, 2009). The study awaits peer review, but it raises intriguing questions about the nature of the achievement gap.*

---

*Equally intriguing is the performance of some schools serving low-income students that have created a "culture of high expectations." At Los Altos High School in Hacienda Heights, California, for example, the school added extra AP classes and provided support for any student who wanted to attend them. Within one year, the school boosted the Latino AP participation rate from 19 to 33 percent, of a student body 63 percent Latino. See Teicher, 2005 and The Education Trust, 2005.

Twenty-First-Century Employment

The $787 billion American Recovery and Reinvestment Act (ARRA) signed into law in February 2009 was designed to create millions of jobs because jobs are the only way to have sustained prosperity. The act included $48 billion in investments for job training and education, nearly $100 billion for transportation and infrastructure, $20 billion in tax incentives for renewable energy, and more than $41 billion for energy-related programs (PolicyLink and Green For All, 2009). Practically, the funds translate into jobs that will employ people to build, modernize, and retrofit homes; shore up public buildings and schools; refurbish parks; and fortify transit and water systems.

This retrofitting activity is part of what some have called "green jobs," employment aimed at getting the country ready for a new era of energy efficiency. Activists like Van Jones, formerly founder and president of Green For All, and for a time White House Special Advisor for Green Jobs, Enterprise, and Innovation, have been looking for years at how to blend environmental protection with solutions for long-time unemployed or underemployed minorities. Long before the ARRA was enacted, they had begun envisioning a new sector of employment (see Figure 4-5), and contributed to passage of the Green Jobs Act in 2007. Of course, not all green jobs are good jobs, and hard work will be needed to ensure that recovery dollars are used for employment that is both green and good.

It will also be important to put those dollars to work for the chronically unemployed, not just those who for the first time lost their job in the recession. Responding to the calls of equity advocates, the Obama administration refined how the funds should be used, issuing sweeping guidelines specifically encouraging projects that support "equal opportunity laws and principles, support small businesses including disadvantaged business

FIGURE 4-5. Potential New Green Jobs in the U.S. in 2018, 2028, 2038

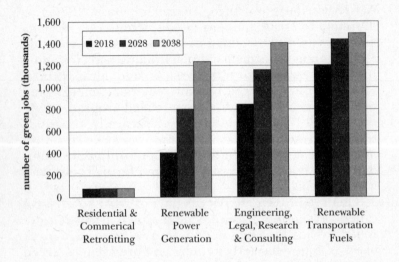

enterprises, engage in sound labor practice, promote local hiring, and engage with community-based organizations."[13] While community groups have been doing the bulk of the pioneering advocacy and training for green jobs, some cities are also taking the initiative. For example, the Chicago Climate Action Plan (CCAP) works with the city's most underprivileged populations, training workers to make buildings more energy-efficient, helping to spur investments in clean and renewable energy sources, improving transportation options, and reducing waste and industrial pollution (PolicyLink and Green For All, 2009). In another innovative approach, Kansas City, Missouri, has decided to invest $200 million of its stimulus cash into revamping and "greening" a single 150-block section of the city that is home to many low-income African Americans. The targeted effort will focus on weatherizing homes, creating and expanding "green job" training, improving public transit, and planting vegetation for a "green sewer" project.[14] To tap into the broad potential of a green economy, however, a sustainable approach is needed to pass on new technology-oriented skills to previously excluded groups.

Community colleges are a major piece to this puzzle. With costs at traditional four-year colleges escalating, many students are rediscovering the benefits of a community college education. Community colleges have historically provided a bridge to opportunity for disadvantaged groups. For example, 75 percent of all African Americans, Latinos, and Native Americans who pursue higher education in California start their journey in a community college (California Tomorrow, 2006). However, years of neglect and financial cutbacks have severely limited the ability of community colleges to provide the high-quality training and workforce education programs that are needed for the future. A substantial and immediate infusion of new federal dollars should help provide states and municipalities with the resources they need to make community colleges engines for the twenty-first-century economy. In July 2009, President Obama announced just such an initiative, saying that he will pour $12 billion into revitalizing the community college system over the next ten years. Of those funds, $2.5 billion would be spent on new community college facilities and $9 billion would go toward boosting graduation rates and better preparing students for twenty-first-century jobs (Rutenberg, 2009).

In California, a network of 110 community colleges provides major opportunities for the expansion of job training for low-income people. PolicyLink, headed by coauthor Angela Glover Blackwell, has been working to raise awareness of the opportunities for work in the infrastructure sector, the profile of which has been elevated as states try to secure federal stimulus funds with projects that are "shovel-ready." As the green economy takes off, major innovations and new occupations are expected to emerge in infrastructure. Community colleges are primed to be effective workforce partners, and model programs are emerging though they remain small in scale compared to the potential demand.

At the Los Angeles Trade-Technical College, a new Regional Economic Development Institute has launched an Infrastructure and Sustainable Jobs Collaborative. Their mission is "to bring together key public, private and community partners to plan and implement a seamless education, training and workforce infrastructure that connects low income, disadvantaged populations to livable wage jobs with career paths within the energy-utility industry."[15]

One company, Pacific Gas & Electric Company (PG&E), through its PowerPathway initiative, is collaborating with local organizations and community colleges to identify and train low-income individuals for high-paying careers in the energy sector, building on its current apprentice line worker program. Already, 400 apprentices are in the pipeline, and company officials say they hope to add another 115 to 120 new line workers a year.[16]

In another effort, the Silicon Valley Leadership Group has been training students to install solar panels. A collaboration between industry and community colleges in the Bay Area, the program helps students get certified in the solar photovoltaic industry. A third of California's 772 solar companies are in the Bay Area and the industry is expecting to expand significantly over the next few years, adding another 5,000 jobs to an industry that already employs approximately 17,000 people statewide. Almost half the new jobs are expected to be in the Bay Area (PolicyLink, 2009). Labor unions, especially the International Brotherhood of Electrical Workers (IBEW), are doing similar work with solar panel installation.

The Recovery Act provides a once-in-a-generation opportunity to rebuild America from the ground up, with equity as a guiding framework. As Van Jones has put it, this is the moment to "retrofit, reboot, and reenergize a nation" (Jones, 2008: 8). The act also represents the direction of the twenty-first-century economy, but it is important to note that, although green sector work represents exciting growth, the bulk of projected new jobs in the U.S. economy will be outside of the green sector in very low- and very high-wage positions (see Table 4-1).

Overall, new employment growth is expected to follow two tracks. At the top: registered nurses, postsecondary teachers, accountants, and computer software engineers. At the bottom: retail salespersons, cooks and fast-food workers, home care workers, janitors, waiters, and child care workers, who provide services for those at the top. A special challenge here is getting workers from the bottom to the top. Making that leap requires skill upgrades that can be costly—and this is where affordable community college becomes so important.

The unifying principle here is that the divide must be bridged between high-wage, high-skill work and, well, the opposite. Sometimes this will mean universal policies, like the Earned Income Tax Credit, and if efforts are to be truly useful, it will sometimes mean particular policies, like opening more jobs for ex-convicts. The strategies are many, but underlying a vision of real opportunity must be an analysis of where the economy is headed.

Immigration Reform and Immigrants

As noted earlier, the talents and energies of every single person will be needed to help set America on the road to recovery and sustainability. Now is not the time to divide our fates, but to conquer our fears and come together to make this country stronger for everyone. Even more today than ever before, immigrants have a vital role to play in the continuing story of America.

Large numbers continue to come. Every year, about 1.5 million people resettle in the United States to live and work. The largest single group, comprising about 40 percent, comes from Mexico (Sen and Mamdouh, 2008). As can be seen in Figure 4-6, the percentage foreign-born is still below the peak achieved in the late nineteenth and

TABLE 4-1. Projected Occupational Growth in the U.S. Economy Top Twenty Occupations, 2006–2016

Occupation Title	Employment Change, 2006–2016	2006 Median Earnings Quartile Rank	Required Training
Registered nurses	587,000	Very High	Associate degree
Retail salespersons	557,000	Very Low	Short-term OTJ*
Customer service representatives	545,000	Low	Moderate-term OTJ
Combined food preparation and serving workers, including fast food	452,000	Very Low	Short-term OTJ
Office clerks, general	404,000	Low	Short-term OTJ
Personal and home care aides	389,000	Very Low	Short-term OTJ
Home health aides	384,000	Very Low	Short-term OTJ
Postsecondary teachers	382,000	Very High	Doctoral degree
Janitors and cleaners, except maids and housekeeping cleaners	345,000	Very Low	Short-term OTJ
Bookkeeping, accounting, and auditing clerks	264,000	Low	Moderate-term OTJ
Nursing aides, orderlies, and attendants	264,000	Low	Postsecondary vocational award
Waiters and waitresses	255,000	Very Low	Short-term OTJ
Child care workers	248,000	Very Low	Short-term OTJ
Executive secretaries and administrative assistants	239,000	High	Work experience in related field
Accountants and auditors	226,000	Very High	Bachelor's degree
Computer software engineers	226,000	Very High	Bachelor's degree
Landscaping and groundskeeping workers	221,000	Low	Short-term OTJ
All other business operations specialists	218,000	Very High	Bachelor's degree
Elementary school teachers, except special education	209,000	High	Bachelor's degree
Receptionists and information clerks	202,000	Low	Short-term OTJ

Source: Bureau of Labor Statistics, Occupational Outlook Handbook, 2008–2009; ftp://ftp.bls.gov/pub/special.requests/ep/OPTDdata/optd.txt

*OTJ is an acronym for On The Job.

FIGURE 4-6. Percent of U.S. Population Foreign-Born, 1850–2007

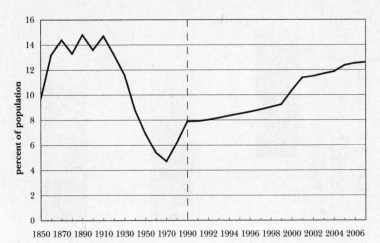

year (data by decade from 1850 through 1990, then by year through 2007)

early twentieth centuries, but the increases over the past thirty years have been dramatic.

The sharp fall prior to this, during the first half of the century, was due to the tightening of immigration restrictions via the quota system of 1921 and the 1924 Immigration Act, both of which also worked to limit immigration from areas other than Great Britain and Northern Europe, partly because of racial animus toward those from other parts of Europe and the rest of the world. The steady decrease in the percentage of foreign-born was turned around only after a new immigration law in 1965 relaxed restrictions, particularly on immigrants from Latin America and Asia.

The impacts of this relaxation can be seen in the change in the composition of the foreign-born between 1970 and 2007 depicted in Figure 4-7: the Latino, black, and Asian shares of this population grew substantially between 1970

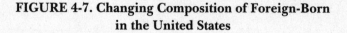

FIGURE 4-7. Changing Composition of Foreign-Born in the United States

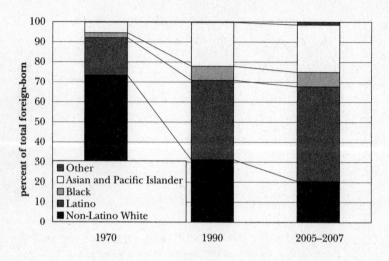

and 1990, with Latinos continuing to become a larger share of the population through 2007.

Immigrants are also varied by their tenure in America. The Migration Policy Institute compiled national data, which is displayed in Figure 4-8. The plurality of immigrants migrated in the nineties, with about one-quarter of immigrants arriving in the eighties and another quarter during the current century. The widespread image of newcomers as recent arrivals does not match up with the facts on the ground, and the concerns that are raised by focusing just on newcomers can be misleading. For example, many are concerned that immigrants tend to not speak English. As shown in Figure 4-9, in 2007, over half of immigrants over the age of five did not speak English "very well" (the highest proficiency you can achieve aside from exclusively speaking English). But what happens if we consider proficiency by how recently immigrants arrived in the country? Here we find significant progress

FIGURE 4-8. Recency of Immigration, 2008

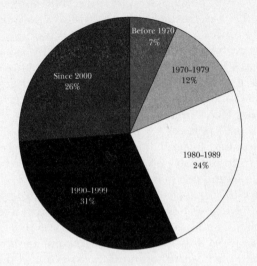

FIGURE 4-9. Limited English Proficiency Among
Immigrants, Ages 5 and Older

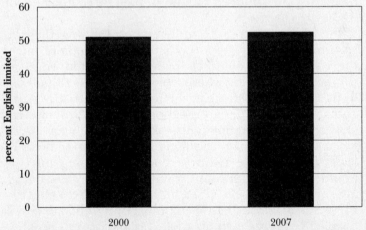

The term limited English proficiency refers to any person aged 5 or older who reported speaking English "not at all," "not well," or "well," on their survey questionnaire. Individuals who reported speaking only English or speaking English "very well" are considered proficient in English.

over time. In 2007, while only 36 percent of immigrants aged five or older who arrived since 2000 spoke English "very well" or exclusively, that figure was 45 percent for 1990s immigrants, 49 percent for 1980s immigrants, and 62 percent for pre-1980s immigrants. And if asked about who speaks English "well" or better—probably a better standard given a tendency of language learners to rate their skills modestly—we find that the figures jump to 56 percent for 1990s immigrants, 67 percent for 1980s immigrants, and 81 percent for pre-1980s immigrants.[17] Immigrants do need greater language skills to integrate into the American mainstream, but they understand this better than anyone and are making progress.

Despite the progress, the children of immigrants are often in precarious positions. More than one in five American youth are children of immigrants, a ratio that increases to one in four if only looking at low-income children. The Migration Policy Institute found that two out of three children who have an undocumented parent live in families with mixed status. As a result, parents or siblings might be deported, a destabilizing event. Prioritizing youth means caring for the children of immigrants, three-quarters of whom are citizens.[18]

But while Americans typically support children, they are less unified in their support of immigrants. And of course, there's even less tolerance for undocumented workers, who may number anywhere from 7 million to 13 million. Reflecting the stalemate at the federal level, many states and about forty cities adopted policies to rid themselves of undocumented immigrants—often by creating a "harsh social and legal climate, claiming that they had to do so in order to secure the country's borders because Congress would not act. At last count, a hundred more were debating similar proposals." (Sen and Mamdouh, 2008: 210–211). A heavy focus has been on barring undocumented people from receiving public benefits and driver's licenses. As of 2007, only seven states still allowed undocumented people to obtain driver's licenses. Enforcement mechanisms, such as workplace raids, have resulted in a seven-fold increase in arrests of undocumented workers (Sen and Mamdouh, 2008).

The lack of action at the federal level has left states, regions, and cities to make their own law—and while there are plenty of negative instances, there are also positive examples. Immigration remains a largely urban phenomenon, and so it's in major cities like Chicago, New York, Miami, Los Angeles, and, increasingly, places like Las Vegas, Denver, and Atlanta where immigrant policy is being built from the ground up. Chicago has been the frontrunner in immigrant policy—with a special focus on integration. There, the Illinois Coalition for Immigrant and Refugee Rights (ICIRR) has been encouraging even noncitizen immigrants to become civically engaged, working to get out the vote of citizens even when they themselves cannot vote.

Some analysts, such as Mark Krikorian, an advocate of restricted immigration, have problems with legal immigration as well. In a column entitled "Legal, Good/Illegal, Bad? Let's Call the Whole Thing Off," he has argued that legal immigration creates the framework and infrastructure for illegal immigration (Krikorian, 2007). Our own view is clear: immigrants help to revitalize inner-city and other communities, are creating a new civic life, and are here to stay. Their success will be our success.

While immigration policy and immigration integration are intertwined, separating the two should help create clarity. The question that confronts us is how best to facilitate the economic and social integration of immigrants into the United States, particularly given their relatively large numbers and, even more important, particularly given the fact that their contributions matter even more in these times. One could even argue, as Van Jones does in Box 4-3, that the revitalized immigrants' rights movement is part of today's civil rights movement, "pulling the nation to a higher level of fairness and inclusion" (Jones, 2006).

Box 4-3. Shout "VIVA!" Anyhow:
On Being Black at a Latino March*

At the May 1, 2006 *Diá Sin Inmigrantes* / Day Without Immigrants march in San Francisco, I saw a beautiful, exciting and hopeful vision of the future of this country.

I also caught a glimpse of a familiar past, fading away. And I shed a few tears for both.

From the moment I climbed aboard the BART subway cars Monday morning, I knew this May Day march and rally would differ from the Bay Area's usual protest fare. The trains headed into downtown San Francisco were filled with working-class Latinos, all wearing white; most had kids in tow.

A Different Kind of Rally

There were few protest signs or banners. But the stars and stripes were everywhere. One tyke on my train kept trying to poke his cousin with a little American flag.

Some of the teeniest kids were wearing their older sibling's white Tees—with their shirt hems hanging down past their knees. The children were all well-scrubbed and happy . . . and very proud.

So were their parents. They knew they were part of something new, and big, and promising.

The bright mood contrasted starkly with the dreary atmosphere that chokes most protests nowadays. On this march, I saw no resigned shuffling of already-defeated feet. No sea of scowls. Nor could I spy a single person-dragging behind her the weighty conviction that resistance—though obligatory—was futile.

To the contrary. Beaming, brown-skinned families walked off those trains with their heads held high. Sure, they may have been poor, facing tough challenges in the near term. But they stepped like they were marching into a future of limitless promise and potential.

Their optimism brought tears to my eyes. And not only for the obvious reasons.

Mourning Black America's Setbacks

Deep inside, I was grieving for my own people. I wished that my beloved African-American community had managed—somehow—to retain our own sparkling sense of faith in a magnificent future. There was once a time when we, too, marched forward together—filled with utter confidence in the new day dawning. There was a time when we, too, believed that America's tomorrow held something bright for us . . . and for our children. Those times will come again.

But today it seems that too many of those dreams have been eaten away by the AIDS virus, laid off by downsizers and locked out by smiling bigots. Too many of those dreams have been felled by assassins, shot up by gang-bangers and buried in a corporate-run prison yard. When Katrina's floodwaters washed our problems back onto the front pages, the once-mighty Black Freedom Movement could not rise even to THAT occasion. Our legendary "Movement" has collapsed—with our "spokespersons," both young and old, trying somehow to live off our past glories.

In the meantime, the white-shirted future was pouring itself down Market Street—chanting "*Si, Se Puede!*"

It was painful. I found myself praying that someday my Black community will recover our momentum and march like this again. I felt all the emotions of being at a funeral and of being present for the birth of a new life, all at the same time. All I could do was sigh and wipe my tears on my sleeve.

But it didn't take long for my feelings of solidarity to

trump my sorrows. Thousands of people were standing up, here and across the United States, for their right to live and work in dignity in this country. Deep in my bones, I felt their pain, knew their hopes and affirmed their aspirations.

And just as non-Blacks had supported our freedom movement in the last century, I was determined—as a non-immigrant—to give my passionate support to this righteous cause.

Chanting for Justice—in Spanish! (well, kind of . . .)

So I joined the crowds in the street, trying to add my voice to the thunderous chants. But I quickly discovered that—all my good intentions notwithstanding—political solidarity is sometimes more easily felt than expressed.

My fellow marchers started roaring out: "*Zapata! Vive! La lucha! Sigue!*"

I was like, Huh? What?

"*Zapata! Vive! La lucha! Sigue!*"

Say what? What are they saying, now?

Then louder, faster: "*LaLuchaSigueSigue! ZapataViveVive! LaLuchaSigueSigue! ZapataViveVive!*"

Whoa, there! What the . . .?

Bewildered, but undeterred, I got myself a "chant sheet." I figured that I could use one of the official written guides to keep me in the know and on track.

Sure enough, the handy leaflet spelled everything out very clearly: "*Las Calles Son Del Pueblo! El Pueblo Donde Está? El Pueblo Está En Las Calles, Exigiendo / Libertad!*"

To me, unfortunately, those words looked precisely like alphabet soup. I found myself desperately trying to remember back to 11th grade, wondering what sound an "x" makes in Spanish.

Finally, I had to face the sad truth about myself: I had B.S.-ed my way through all my high school and college language requirements. Now, I had to admit that Mrs. Savage (from fourth period Español) had been right: I really HADN'T cheated anyone—but myself.

And now I had to accept the miserable results: as an utterly monolingual English speaker, I wasn't even knowledgeable enough about the Spanish language to shout out simple phrases, during most of the protest.

Okay, I told myself. Fine. I decided instead to just walk cheerfully along, clapping in time with the drummers. But even some of the Latin rhythms were unfamiliar, strangely syncopated. I couldn't always find the beat, despite my best efforts. (Suddenly, I was filled with all this love and sympathy for all those a-rhythmic white folks whom I used to make fun of at Black rallies, parties and churches. I AM SO SORRY, Y'ALL!)

Well, needless to say, I was on the verge of giving up. Then I found a solution: I would simply listen for any chant that had the word "VIVA!" in it. For some reason, there were lots of chants with that word in it. And then, whenever appropriate, I would just raise my fist and shout—"VIVA!"—along with the crowd, as loud as I could.

And that was pretty much all I could do. I did it for a few hours, then went home. I hope it was enough. Because, despite feeling somewhat out of place, I was absolutely thrilled to see my sisters and brothers, taking the future into their own hands.

Perhaps Brown Power Can Save America—
Including Black America?

By simply standing up for their own kids and grandparents—for their own dignity and futures—activist Latinos today are pulling the nation to a higher level of fairness and inclusion.

They are posing a simple and devastating question: should U.S. society continue to profit from the labor of 11 million people—many of whom pick our fruit, nurse our children, clean our workplaces—without embracing them fully, without honoring their work, without extending to them the same rights and respect we would want for ourselves?

Can we countenance or tolerate a Jim Crow system—in brown-face—with a shunned tier of second-class workers, enriching society but lacking legal status and protections?

Or are we willing to change our laws—and change our hearts—to embrace those upon whom our economy has come to rest? This is a simple moral challenge. The right answers are not easy, but they are obvious.

I know that there will be a backlash (there always is when people push for fairness), even coming from some Black folks. But I also know that the Latino-led struggle for justice and inclusion offers hope to all of us. A national conversation about the true meaning of dignity, equality, opportunity and fair play in the modern economy can ultimately benefit every American community.

I am confident that it will.

Because during the two prior centuries, it was the African-American community that performed this service for the country. And we paid a high and awful cost in blood and martyrs. Unfortunately, we did not achieve all of our aims. But we did tear apartheid from the pages of U.S. law books.

And in the course of that struggle, we did improve the lot of all Americans—expanding social programs, democratic rights and social tolerance for all people. And our efforts opened the doors for today's equality struggles. Our marching feet moved the whole nation forward.

Of course, I cannot help but mourn the loss of a Black community strong enough to put this nation on its back, and carry it forward, step by step, toward justice . . . as we once did. But my pain only amplifies and underscores my joy that this marvelous new force HAS arisen, one that is capable—in this tough, new era—of deepening and extending the struggle to transform America.

Strong brown hands have grabbed a hold of the U.S. flag. And they are pulling it away from those who have monopolized it, from bullies who have abused the nation's symbols for their violent and illegitimate ends.

I am glad. Because only a mass movement with broad shoulders—and rough hands—will have the power to win the coming tug-of-war for the heart and soul of this country. The Latino community has birthed just such a movement.

Someday, I know that my own people will recover our strength, and rejoin them on the front-lines. And in the meantime: Latinos and other immigrant communities are starting to raise core questions about their own children's access to education, health care, jobs and safety.

As they do so, if history is any guide, every American community will benefit greatly from their efforts. Including my own.

---

*This article was written by Van Jones, the founder and former president of Green For All, who later served for a short time as White House Special Advisor for Green Jobs, Enterprise, and Innovation. It originally appeared in the *Huffington Post* on May 3, 2006.

To start with, we should ensure that the children of immigrants, who are often U.S.-born, receive adequate public education and services, even when their parents have uncertain legal status.* It is also necessary to extend the school day to give students the time to learn both English and academic subjects and improve academic assessment tools for English learners so that they can be appropriately placed by ability (Fix and Zimmerman, 2000: 41).

Adults also have learning needs. Like their children, immigrants who learn English are more likely to succeed. Again, community colleges play a role in preparing immigrant adults for the workforce. A recent report examining the opportunities and barriers to immigrant integration in Los Angeles County found that a lack of English skills was one of the greatest impediments to job advancement and that there is a "striking shortage" of English-language programs to meet the need (Pastor and Ortiz, 2009). The report, commissioned by the California Community Foundation, called for more English classes, job training, and leadership development programs to help immigrants acquire the skills to keep California economically competitive. In terms of modeling what is needed, the report pointed to a collaborative effort between the Santa Ana Chamber of Commerce and the Rancho Santiago Community College District to teach English to 50,000 Santa Ana workers by 2010.

Other community-based institutions are important to immigrant assimilation. Legal centers can provide advice on immigration, but also on tenants' rights and other skills needed to navigate in the U.S. political system. Community health centers can provide preventive education and ensure quick access to those who may lack insurance. Pastor and Ortiz (2009) also argue that local planning agencies could commit to involve all residents in neighborhood design efforts; there are no restrictions imposed in such processes regarding citizenship, and such

---

*In New York, for example, 70 percent of families with children headed by undocumented immigrants have children who are citizens. See Fix and Zimmerman, 2000: 15.

exercises could be active training ground for an engaged future citizenry.

The same report makes a seemingly offbeat recommendation with respect to immigrant integration: step up investments in the well-being of African Americans. The authors argue, however, that black communities are receiving a good share of immigrants and their service organizations are supporting them. Moreover, investing in the black community will defray tension around economic competition. Sadly, blacks have remained at the bottom of the socioeconomic scale, even with mass immigration, so making an investment in the black community will lift minority communities from the bottom. This is exactly the sort of intersectional thinking that makes racial equity good for everyone and not just a particularistic plea.

Finally, immigration policy will also need to be remedied. Integration policy, while distinct from immigration, is still affected by it. For example, unauthorized immigrants will continue to be harassed and sometimes deported as a result of Immigration and Customs Enforcement raids until there is a more humane and consistent law. And so, any immigration policy needs to have at its heart a pathway to citizenship for the millions working and living in the shadows. Such a policy would alleviate exploitation at the bottom of the labor market, thereby raising wages, and contribute a new, engaged workforce to the American enterprise. Inevitably, more secure borders will be part of a package, too, and racial equity proponents will have to monitor implementation to make sure it is evenhanded and humane.

In the meantime, the work of community groups will help fill the gap. Labor unions can continue standing against workplace raids, community health centers can continue preventative education for those lacking health insurance, and legal centers can continue advising immigrants on their rights as tenants. And, at the highest levels of national policy, perhaps Barack Obama, the son of an immigrant, can help steer the Congress to a reform worthy of an open and good-hearted nation.

Incarceration and Prisoner Reintegration

The United States locks up more of its citizens than any other country in the world. Despite being home to only 5 percent of the world's population, the nation houses 25 percent of the world's prisoners.[19] Our criminal justice system also disproportionately affects communities of color. As Figure 4-10 illustrates, the percent of adult males held in federal or state prisons and local jails is drastically higher for black and Latino males relative to white males. Despite the leveling out of rates in recent years, nearly 5 percent of all black and 2 percent of all Latino adult males were imprisoned in 2007, compared to less than 1 percent of white adult males.

Racial inequities contribute to the disparity. According

FIGURE 4-10. Percent of Adult Males Held in Federal or State Prisons and Local Jails, 1999–2007

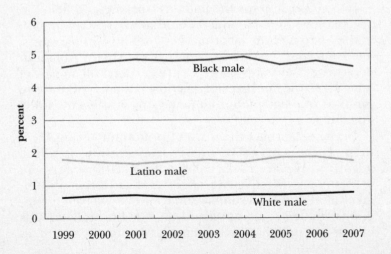

to a recent report from the National Council on Crime and Delinquency (NCCD), there is a misconception that the overrepresentation of youth of color in the criminal justice system is due to their committing more crimes relative to white youth; at the national level, white youth actually make up a majority of the juvenile court referral population across all offense categories (personal, property, drug, and public order). While African American youth comprise 30 percent of the juvenile court referral population, they are overrepresented in the detained population at 37 percent (National Council on Crime and Delinquency, 2007). In an analysis of national and state data, researchers at NCCD found that between 2002 and 2004, African Americans represented 16 percent of the U.S. youth population under the age of 18, constituted 28 percent of all the young arrested, 37 percent of those detained in juvenile jails, and 58 percent of all juveniles sent to adult prison (National Council on Crime and Delinquency, 2007). Another study showed that young white men charged with violent offenses have an average imprisonment of 193 days after trial; for African American and Latino youth, the figures are 254 and 305 days, respectively (Marable, 2000: 7). Similarly, black adults receive longer sentences than whites for convictions for the same crime, even when whites have more past offenses (The Sentencing Project, 2008).

Changing course on the criminal justice front will require a rethinking of current strategies as well as political courage. And while significant progress remains to be made, the introduction of Senator Jim Webb's National Criminal Justice Commission Act of 2009 marks a step forward in the right direction. The act calls for the creation of a blue-ribbon commission to begin an eighteen-month "top-to-bottom review of our entire criminal justice system."[20] If enacted, the commission, through its findings, could go a long way to creating a more equitable approach to incarceration and criminal justice. Indeed, tackling the entry side is critical to any notion of reform.

But addressing the challenge of incarceration must go beyond the entry side. Prisoners who have served their time must also be supported in returning to community life. Reengaging ex-offenders with the workforce is not charity, but good business and sound urban policy.

After all, recidivism is expensive: In a study of Pennsylvania and racial disparities in the Pittsburgh labor market, taxpayers in the state were said to pay about $40,000 annually for a state prisoner, $18,000 annually for a county prisoner, and for elderly prisoners in failing health, costs can increase to $100,000 (Benner and Fox, 2009). All this is occurring against a background of already stretched finances. Researchers at the University of Pittsburgh found that more than half of the municipalities in the ten-county southwestern Pennsylvania region face structural deficits and many communities borrow heavily to plug the gap in their budget. The Pittsburgh region has the highest levels of interest debt expenditure per capita compared to fourteen other benchmark cities identified by the University of Pittsburgh– and Carnegie Mellon–linked Pittsburgh Regional Indicators Project, spending more than $350 annually for every man, woman, and child living in the region simply to pay the interest on municipal debt. The highest levels in the region are in Allegheny County ($473) and Beaver County ($494), the two counties that also have the highest concentrations of African Americans and poverty.[21]

Higher rates of incarceration ultimately lead to a vicious and costly cycle, especially since a prison record greatly reduces employment opportunities. Indeed, one study has concluded that criminal convictions are "virtually impossible to overcome" for black men seeking employment (Pager, 2007). The concentrated pockets of unemployment to which ex-felons contribute also increase state and local government's share of social services payments, from income support to health care. Many studies have shown a correlation between unemployment and rates of mental health problems (Center on Race and Social Problems, 2007). Again, referring back to Pennsylvania as an example, African Americans were found to have a higher rate of serious mental illnesses such as depression and are over-represented in the utilization of mental health and drug abuse services compared to whites. In Allegheny County (which includes Pittsburgh and its suburbs) blacks make up as much as 30 percent of the clients for such services, but only 12.4 percent of the population (Center on Race and Social Problems, 2007: 42).

A notable program that deals directly with these particular issues of integration is under way in Arizona. Called "Getting Ready," the philosophy behind the program is that preparation for reentry begins from the day an individual steps inside prison. In contrast to most correctional facilities, where staff exercises complete control over prisoners, Getting Ready mimics the choices and incentives of the outside world. Prisoners are empowered to take control of their own lives and are given more responsibility in prerelease preparation. State inmates at any custody level can opt in to the program. In this "parallel universe," prisoners are also given access to real-world job training and educational opportunities and are encouraged to earn high school equivalency diplomas and to work full-time. To ensure success and sustainable wages after inmates are released, job training and employment behind bars are aligned with actual Arizona industries.

Instituted in 2004, Getting Ready reports reduced recidivism rates, and that its graduates are 35 percent more successful in the community than nonparticipant inmates of comparable risk. In addition, inmate-on-inmate violence is down by 37 percent, inmate-on-staff assaults by 51 percent, and inmate suicides by 33 percent. In 2008, the program was recognized for its pioneering approach by the Ash Institute for Democratic Governance and Innovation at Harvard University and was given $100,000 toward dissemination and replication around the country.[22] In 2008,

Congress also signaled a much-welcomed change in policy by passing the Second Chance Act, which authorizes resources for new efforts and research on reentry issues.

Our strategies to address incarceration and prisoner reentry must tackle an illogical criminal justice system that overimprisons inner-city residents and underdelivers on rehabilitation and reentry opportunities. For example, the country needs to reconsider the harsh sentences handed down to nonviolent offenders who would benefit from drug treatment rather than jail time. Federal laws that punish crack cocaine users and dealers far more severely than the users and traffickers of powdered cocaine should be amended since there is no pharmacological difference between the two drugs and the disparities only serve to widen the criminal justice system's unequal treatments of blacks and whites. There was some progress in 2007 when the U.S. Sentencing Commission decided to diminish the differences in crack cocaine sentencing; it is estimated that the decision late that year to make the lighter sentences retroactive will affect over 19,000 inmates. And, in a reflection of the racial character of the crack differential, nearly 90 percent of those affected were African American.[23]

And it's not just drugs and sentencing. The juvenile justice system, which has become a feeder system for prisons, should become less punitive and focus more on rehabilitation and reentry. States should restore voting rights for ex-felons to ease their reintegration back into their communities and provide ex-offenders with a sense of belonging, citizenship, and responsibility. Effective education campaigns can marshal the public will for such reforms. In 2002, Connecticut repealed a law that stripped felons on probation of their right to vote (Zielbauer, 2001). The state now allows felons on probation and parole to vote, which provides an opportunity for ex-felons to civically engage with their communities.

Criminal justice reform may be one of the toughest areas for enacting change and one of the biggest leadership challenges. The federal government should set the

tone for equitable and fair policies in this arena. Ways must
be developed to frame the issue to enable all Americans
to acknowledge and recognize the crisis as one of shared
concern. For starters, any campaign to lead such a movement can be more effective by emphasizing that closing the
racial gap in criminal justice outcomes will yield financial
benefits for everyone in the community by lowering prison
construction and maintenance costs, easing the pressures
that fragment families and neighborhoods, and enabling
more people to contribute to the local economy and its tax
coffers.

Healthy Metropolitan Communities

Not too many years ago, it might have sounded like a fan-
tasy to speak of livable American cities. Our cities, symbols of urban blight and racial isolation, were neglected
and left to decay. At the same time, the suburbs were
once mainly white and often wealthy, not places having
to struggle with poverty and crime as they are today. The
stereotypical differences between suburbs and cities are
blurring, and a unique opportunity exists to rebuild our
metropolitan communities into places of inclusion and
opportunity for all.

Many cities are on the upswing, as young professionals, well-heeled families, and empty nesters rediscover the
advantages of urban living. But urban revitalization has not
benefited everyone. In some cases, longtime disparities of
race, class, and geography have been exacerbated. Further,
even as some cities emerged from decades of disinvestment
and neglect, others have continued to languish and be left
behind. For them it is not that easy to scrub off the legacy
of "white flight" and sprawl.

As a Chicago community organizer, Barack Obama wit-
nessed firsthand the flip side of sprawl in the abandoned
and broken neighborhoods on the city's South Side. And as
an organizer working for the Gamaliel Foundation, which
advocated for a more comprehensive approach to regional

equity, he no doubt embraced the view that an impoverished inner city affects the health of the greater whole.
Today, many are pointing to Detroit as one of the more
stubborn cases of urban decline. We should not forget that
the strength of greater Detroit is linked to the strength of
Detroit itself. In December 2008, the median price of a
house sold in Detroit was $7,500. One-third of the popu-
lation lives in poverty and almost 50 percent of children
are in poverty (Jones, 2009). Only about one-quarter of
Detroit's high school students graduate on time (Fields,
2008). About 550,000 residents, over half of the city's total
population, lack ready access to healthy foods, with a pre-
ponderance of liquor stores, gas stations, and convenience
stores serving as the city's food stamp retailer[24] in a city
where 30 percent of residents are on food stamps.[25]

The strength of our suburbs also contributes to the
health of our metropolitan regions. Unfortunately, many
suburbs are struggling, particularly in the wake of the foreclosure crisis. In Clayton County, Georgia, for instance,
which encompasses many of Atlanta's southern suburbs,
the foreclosure rate was twice as high as that in Atlanta
(Katz and Bradley, 2009).

Researchers at the Brookings Institution have argued
that the United States has become a "MetroNation," with
our economic competitiveness inextricably tied to the fates
of our cities and surrounding suburbs. If this is so, then
renewing America's vitality begins in metropolitan communities. The nation's policies must ensure that people can
connect to opportunity no matter where they live. To do
this, attention must be paid to the infrastructure and transportation networks that speed the movement of goods and
people but to do so in a way that promotes good health.
Physical environments where people live must include
decent housing, safe parks, clean air, and access to healthy
foods. Finally, investments in people must ensure that all
have access to quality education and jobs that pay livable
wages.

Outlined below are some of the priorities that will be

key to revitalizing metropolitan communities so that all can participate and prosper in the twenty-first century.

Transportation. To remain competitive, America needs to rebuild its crumbling infrastructure and create fresh transportation options. This time, we need to do so in a way that doesn't shortchange low-income people. Priority must be given to those projects that will help ease the transportation burden of low-income people in literally getting to jobs and in training them for the jobs, as noted earlier. In short, it is time to think innovatively. As President Obama said, our challenge is "not just fixing old transportation systems but it is also imagining new transportation systems." We should be thinking regionally about how we plan our transportation infrastructure, he said, adding, "the days where we're just building sprawl forever, those days are over."[26]

More findings indicate the critical importance of living next to public transportation. Health benefits can be gained by avoiding exposure to heavy traffic, and economic benefits can also result. Americans living in areas served by public transportation save $18 billion annually in congestion costs. Transit riders also save about $1,400 in gas per year. In addition, transit availability can reduce the need for an additional car, a yearly expense of $6,251 in a household budget (American Public Transportation Association). People who live in cities with well-established rail transit systems spend about 12 percent of their total household expenditure on transportation, compared to almost 15 percent for people who live in cites that lack rail systems (Litman, 2004). In contrast, the poorest fifth of Americans spend 42 percent of their annual household budget on the purchase, operation, and maintenance of automobiles (Surface Transportation Policy Project Fact Sheet). Low-income workers who use public transit to commute to work spend on average about 7 percent less of their income on transportation (Sanchez, Stolz, and Ma, 2003).

Transportation obviously has implications for jobs and housing, and new research is emerging to show the connections between transportation and health (PolicyLink and Prevention Institute, 2009).

Broad thinking is needed to create innovative transportation policies that can improve people's lives. This book supports a multipronged approach that recognizes the overlap between transportation and other issues. In a good sign, the Obama administration announced a partnership between the U.S. Department of Housing and Urban Development (HUD) and the U.S. Department of Transportation to help expand choices for affordable housing and transportation, recognizing that too many people are paying too much for these basic needs.[27] The Environmental Protection Agency later joined this partnership in a broader effort to create livable communities that promote equitable development while simultaneously addressing the challenge of climate change.[28]

Access to Grocery Stores. The health of a community is directly related to the environment that surrounds the community. In the past, this issue was addressed under the rubric of environmental justice. Clean air and water are a universal right. But there is another issue that is affecting community health: a notable lack of access to healthy foods.

Many low-income communities of color lack grocery stores that provide access to healthy foods. A growing number of studies suggest that this situation is contributing to rising rates of diabetes and obesity (PolicyLink, UCLA Center for Health Policy Research, and California Center for Public Health Advocacy, 2008). Fortunately, awareness of this issue is growing. Strategies and approaches are emerging to help attract grocery stores to disadvantaged neighborhoods. These strategies not only increase health benefits, but also increase economic opportunities in the form of jobs.

One example of such an approach is the Pennsylvania Fresh Food Financing Initiative—a public-private partnership created as part of the state's 2004 economic stimulus package. In four years, it has shown impressive results, helping to develop 68 supermarkets and fresh food outlets in underserved rural and urban areas throughout the state and creating or retaining 3,700 jobs. Just $30 million in state seed money has already leveraged an additional $165 million in private investment.[29] The program continues to dramatically improve access to healthy food statewide, while also driving meaningful, long-term economic development. Advocates are now calling on the federal government to use the Pennsylvania program as the model for a national initiative to improve children's health, create jobs, and spur economic development nationwide.

Protecting Against Displacement. Sprawl has caused problems, to be sure, including increased segregation, higher transportation costs, and negative impacts on both the environment and economic opportunity. But it's also the case that in the last decade the revitalization of cities has led some to be concerned about "gentrification" and displacement and has fostered alternative models of economic growth.*

Whereas redlining—so-called because banks literally drew circles in red ink around minority neighborhoods to which it would not extend loans—has technically ended, gentrification is now using the market to direct where minorities can, and more specifically, cannot live. The new hot spot for yuppies is the central city. High incomes allow them and developers to price out previous low-income tenants and their landlords. In strong market cities, new construction favors wealthy residents. Thus, properties are rebuilt into upper-end housing and lower-income residents get displaced. In the Bay Area, San Francisco, emerging now as a sort of boutique city, was the only county of nine

---

*Equitable development is an approach used by PolicyLink that offers policies and practices that enable low-income and low-wealth residents to stay in their communities and participate in and benefit from economic activity.

to see increases in their white population since 2000 (Pastor, 2008).

While hard data on displacement and gentrification is scant—there are many proxies such as housing cost, neighborhood income, neighborhood demographics—the anecdotal evidence is compelling. In 2007, under the Right to the City Alliance, which included allies in Boston, Washington, D.C., Los Angeles, Miami, New Orleans, New York City, Providence, and the San Francisco Bay Area, low-income residents across the country asserted that they were entitled to return to the city. It's not that the members of the Right to the City Alliance necessarily dislike higher-income residents; they just want to be able to live the same or a better lifestyle as before gentrification. But instead, lower-income residents usually get moved to whatever leftovers the city or region has to offer.

Equitable development has emerged as an approach forged by PolicyLink that connects the smart-growth movement with this effort to prevent smart growth from becoming exclusive growth. Although smart growth has sometimes found its realization in newly created places like Seaside, Florida (the infamous location of the movie *The Truman Show*), older urban-core neighborhoods would seem to make smart growth even smarter. Inner cities, after all, have grids with memories of days when street-oriented porches and mixed-income living were the norm, not the latest fad in urban planning. While streets are often dilapidated in the urban core, transit systems are already at work, reducing the high transportation expenditures of low-income residents. Steering more investment into transportation upgrades instead of sprawling highways will serve more, and poorer, people while still drawing wealthier folks back to the city. And steering development inward can preserve precious farmland and open space as well as reduce our global carbon footprint.

PolicyLink has consistently attempted to connect equity to smart growth. In their first Funders' Network translation paper on social equity and smart growth in 1999, the text was long on hope but short on evidence. Only five years later, however, PolicyLink issued a second edition of the paper that provided a plethora of examples that included region-wide affordable housing, equitable transportation, "fix-it-first" infrastructure spending, and better land use in places as diverse as Boston, Atlanta, Detroit, San Diego, and the Bay Area (Blackwell and Fox, 2004). An ally of PolicyLink, the East Bay Alliance for a Sustainable Economy (EBASE) has chronicled community benefits agreements (CBAs), which are now used around the country to hold development—like high-rise lofts and towering office buildings—accountable to existing residents (EBASE, 2008). Equitable development has joined with smart planning to create a message of hope, a style of inclusion, and a frame that suggests that competitiveness and cohesion can go together.

Some say that smart planning and social inclusion are luxuries the nation can ill afford as it works its way through a crisis—or in general, for that matter. This is exactly wrong: contrary to traditional economics and popular discourse, research has shown that those metros that make more progress on reducing poverty, segregation, and inequality actually grow faster and stronger, an argument for equitable growth to which we return in our concluding chapter (Pastor and Benner, 2008).

Putting It Together. Without careful planning, our cities will soon return to the segregation and disparities of the past, but with a twist: wealthy whites living in sparkling downtowns and the poor isolated and struggling in aging, underserved suburbs, similar to Paris. But as that city's recent riots made clear, the comparison is hardly flattering and consigns low-income people, immigrants, and people of color to disinvested outskirts that offer little opportunity and even less hope for the future.

Now is the time to reimagine our metro areas, and President Obama, so far, seems up to the challenge of sparking our imagination. During his candidacy, in a speech he made to the U. S. Conference of Mayors, he said, ". . . we also need to stop seeing our cities as the problem and start seeing them as the solution. Because strong cities are the building blocks of strong regions, and strong regions are essential for a strong America."[30] To implement this vision, the White House now has an Office of Urban Affairs that takes an explicitly regional approach.[31]

A national movement is also afoot, as evidenced by the turnout of close to 2,000 people at the 2008 PolicyLink summit linking equitable development and smart growth. Americans are looking for opportunities to connect around shared issues. Building healthy metropolitan communities may just be one way to reach that higher common ground.

Climate Change and Equity

In the previous edition of this book, environmental justice was identified as one of the challenges for the new millennium. These issues, however, have escalated and intensified as part of a broader concern about climate change and its impact on low-income communities. The issues surrounding climate justice are in the nascent stages of being quantified, but the warnings indicate the proliferation of existing environmental justice issues for communities of color. Several reports recently published paint an alarming picture. A study by the Environmental Justice and Climate Change Initiative (EJCC) reports on the health, economic, and community impacts of climate change on African Americans. EJCC notes that increased exposure to toxic air pollutants, economic hardships related to rising fuel costs, and heat-related deaths are just the beginning of the many climate hardships that low-income communities will face (Hoerner and Robinson, 2008).

The African American community—despite their low levels of contribution to global warming relative to non-Hispanic whites—will be unduly affected in a multitude of ways. For example, the rise in temperatures caused by climate change could increase the number and magnitude of hurricanes and tropical storms. What is most concerning is that six of the states within the Atlantic hurricane zone have the highest share of African Americans in the United States (Hoerner and Robinson, 2008). Their vulnerability to these types of disasters coupled with their economic vulnerability worsens the outlook for African Americans. EJCC reports that the rise in unemployment due to price shocks in the energy market will only exacerbate unemployment among a group that is consistently troubled by high unemployment rates.

Another recent study about the inequalities of climate change further elaborates on the realities of climate change's disproportionate impacts on low-income communities and communities of color (Morello-Frosch et al., 2009). In a report titled *The Climate Gap*, researchers analyze data for California to paint a picture of the health and economic consequences of climate change for the state. The findings, consistent with EJCC's report, echo similar concerns for low-income communities of color. These concerns span extreme heat waves, health hazards from increased air pollution, changes to the prices of basic necessities, changes to job opportunities, and changes to the price of extreme weather insurance.

For example, five of California's smoggiest cities, which are also home to the state's highest shares of people of color and low-income individuals, are projected to have the highest ambient ozone increases. There will be health and financial implications for low-income communities of color, forcing them to spend a greater share of their income on basic necessities such as food, water, and electricity as the price of these goods continues to rise. They will also have less disposable income to spend on insurance to protect them against a growing number of extreme weather events projected to occur. And industries such as agriculture and tourism, which in California contain jobs mostly held by low-income people of color, may be hardest hit by climate change. The researchers argue that the agricultural sector—already characterized by job insecurity, low wages, seasonal work, and a workforce that is 77 percent Latino—will be hard hit as changes to weather increase the industry's volatility.

The findings from recent research on climate justice find that the risk for low-income populations and communities of color is very real. The problems of climate change and heat will permeate cities. Central cities will be forced to contend with the urban heat island effect, which occurs when the built concrete and asphalt environment actually traps heat and increases temperatures in central cities. In some places, urban heat islands are nearly 5 degrees Fahrenheit higher than surrounding areas. Heat also releases allergens, including pollen and mold, triggering conditions such as asthma in children (Lin, 2008).

Research has also shown that heat waves are most dangerous for socially isolated people and people of color. In 1995, a dramatic heat wave in Chicago caused the deaths of approximately 739 people and thousands of heat-related illnesses. Many of those who died were low-income, elderly, ill or bedridden, living alone, isolated, and without an air conditioner (Klinenberg, 2002). Having an air conditioner would be a simple coping mechanism for heat waves; however, research has shown that African Americans in the Los Angeles region have less access to air conditioning relative to the general population (Morello-Frosch et al., 2009; U.S. Census Bureau, 2004). Researcher Eric Klinenberg, who investigated the 1995 heat wave in his book *Heat Wave: A Social Autopsy of Disaster in Chicago*, observed that many of the African Americans who died lived in crumbling, disinvested neighborhoods that lacked infrastructure such as good transportation or recreational facilities that could have served as cooling centers during the crisis. These social factors and others will come into play in determining who suffers most from the effects of global warming. And in areas where severe heat waves already occur, they will intensify in magnitude and duration.

Overall, these studies paint a stark picture of what's to come for low-income communities of color. These communities will be the ones with the least resources to respond to extreme or irregular weather events. Some may be forced to choose food over paying the heating bill, or to choose gas over air conditioning. Others may not have adequate health care to access services related to heat effects or a rise in disease related to climate change. Drinking-water quality could be affected in communities that may already lack access to water that meets basic sanitation standards.

Today, there does not exist widespread recognition that these problems affect various groups differently or that a different set of solutions can promote a different set of social goals. The solutions that are used to address climate change will profoundly impact people of color and low-income communities. In many ways, these communities will serve as a measure of how effective our solutions really are.

Going forward, the consequences and indirect impacts of new regulations and mandates to address climate change will need to be analyzed through an equity lens to ensure that the climate gap does not worsen disparities for low-income communities of color. Efforts to minimize greenhouse gases should prioritize cutting emissions in neighborhoods that are overburdened with air toxics first; many have argued that the current policy fascination with cap-and-trade mechanisms runs the risk of ignoring this important externality (something which seems much less "external" for communities living near refineries and other emitters of greenhouse gas emissions, and other toxics).

Other parts of our strategy to address climate change could expand investments in retrofitting older buildings and homes that were constructed in the 1950s and 1960s to be more energy-efficient. This green-collar economy is inextricably linked with public investments in areas such as transportation, land use, and housing, and prioritizes the older urban and inner-ring suburban areas where many people of color live. By pulling together environmental issues, the move toward energy independence, and economic development under the rubric of the equity movement, America can finally break free from its most intractable problems.

Conclusion

The climate challenge helps illustrate how the issues of racial equity facing America in the twenty-first century may be different, deeper, and more complex than the questions of overt discrimination that occupied attention in an earlier era. We need to look for universal gains and principles—such as everyone's right to a clean environment or the common interest in metropolitan sprawl—but we must also understand and address the specific issues affecting different ethnic groups. Policy recommendations will require serious research and honest debate rather than a simple attachment to old remedies.

Most of all, these urgent issues will require a new form of leadership, one that recognizes race but is not fixated on it, one that crosses boundaries but stays rooted in community, one that embodies a broad moral vision but has a pragmatic program for making sure all Americans prosper. It is to this discussion of leadership that we now turn.

Notes

[1] See *One in 100: Behind Bars in America 2008*, PEW Center on the States, 2008, http://www.pewcenteronthestates.org/uploadedFiles/One%20in%20100.pdf.

[2] Building Resilient Regions comparative cities database. Analysis by the Program for Environmental and Regional Equity (PERE).

[3] See *MetroNation*, Metropolitan Policy Program, Brookings Institution, 2007.

[4] President Barack Obama, speech to a joint session of Congress, February 24, 2009, www.whitehouse.gov/the_press_office/remarks-of-president-barack-obama-address-to-joint-session-of-congress.

5 See Michael Rebell's draft paper presented at the 2008 Symposium on Comprehensive Educational Equity, "Overcoming the Socioeconomic Barriers to School Success," Teachers' College, Columbia University, November 17–18, 2008 at http://devweb.tc.columbia.edu/man ager/symposium/Files/116_Rebell_Implementing%20Comp%20%20 Edu%20Equity%20Draft%2011–12–08%20doc.pdf. The paper covers a range of cases, including the 2003 New York Court of Appeals' decision upholding that New York schoolchildren are constitutionally entitled to the "opportunity for a *meaningful* high school education." Cited with the permission of the author.

6 See text of speech on urban poverty at http://www.barackobama .com/2007/07/18/remarks_of_senator_barack_obam_19.php.

7 From "Comprehensive Educational Equity: The Path to Meaningful Opportunity for Excellence," notes prepared by Edmund Gordon for the 2008 Teachers' College Educational Equity Conference. Used with the permission of the author.

8 Speech on urban poverty accessible at http://www.barackobama .com/2007/07/18/remarks_of_senator_barack_obam_19.php.

9 Ibid.

10 See *Diplomas Count 2008: School to College*, special edition of *Education Week*, June 5, 2008.

11 Tabulations by the Program for Environmental and Regional Equity (PERE) of IPUMS 2005–2007 Pooled ACS data.

12 See Steele and Aronson (1995) and the popular review of this research in Sharon Begley, "The Stereotype Trap," *Newsweek*, November 6, 2000, pp. 66–68.

13 As indicated in a cover letter from Peter Orszag, director of the Office of Management and Budget, April 3, 2009, accessible at http://www .recovery.gov/sites/default/files/m09–15.pdf.

14 For more information, please see http://www.niemanwatchdog.org/ index.cfm?fuseaction=ask_this.view&askthisid=00415.

15 LA Infrastructure and Sustainable Jobs Collaborative, Regional Economic Development Institute, Los Angeles Trade-Technical College, http://www.lattc.edu/dept/lattc/REDI/Utility.html.

16 As noted in a press release, "Pacific Gas and Electric Company Launches Workforce Development Program," January 14, 2008, accessible at http://www.pge.com/about/news/mediarelations/newsreleases/ q1_2008/080114.shtml.

17 Tabulations by the Program for Environmental and Regional Equity (PERE) of IPUMS 2007 ACS data (nationwide).

18 The Migration Policy Institute, Children and Family Policy, http:// www.migrationinformation.org/integration/children.cfm.

19 National Criminal Justice Commission Act of 2009, http://webb.senate .gov/email/criminaljusticereform.html.

[20] Senator Webb's National Criminal Justice Commission Act of 2009 Fact Sheet, http://webb.senate.gov/email/incardocs/FactSheeti.pdf.

[21] Compiled from U.S. Census Bureau Census of Local Governments 2002, as reported at http://www.pittsburghtoday.org/web/indicators .jsp?cat=6.

[22] http://www.allbusiness.com/crime-law-enforcement-corrections/correc tions-prisons/11554234-1.html.

[23] See "Sentencing Commission Narrows Crack/Cocaine Disparity," Public Welfare Foundation Newsroom, December 12, 2007, http://www .publicwelfare.org/Newsroom/NewsDetails.aspx?newsid=16.

[24] See, Mari Gallagher Research & Consulting Group, *Examining the Impact of Food Desserts on Public Health in Detroit*, 2007, http://www.mari gallagher.com.

[25] Andrew Grossman, "Shopping Becomes a Challenge as Auto-Industry Collapse Adds to City's Woes," *Wall Street Journal*, June 17, 2009.

[26] Both quotes are from President Obama speaking at a town hall forum in Ft. Myers, Florida. See Kaid Benfield, "President Obama: 'The Days Where We're Just Building Sprawl Forever, Those Days Are Over," February 11, 2009, http://www.worldchanging.com/archives/009420 .html.

[27] See Department of Transportation press release, "HUD and DOT Partnership: Sustainable Communities," March 18, 2009, available at http://www.dot.gov/affairs/dot3209.htm.

[28] http://yosemite.epa.gov/opa/admpress.nsf/0/f500561fbb8d5a08852575 d700501350?OpenDocument.

[29] See the PolicyLink Web site, http://www.policylink.org/HealthyFood Retailing.

[30] Organizing for America, "Barack at the Conference of Mayors Convention in Miami, FL," June 21, 2008, http://my.barackobama.com/ page/community/post/stateupdates/gG5R7x.

[31] The White House, Urban Policy, http://www.whitehouse.gov/issues/ urban_policy.

References

Aarons, Dakarai. 2009. "President Envisions Anti-Poverty Efforts Like Harlem's 'Zone.' " *Education Week*, March 11.

American Public Transportation Association. Press kit accessible at http:// www.apta.com/media/releases/070618_dump_the_pump.cfm.

Benner, Chris, and Radhika Fox. 2009. *Inclusion in the Workforce: Positioning the Pittsburgh Region to Prosper and Compete*. Pittsburgh: Sustainable Pittsburgh.

Blackwell, Angela Glover, and Radhika Fox. 2004. *Regional Equity and Smart Growth: Opportunities for Advancing Social and Economic Justice in America*. Funders' Network for Smart Growth and Livable Communities, Translation Paper 1, Edition 2. http://www.fundersnetwork.org/usr_doc/Regional_Equity_and_Smart_Growth_2nd_Ed.pdf.

California Tomorrow. 2006. *California's Gold: Claiming the Promise of Diversity in California's Community Colleges*. San Francisco: California Tomorrow.

Cech, Scott J. 2008. "P-16 Councils Bring All Tiers of Education to the Table." *Education Week*, June 5.

Center on Race and Social Problems. 2007. *Pittsburgh's Racial Demographics: Differences and Disparities*. Pittsburgh: Center on Race and Social Problems.

Dillon, Sam. 2009. "Study Sees an Obama Effect as Lifting Black Test-Takers," *New York Times*, January 23, 2009.

Dobbie, Will, and Roland G. Fryer, Jr. 2009. "Are High-Quality Schools Enough to Close the Achievement Gap? Evidence from a Bold Social Experiment in Harlem." Harvard University, http://www.economics.harvard.edu/faculty/fryer/files/hcz%204.15.2009.pdf.

Dounay, Jennifer. 2008. "The Three A's of Successful P-16 Reform." *Education Week*, June 5.

EBASE (East Bay Alliance for a Sustainable Economy). 2008. "Building a Better Bay Area: Community Benefit Tools and Case Studies to Achieve Responsible Development." September.

Education Trust. 2005. *Gaining Traction: Gaining Ground*. Washington, DC: Education Trust. November.

Ellison, Jesse. 2009. "The Refugees Who Saved Lewiston." *Newsweek*, January 26.

Fields, Gary. 2008. "The High School Dropout's Economic Ripple Effect." *Wall Street Journal*, October 21.

Fix, Michael, and Wendy Zimmerman. 2000. "The Integration of Immigrant Families in the United States." Citizens' Commission on Civil Rights Biennial Report on Federal Civil Rights and Enforcement.

Gordon, Edmund W., Beatrice L. Bridglall, and Aundra Saa Meroe. 2005. *Supplementary Education: The Hidden Curriculum of High Academic Achievement*. Lanham, MD: Rowman & Littlefield Publishers.

Hoerner, Andrew J., and Nia Robinson. 2008. *A Climate of Change: African Americans, Global Warming, and a Just Climate Policy for the U.S.* Environmental Justice and Climate Change Initiative (EJCC). http://ejcc.org/climateofchange.pdf.

Jencks, Christopher, and Meredith Phillips. 1998. "America's Next Achievement Test: Closing the Black-White Test Score Gap." *American Prospect* 9 (40): 44–53.

Jones, Tim. 2009. "Detroit's Outlook Falls Along with Home Prices." *Chicago Tribune*, January 29.

Jones, Van. 2006. "On Being Black at a Latino March." *Huffington Post*, May 5.

———. 2008. *The Green Collar Economy*. New York: HarperCollins.

Katz, Bruce, and Jennifer Bradley. 2009. "The Suburban Challenge." *Newsweek*, January 26.

Klinenberg, Eric. 2002. *Heat Wave: A Social Autopsy of Disaster in Chicago*. Chicago: University of Chicago Press.

Krikorian, Mark. 2007. "Legal, Good/Illegal, Bad? Let's Call the Whole Thing Off." *National Review Online*, June 1.

Lin, Serena. 2008. *Understanding Climate Change: An Equitable Framework*. Oakland, CA: PolicyLink.

Litman, Todd. 2004. *Rail Transit in America: A Comprehensive Evaluation of Benefits*. Victoria Transport Policy Institute. October 25. Accessible at http://www.apta.com/research/info/online/documents/rail_transit_summary.pdf.

Marable, Manning. 2000. "Facing the Demon Head On: Institutional Racism and the Prison Industrial Complex." *Southern Changes* 22(3): 4–7.

Morello-Frosch, Rachel, Manuel Pastor, Jr., James Sadd, and Seth B. Shokoff. 2009. *The Climate Gap: Inequalities in How Climate Change Hurts Americans & How to Close the Gap*. The College of Natural Resources at the University of California, Berkeley, and the University of Southern California Program for Environmental and Regional Equity.

National Council on Crime and Delinquency. 2007. *And Justice for Some: Differential Treatment of Youth of Color in the Justice System*. Oakland, CA: National Council on Crime and Delinquency.

Oakes, Jeannie and Marisa Saunders, eds. 2008. *Beyond Tracking: Multiple Pathways to College, Career, and Civic Participation*. Cambridge, MA: Harvard Education Press.

Orfield, Myron. 1997. *Metropolitics: A Regional Agenda for Community and Stability*. Washington, DC: Brookings Institution Press.

Pager, Devah. 2007. *Marked: Race, Crime, and Finding Work in an Era of Mass Incarceration*. Chicago: University of Chicago Press.

Pastor, Manuel. 2008. "State of the Region: The New Demography, the New Economy, and the New Environment." Program for Environmental and Regional Equity and the Bay Area Social Equity Caucus (SEC). Presented at the SEC 10th Anniversary State of the Region Conference, December 15, 2008.

Pastor, Manuel, and Chris Benner. 2008. "Been Down So Long: Weak-Market Cities and Regional Equity." In Richard M. McGahey and Jennifer S. Vey eds., *Retooling for Growth: Building a 21st Century Economy in*

America's Older Industrial Areas. Washington, DC: Brookings Institution Press.

Pastor, Manuel, and Rhonda Ortiz. 2009. *Immigrant Integration in Los Angeles: Strategic Direction for Funders*, The Program for Environmental and Regional Equity (PERE).

PolicyLink. 2009. *Community College Pathways Out of Poverty for Vulnerable Californians*. Oakland, CA: PolicyLink.

PolicyLink and Green For All. 2009. *Bringing Home the Green Recovery*. Oakland, CA: PolicyLink and Green For All.

PolicyLink and Prevention Institute. 2009. *The Transportation Prescription: Bold New Ideas for Healthy, Equitable Transportation Reform in America*. Oakland, CA: PolicyLink.

PolicyLink, UCLA Center for Health Policy Research, and California Center for Public Health Advocacy. 2008. *Designed for Disease: The Link Between Local Food Environments and Obesity and Diabetes*. Oakland, CA: PolicyLink. April.

Rouse, C. E. 2005. "The Labor Market Consequences of an Inadequate Education." Princeton University and NBER. Preliminary paper prepared for the Equity Symposium on "The Social Costs of Inadequate Education" at Teachers' College, Columbia University.

Rutenberg, Jim. 2009. "Obama Plans New Funds for Colleges." *New York Times*, July 15.

Sanchez, Thomas W., Rich Stolz, and Jacinta S. Ma. 2003. *Moving to Equity: Addressing Inequitable Effects of Transportation Policies on Minorities*. A Joint Report of the Civil Rights Project at Harvard University and the Center for Community Change. Cambridge, MA: Civil Rights Project at Harvard University.

Sen, Rinku, and Fekkak Mamdouh. 2008. *The Accidental American: Immigration and Citizenship in the Age of Globalization*. San Francisco: Berrett-Koehler Publishers.

The Sentencing Project. 2008. *Reducing Racial Disparity in the Criminal Justice System: A Manual for Practitioners and Policymakers*. 2nd ed. Washington, DC: Sentencing Project.

Skocpol, Theda. 1991. "Targeting Within Universalism: Politically Viable Policies to Combat Poverty in the United States." In Christopher Jencks and Paul E. Peterson, eds., *The Urban Underclass*. Washington, DC: Brookings Institution Press.

Steele, Claude M., and Joshua Aronson. 1995. "Stereotype Threat and the Intellectual Test Performance of African-Americans." *Journal of Personality and Social Psychology* 69 (5): 797–811.

Surface Transportation Policy Project. *Transportation and Poverty Alleviation Fact Sheet*. Accessible at http://www.transact.org/issues/intro_elc.asp.

Teicher, Stacy A. 2005. "Schools Build 'Cultures of Excellence.'" *Christian Science Monitor*, December 8.

U.S. Census Bureau. 2004. *Current Housing Reports: American Housing Survey for the Los Angeles-Long Beach Metropolitan Area, 2003*.

Viadero, Debra. 2007. "Low-income Students are Public School Majority in South, Study Finds." *Education Week*, October 30.

Wilson, William Julius. 1999. *The Bridge over the Racial Divide: Rising Inequality and Coalition Politics*. Berkeley: University of California Press.

———. 2009. *More Than Just Race: Being Black and Poor in the Inner City*. New York: W. W. Norton.

Zielbauer, Paul. 2001. "Felons Gain Voting Rights in Connecticut." *New York Times*, May 14.

5

New Leadership for the Twenty-First Century

Addressing the dysfunction of racial inequity is not an easy task. Tackling climate change in a way that acknowledges the legacy of environmental injustice will require both thought and struggle. Making education function in a way that engages students, their parents, and communities will be a challenge. Persuading Americans that immigrants add far more to this country than they subtract will require bold, visionary appeals to surrender old prejudices for a better tomorrow. Lifting up the issues of excessive incarceration will raise hackles and attempting to link city and suburb in a metropolitan whole runs against decades of segregation and abandonment.

Taking on all these issues at the same time is even harder—and it will require a new sort of twenty-first-century leadership. But what does that leadership look like, how does it work, and how can we develop it?

This chapter suggests that the answers to these questions can be found by shifting our zoom lens to wide-angle, and focusing not only on the role of our policymakers in this new political arrangement, but also on that of our grassroots leaders. The election of Barack Obama is important, but it is also the culmination of the social justice movements of the 1960s and 1970s that challenged leadership to expand opportunity for all. In a nation where no one group will be a majority, national leadership must collaborate with a disparate group of actors and articulate a vision for a fairer, more just, and more productive society. Yet it is on the local level that inequity most deeply resonates—crumbling sidewalks in Detroit, diesel pollution in West Oakland, and lack of sufficient transit for low-income Atlanta—and where solutions are best identified.

The Leadership Learning Community has outlined the challenges ahead, in which twenty-first-century leaders must be prepared to lead under conditions of globalization, increasing stress on the environment, increasing speed and dissemination of information technology, enhanced diversity, rapid change, unprecedented complexity, growing interdependence, and an ever-widening gap between the haves and have-nots (Meehan, Perry, and Reinert, 2009). And it is a full suite of leaders—from the grass roots to the grass tops—that will be necessary to undo decades of bad policies and produce viable, sustainable change.

This generation of leaders will have to prepare itself to deal with a stew of complicated issues, made all the more vexing because there is no precedent upon which it can rely for guidance. No previous generation of American leadership has ever had to tackle so much so quickly. To quote the mantra of civil rights activist Jesse Jackson, Sr.: "You can't teach what you don't know; you can't lead where you don't go." The past few chapters of *Uncommon Common Ground* aimed to shine a light on the "knowing"; this chapter aims to spotlight the "going," which is the actual process of leadership and its development.

Here, in a nutshell, is what America's leaders must confront:

1. *Increasing racial and economic disparities.* In October 2009, the U.S. Labor Department reported the highest unemployment rates since the sharp downturn of the early 1980s: 10.2 percent of the labor force looking for work, and even more too discouraged to keep searching. At the same time, African Americans and Latinos were facing unemployment rates of 15.7 and 13.1 percent respectively.[1]

2. *The so-called "browning of America" and the array of issues affiliated with the rapid demographic shifts in cities, suburbs, and rural areas.* Most significantly, racial dynamics are no longer just black-white: South Los Angeles, for example, has experienced a surge in Latino immigrant populations where African Americans had been the majority, and churches and other institutions that have long served the needs of African American communities are pressed to serve the diverse and sometimes conflicting needs of immigrant populations. They, along with other community leaders, will have to help reconcile differences among groups, and build infrastructure and programs that will improve everyone's standard of living.

3. *The interconnectedness of issues and their solutions.* Today's society presents a modern-day "chicken-or-egg" syndrome. For example, educational achievement is linked not only to teachers and parental involvement, but also to improving community conditions such as reducing violence and increasing access to health care. It would be shortsighted to create jobs without examining unequal educational opportunities and the lack of efficient public transportation.

4. *The changing electorate.* Barack Obama's presidential campaign mobilized voters in a way this nation has never seen. We saw an unprecedented jump in the numbers and enthusiasm of youths and racial minorities. At the same time, political leaders are hard-pressed to garner widespread support for measures that directly address racial inequality.

5. *Globalization*. Looking beyond one's immediate sphere and geographic location is a must in this new century. Garment workers in North Carolina no longer compete only with garment workers in California or New York, but in Guatemala and Vietnam as well. Globalization has enormous implications for all leaders who are working toward racial equity. The political backlash against globalization has led not only to civic protests but also to debate about how to make international institutions more accountable. As economies across the world become increasingly interconnected, leaders must expand their global vision and understanding.

Leadership for Changing Times

Leaders for racial equity have and will come in different shapes and sizes, hailing from the religious, labor, business, and political spheres. The paths of prominent leaders such as Martin Luther King, Jr., César Chávez, and Philip Vera Cruz are good road maps, but there are also large numbers of less well-known community leaders who have taken on the often tricky and sometimes even dangerous task of fighting for racial justice and equality. (See Box 5-1 for an example; and see also Kwoh and Leong, 2009, for additional civil rights stories.)

With the emerging trends and barriers facing leaders in the new millennium, the qualities of good leadership need refining and updating. A leader in the twenty-first century should be a problem solver, a lifelong learner, and an ethical example for others. To lead, one should have a penchant for action as well as a commitment to reflection and collaboration.

In a 2005 publication, the Asian Pacific American Legal Center (APALC) described this new brand of leadership as:

Box 5-1. California Indians and the Civil Rights Movement

The American Indian community of California of the 1960s, in all of its diversity of tribes and places of origin, was acutely aware of the civil rights movement as it appeared in California and on television. The inspirational oratory and heroic actions of Martin Luther King, Jr., César Chávez, and Philip Vera Cruz fell on fertile ground all across California Indian country. It fostered an emerging sense of identity and energy that led to significant progress on several fronts. Symbolically, the term Native American began to supplant the previously used term of American Indian as the appropriate form of reference for a more proactive and assertive collective identity. This new approach of activism proved to be effective.

Signs of progress were seen all across California. In 1967, a state legislative commission was established for a redressing of historic grievances in response to an outcry from California tribal leaders. The central issue to be considered during this time was the destructive impacts of a cessation of federally supported Indian services, which left almost one-third of California's tribal governments to collapse across the state. Within the community, California Indian-controlled organizations were established to advocate for the expansion of tribal opportunity, economic development, and health care. Statewide organizations that emerged from this new activist era include the Inter-Tribal Council of California, the California Rural Indian Health Board, the California Indian Manpower Consortium, and California Indian Legal Services, all of which remain operational today.

The link between the Native Americans and their tribal lands is immutable and unchanging as a source of identity and strength. Compared to tribes in other parts of the country, tribes in California maintained control over a relatively small land base made up of four larger reservations and numerous small *rancherias* spread across the state. The relocation of thousands of American Indians to California from reservations in rural America created a new population of American Indian people in urban California centered on cities such as San Jose, Oakland, San Francisco, and Los Angeles. These "Urban Indians" clustered around support programs such as the Friendship House in Oakland and the San Francisco Indian Center.

After the loss of federal recognition in the 1950s and 1960s, the collapse of many tribes compounded issues regarding the failed treaty process of the 1840s and increased the number of federally unrecognized California Indians. The result of all this displacement was a unique form of civil rights activism by American Indians in California to "reclaim the land." During this era, Indian activists successfully occupied, reclaimed, and acquired title to lands in Sonoma County and Yolo County, which are now home to the prominent Native American academic institutes Ya-Ka-Ama Indian Education and D-Q University.

Although not all efforts were successful, solidarity was established within various tribes in California. Such examples include: in Summit City, California, the attempts to reclaim a condemned housing compound near a federal dam at Toyon—a Native American territory—ultimately failed, but unity was accomplished; and in San Francisco, probably the most spectacular of these efforts was the takeover of Alcatraz Island on November 24, 1969. The resulting 557-day occupation of this island was a galvanizing event in the California American Indian community that was viewed by the whole nation. It was an act of civil disobedience that forged lasting bonds of cohesion among those who participated, regardless of their tribal membership or even the federal status their tribe held. The American Indian civil rights movement had found new strength by establishing partnerships within its own community—marking a new era of emerging identity.

—Written by James Allen Crouch,
executive director of California
Rural Indian Health Board, May 14, 2009.

1. Committed to social justice, equality, inclusion, and the empowerment of disenfranchised communities.
2. Embracing the intersectional nature of individuals' identities, including race, ethnicity, class, gender, and sexual orientation.
3. Promoting the ability to work from a multigroup perspective, understanding the needs of each group, and bridging them to work toward the greater good for everyone.
4. Seeking to cross boundaries of race, ethnicity, class, gender, sexual orientation, and other divides, as well as sector, discipline, profession, and geography.
5. Recognizing that effective solutions need to be generated by and in conjunction with those closest to the issues.

Below, we explore how these characteristics apply to four areas of rapid change: the new economy, the new demography, the new geography, and the new technology. We use these categories only as a means to organize thoughts, not as restrictive groupings; as we will see, the qualities of good leadership cut across all these areas, and leaders will need to integrate agendas in these areas in their practice. We conclude this section by briefly touching on the capacities that communities and leaders need before turning in the close of the chapter to how such capacities can be developed through leadership programs, mentoring, and other avenues for growth.

Leadership in the New Economy

The biggest obstacle to effective leadership is the recession of 2008–2009, which has had a direct impact on racial justice efforts. An extreme, fundamentalist approach to capitalism has led to widening inequality over the past thirty years. In April 2009, *The Economist* reported that in "1979, 34.2 percent of all capital gains went to the top 1 percent of recipients; by 2005, the figure was 65.3 percent."[2] Excessive debt, speculative buying, unshared economic prosperity, and excessive greed have all widened economic and racial disparities. A *Washington Post* article says, "The gap between the wealth of white Americans and African Americans has grown. According to the Federal Reserve's Survey of Consumer Finances, for every dollar of wealth held by the typical white family, the African American family has only one dime."[3] The actual wealth gap may actually be worse because the Federal Reserve survey was completed in 2007 before the financial meltdown in 2008.

Consequently, it is incumbent upon leaders to understand that simply restimulating the economy without changing the growing patterns of inequality will only lead us right back to where we started in a few years' time, and again and again. Regulating the markets is not enough. The question is not, as some pundits suggest, between socialism and capitalism, but this: in what form does our economic system reduce inequalities and work for all Americans?

As mentioned in Chapter 4, in times like these, many people subscribe to the false belief that *any* growth is good and that equity is a luxury. So, trying to insert a new analysis and policy framework among loud voices and scrambling strategists requires voices that are clear and which lift up what works rather than merely pointing out what does not. By now, it's clear that trickle-down economics failed America; what's more important is highlighting how living wage laws, community benefit regulations, and expansions in health care will strengthen, not weaken the nation. Leaders need to come to the table with a viable economic alternative. This will take research and some appropriate expertise, but it's also about vision. Leaders will need to move from a demand for economic justice—that is, a redistribution after the fact—to the notion that we can and should create a just economy, one in which the initial outcomes reward the energy, enthusiasm, and creativity of working people.

In short, as the American economy reboots to version 2.0, it should upgrade to a model based on rebuilding with equity.

This will be a particular challenge in an integrated world economy where neighborhood economic analyses are complexly interrelated with international trends. For example, the aforementioned garment workers—largely people of color—are among the working poor in the United States, in some measure because they are competing with even more poorly paid workers in other countries. Leaders will be unable to affect and improve the working and health conditions of garment workers without a global understanding of change in this industry. What interests push against a higher minimum wage? What dynamics in the market produce very high-and very low-wage work and how can we change that? How does one raise wages without pushing businesses toward off-shoring or plant closures? And if a job is off-shored, how does that affect the workers and minorities of other countries? Why are jobs, especially good jobs, outside of poor communities? Why are mixed-income communities difficult to create?

When leaders promise diversity and equity but the inner city remains poor and the downtown becomes a playground for urban professionals, resentment grows. Leaders of multiethnic coalitions need to have a larger commitment to both visualizing and achieving inclusive economic growth for their regions and for the nation.

Leadership, New Politics, and New Demography

Leadership will be challenged on how to tackle the issue of race with the first African American to be elected president. Complexities will arise in uniting the diverse mosaic of groups struggling for social justice.

In March 2009, the *Los Angeles Times* reported that conservative legal foundations and the Republican governor of Georgia filed briefs in the U.S. Supreme Court challenging key parts of the Voting Rights Act, citing among other things, high black turnout in the fall election.[4] The conservative groups believed that Obama's victory heralded the emergence of a color-blind society in which special legal safeguards for minorities are no longer required.

In its June 2009 decision, the Supreme Court sidestepped a challenge to a key provision of the Voting Rights Act. In the case of *Northwest Austin Municipal Utility District Number One v. Holder*, a Texas water district argued that Section 5 of the Voting Rights Act is unconstitutional and should be declared invalid. The section requires state and local governments to preclear changes in electoral procedures with the federal government. Section 5 applies in areas that have been historical bastions of discrimination, including many states and municipalities in the South as well as some in California and New York. The Court avoided making a ruling on whether Section 5 is constitutional, but provided the water district and similar municipal jurisdictions with an option to bail out from the provision if the municipality could demonstrate a clean track record with regard to restricting voter rights in the previous decade.[5] While this key provision of the Voting Rights Act remains, how long the Court will allow Section 5 to remain in place is open to question.

In any case, the suggestion by conservative groups to take away a crucial protection of a basic democratic right based on the victory of a black presidential candidate reflects a renewed belief in color-blind politics, a belief that is gaining popularity beyond conservative circles. It is paramount that we remember that one person's achievements are not an accurate indicator of the collective racial, economic, and educational experience of diverse Americans. Leaders must again rise to the challenge of bringing racial justice issues to the forefront.

Of course, the question of how much to emphasize race and racial differences runs through nearly every aspect of policymaking and coalition building in this country, with one line of thought suggesting that we would be better off with universal appeals for, say, more education or more economic growth, with the hope that this would have particularly important benefits for racial minorities.

In our last book, we offered a simple phrase to capture our own approach: "you need to get race up front to get race behind." In our experience as organizers of community groups, professionals, and policymakers, those groups that do not discuss racial tensions and differences early on eventually find such conversations forced upon them as they come to key strategic political and policy discussions. On the other hand, those groups that do take account of race and racism early are better prepared—and seem to focus on the universal issues with an ease and trust not evidenced by those who have avoided the topic.

It's because of trust built through long-term relationships, based on an understanding of each others' issues and sustained through sometimes highly uncomfortable conversations, that we get down to root problems, cultural differences, and common but not identical ground. Unaddressed racial tension is the underlying cause of mistrust. This is not about getting beyond race; it's about acknowledging the elephant in the room so that you can move on to other matters.

Of course, one additional challenge in the current period is the lack of a unifying issue around which to focus a vision and rally as in previous decades. In the 1960s and 1970s, the unquestioned goal was ending legalized discrimination. Leaders from all walks of life recognized the need to advocate for laws that created equal opportunity, guaranteed equal rights, and afforded equal access.

Today, the racial equity agenda is more complex and involves the full set of issues reviewed in Chapter 4. Achieving common ground is difficult, even among those who believe that significant structural barriers that stifle individual efforts are still in place. All too often, different and sometimes competing agendas exist among groups that are separated by race, ethnicity, geography, political view,

---

Box 5-2. Racialized Gang Violence Prevention and Intervention: The Dangers and Opportunities for Progressive Leadership

One of the most complex and consequential issues facing progressive leaders forging multiethnic coalitions is the gang issue, and in particular the impact it has on race and ethnic relations. If racialized gang violence continues to grow, it poses serious threats to efforts to strengthen bonds between racial and ethnic groups, particularly Latinos and African Americans. At the same time, the racialized gang violence problem presents valuable opportunities for diverse communities to come together to pursue meaningful solutions beyond police suppression. Preventing gang violence is a public safety problem that is considered a high priority for many communities.

An example of racialized gang violence is the violence in one region of Southern California in which a multigenerational Latino gang was said to be given a "green light on blacks" by the prison-based Sureños of the Mexican Mafia prison gang, because of an alleged drug theft by an African American gang in the area. In the violence that followed, black gang members were attacked, as well as blacks with no known gang affiliation. Retaliation by the black gang followed, which led to Latino gang members and non–gang-member Latinos being shot. Not surprisingly, the retaliatory attacks by both sides became less careful about whether the target was a gang member or not. And when community members saw innocent people getting shot, understandably the fear and animosity toward the other racial group began to spread.

So while the violence might begin between gang members, increasingly the harm is visited upon persons who are not involved with gangs. It claims innocent lives, fuels interracial violence in schools and communities, deepens fear and discord among the involved racial and ethnic groups, and is perpetuated by prison-based gangs.

It is important, however, to place the issue in perspective. Most gang violence continues to be intraracial or intraethnic—violence among people of the same racial or ethnic identity. Some analyses of gang homicide data in the city of Los Angeles suggest that 90 percent of cases are intraracial. However, the gang violence between people of different racial and ethnic identities is occurring more frequently, and there are many neighborhoods that are dominated by a given gang with racial animus. For example, in Los Angeles County, racial and ethnic hate crimes carried out by gang members have grown by 38 percent from 2005 to 2007.* Gang-perpetrated racially targeted violence needs to be addressed as part of gang violence reduction efforts, or we will face the danger that it will continue to expand and set back other positive gains in race and human relations work.

—Written by Robin Toma,
executive director of the Los Angeles County
Human Relations Commission, May 5, 2009.

---

*Los Angeles County Commission on Human Relations, Annual Hate Crime Report, 2007, www.lahumanrelations.org.

or "turf" (see Box 5-2 for a look at the black-brown gang issue, for instance). Groups are often divided over their goals and approaches based on ethnic group affiliation; intragroup tensions cloud the vision. Further, these divisions are exacerbated by the economic recession that makes dollars scarce and competition easier than collaboration.

Our past is not all that different from today—and some of that past gives us cause for hope. After the Los Angeles riots in 1992, the MultiCultural Collaborative (MCC) argued that the institutional responses to the crisis were fragmented and often disconnected from the social and economic causes that were at the root of many intergroup and racial conflicts (Choi, Lizardo, and Phillips, et al., 1996). Yet only thirteen years later, Antonio Villaraigosa, the first Latino mayor in L.A. in over 130 years, was elected in a campaign that lifted up common aspirations for education, public safety, and economic betterment. He did this not by avoiding race, but by finding a place for race: he secured election partly because he had been an effective advocate for racial justice in his previous public stances; he invested campaign time and resources to bring together African American and Latino constituencies; and he was seen as someone who understood the racial realities of the city's politics.

A new vision and commitment to racial equity is one that deals with the reality of race but seeks pragmatic solutions. This vision would espouse that racial attitudes may soften over time, but the structural inequality will not evaporate if left uncorrected. Its solutions will come in the form of universal and particular policies that crumble the hidden scaffolding of race in our institutions and erase the conscious and unconscious biases we hold personally.

Another example of leadership in the new demography is the Parent Organization Network (PON) in Los Angeles. United by a common concern for education, African American, Latino, and Asian American parents came together to improve educational outcomes for low-income minority communities. PON was initiated in July 2005 as a collaborative for independent parent organizations by the Los Angeles Multicultural Educational Collaborative (LAMEC) which is made up of the Asian Pacific American Legal Center (APALC), the Los Angeles Urban League (LAUL), and the Mexican American Legal Defense and Educational Fund (MALDEF).

The goal of the Parent Organization Network is essentially to build a movement to transform the public education system through policy reforms. Now, PON has over twenty parent organizations of different racial backgrounds building organizing capacity to improve the public education system in Los Angeles. In 2008, PON held its third countywide summit for more than four hundred community and parent leaders with the theme "Divided No More." It highlighted the need for a multiethnic parent movement and provided interpretation in Spanish, Chinese, and Vietnamese in order to involve all concerned parents regardless of fluency in English.

A particular application of this need for honest dialogue involves black-brown tensions. Of course, some of these tensions are overdrawn: While the media coverage of the 2008 presidential election overheated electoral rivalries between African American and Latino voters, collaboration was actually happening across the nation. According to Rubén Lizardo, associate director of PolicyLink, Latinos and African Americans in Los Angeles and the San Francisco Bay Area have been collaborating on a range of issues affecting their communities, including:

1. Inferior health services and the lack of access to quality health care that also meets diverse culture and language needs.
2. Escalating high school dropout rates and stagnant college participation rates.
3. Deterioration of community supports to vulnerable families that underlie the crisis facing men and boys of color.
4. Higher incidences of living in communities that have become dumping grounds for America's toxic wastes.
5. Higher rates of poverty and exclusion that stem from different structural obstacles to economic opportunity as well as failed federal immigration policies.[6]

Other groups are explicitly advancing black-brown alliances by building cross-racial organizing models from the ground up, such as Community Coalition and Action for Grassroots Empowerment and Neighborhood Development Alternative (AGENDA) in Los Angeles, and Urban Habitat in Oakland. These grassroots organizations have also gathered to share best practices, for example at the PolicyLink 2008 Regional Equity Summit in New Orleans and the 2008 Black-Latino Summit in Los Angeles.

What both Obama and successful leaders in these efforts demonstrate is the ability to lead beyond their constituency—they must be multiethnic and multiracial. In an interview with Stewart Kwoh in January 2001, Craig McGarvey, a former program officer at The James Irvine Foundation, described such leaders as "border bridgers" who must speak to and for their constituents while earning the respect of the constituents of others. "Border bridgers are leaders who move with integrity outside their own circles, always seeking a circle that is broader. They find common ground by setting difference aside and focusing on interests that can be shared."

The growing racial diversity of the United States in general, and in many poor neighborhoods in particular, requires that leaders have both a universal concern for all disadvantaged people as well as an understanding of a particular group's needs. These dual—and sometimes dueling—concerns may lead to situations in which leaders must negotiate how best to bring groups that are in conflict over significant issues together as well as to mitigate disputes over competition for limited resources.

For instance, during the debate over Proposition 187 (1994)—the California ballot initiative that sought to deny welfare benefits, education, health, and social services to undocumented immigrants—the initiative's proponents pitted racial groups against each other, arguing immigrants stole jobs from poor African American workers and overwhelmed an already overburdened social and health service system. The measure failed, in part because African American and other leaders wouldn't bite, and instead worked to convince their own constituents that immigrant struggles were similar to their own experiences and that a pro-immigrant agenda would preserve the civil rights of all Californians.

As Carmen Morgan, director of Leadership Development in Interethnic Relations (LDIR), states: "There is a need for an expanding social justice analysis. Long gone are the days of segregated movements. Today's generation, a generation of multi-identified, class conscious, queer, people of color, expect more intersections, more interplay between these issues. They expect that the identities that shape their experiences will be included in all aspects of their movement building. If existing movements do not address their reality, these young activists will just create their own movements," said Morgan.

She added: "Barack Obama's great appeal to Generation X is due in part to his own complicated set of identities. White *and* black. Holding both Midwest *and* immigrant roots. Raised working class but *also* Harvard educated. These identities coexist to form a more textured canvas. For Generation X'ers, Obama and his election were emblematic of the shift away from the rigid identity politics of the sixties" (Morgan, 2009).

However, in the day-to-day work of movement building, these intersectionalities are harder to address effectively. The passage of California's Proposition 8 on November 4, 2008, brought this challenge squarely into the limelight. Although elated by the election of the nation's first African American president, many progressive activists were shocked by the narrow passage (52 to 48 percent) of Proposition 8, an amendment to the California Constitution that eliminated the right of same-sex couples to marry.

On November 5, a widely reported exit poll seemed to show that 70 percent of California's African American voters supported Prop 8.[7] Immediately, African Americans and other minority communities to a lesser extent became very public scapegoats for the passage of Prop 8 as high-profile gay and often white voices blamed African American homophobia for taking away the rights of gays and lesbians (including rights belonging to African American LGBTs).[8] Subsequent studies and surveys weakened the message: in January 2009, for example, the National Gay & Lesbian Task Force released a study finding that African Americans supported Prop 8 at a much lower level— at no more than 59 percent—and that this support was due in large part to the significantly larger proportion of African Americans who regularly attend church (57 percent versus 40 percent for whites) (Egan and Sherill, 2009).

It has become clear that racial and ethnic minority communities cannot be presumed to support marriage equality simply based on civil rights solidarity. More work needs to be done. Many African Americans believed that support for Prop 8 in their community reflected the failure of the No on Prop 8 campaign to include diverse communities and work with African American LGBTs. And, of course, education within ethnic communities is also critical.

For the Asian and Pacific Islander (API) community, these same concerns also existed and led API activists to organize the community in response. Karin Wang, vice president of the Asian Pacific American Legal Center, says that after thousands of Chinese immigrants protested gay marriage in 2004, API community activists responded by forming API Equality-LA, a new coalition "to raise an alternative voice, one that showed strong API support for the freedom of gays and lesbians to marry and that included both LGBT and allied members" (Chang and Wang, 2009). In Los Angeles, API Equality-LA used multiple strategies to build a strong network of API community groups and individuals in support of marriage equality: one-on-one conversations, outreach at community festivals and through ethnic media, coalition building, and even filing an API-specific amicus brief before the California Supreme Court. The majority of organizations supporting the coalition were "allied," meaning their primary focus was *not* on the LGBT community. Active allied groups included civil rights organizations such as the Asian Pacific American Legal Center (APALC) and the Japanese American Citizens League (JACL), who used the parallels between the past struggles of Asian immigrants against antimiscegenation laws and the current movement for same-sex marriage to persuade API community members to support marriage equality.[9] A November 4, 2008, exit poll found that API voters in Southern California favored Prop 8 by 54 to 46 percent (APALC, 2008)—close to the general vote, but more important, a dramatic shift from the 68 to 32 percent vote in 2000 for Proposition 22, an earlier ballot measure against gay marriage.

According to Wang, API community leaders believe the shift is attributable to the four-plus years of education and organizing efforts launched in response to the anti–gay-marriage protests (Chang and Wang, 2009). But the success is also closely linked to the ability of groups like API Equality-LA and APALC to unite different struggles for equality under one larger vision of justice. For example, throughout its organizing in support of the legal brief, APALC heard many times from API organizations that the link between antimiscegenation and marriage equality was extremely compelling. After Prop 8 passed, civil rights lawyers expressed concern that allowing Prop 8 to stand would set a dangerous precedent by allowing a simple majority vote to strip away fundamental rights of a protected minority. The fear is that Prop 8 will open the door to repealing the fundamental rights of other minority groups (Wang, 2009). This fear was echoed by dozens of leading racial justice, women's rights, and other civil rights groups in challenging the passage of Prop 8. The ability to link the struggles of different communities, either through highlighting parallels or showing broader impact, is exactly the sort of link that is needed to build lasting alliances across seemingly disparate struggles. But there must be sensitivity and understanding in order to bridge the interests of minority groups. What may work for one group may not work for another.

Leadership in the New Geography

To be effective in this new environment, leaders in racial equity must be able to navigate several geographies: local,

regional, and national. For example, after the American
Recovery and Reinvestment Act was passed into law on
February 17, 2009, organizations such as Green For All
and PolicyLink hosted a conference call on February 24,
2009, that attracted thousands who wanted to understand
how to advocate for Recovery Act dollars and bring them
to the inner city. Without community organizers, the dollars would go to the savviest grant writers, not necessarily communities with the greatest need. Organizers bring
knowledge and understanding to the table: neighborhood
advocates understand the specific needs of that community; local organizers understand the needs of the area;
and city, county, and state organizers ensure that money
funds the transportation, health, education, environment,
and employment concerns of people that have limited
power at the decision-making table. But in implementing the Recovery Act, relationships with larger national
bodies are critical. This balance can mean smaller groups
grounded in their neighborhood but attached to larger
umbrella networks—the New World Foundation labels
these anchor organizations, "with the scope, sophistication
and reach to be able to challenge power and policy" (Pastor
and Ortiz 2009: 4). Explicit strategies for scaling up must
be identified and coordinated by leadership if they hope to
affect the racialized structure of America (see Box 5-3 as an
example).

Such larger coalitions can be difficult to organize.
There is an understandable tendency to focus exclusively
in one's own terrain, on one's own issue, or in one's own
racial or ethnic group, but such isolation can detract from
creating a larger impact. "Historical separation, the arti-
ficial parsing of social issues along racial lines, and an
absence of communication and trusting relationships
among activists in different fields frustrate the development of synergistic efforts," said Dayna Cunningham,
executive director of the Community Innovators Lab at
MIT.[10] "Rather than joint strategies to tackle major problems in multidisciplinary ways, problem-solving efforts

Box 5-3. Community Organizing for
Equity in Transportation

In the wake of more than $2 trillion in emergency investments by the federal government in an attempt to reverse the recent economic collapse, voices for equity in the arena of infrastructure investment and environmental sustainability will be more crucial than ever. The application of more than $300 billion in federal transportation money will set the stage for an inside-the-beltway showdown among policymakers, lobbyists, advocates, and the various transportation industries. While the national policy debates will surely raise the visibility of transportation innovations, reinforce the interconnectedness between transportation and climate change, and highlight the transportation needs of new constituencies, there is no guarantee that economic and social equity will be front and center in these debates. Yet, one of the greatest determinants of being able to rise out of poverty is access to quality employment, which equity-based transportation policies can help to provide to the most vulnerable Americans. Many of the communities that are most dramatically falling behind economically are plagued by inadequate, worsening infrastructure. It will be essential that community voices, with the direct knowledge of what is needed on the ground, work in concert with policy advocates to keep ongoing national, state, and local transportation policies focused on these issues.

Organizers have been reexamining transportation policy and its impact on the nation's most vulnerable. From the trailblazing work of Transportation Equity Network to bring tangible outcomes from transportation investment into low-income communities throughout the nation, to locally driven equity coalitions working in dozens of metropolitan regions, to emerging efforts to mobilize around the American Recovery and Reinvestment Act of

2009, leadership across the United States is making the connection between our transportation choices and the quality-of-life outcomes that undergird our economy. An equitable transportation agenda will provide the media, policymakers, and grassroots organizations with a local, state, and federal policy vision to ensure that transportation policy becomes a significant vehicle for addressing inequity across sectors.

Only through authentic community voices aggressively promoting equity outcomes will long-term, fundamental, and equitable reform of federal transportation policy be achieved.

—Written by Dwayne Marsh,
senior director for policy engagement
at PolicyLink, April 21, 2009.

remain fragmented, disparate, and weaker than they need to be," said Cunningham.

But this is exactly why racial equity organizers and advocates need to take geography and scale into account. In our experience, there is more openness to recognizing our intertwined futures the closer we get. And scale is about more than the horizontal dimension of space—it's also about how we connect top and bottom, leaders and communities. Today's business leaders, for example, must be able to move beyond the traditional top-down leadership approach to a more horizontal, collaborative style that has the advantage of being quicker and more inclusive, utilizing diverse ideas and interests to take advantage of opportunities. At the same time, in light of today's economy, they need to deal with the intersection of domestic and global forces. In the context of working for racial justice, collaborative leadership can ensure that the table is inclusive, that developing leadership occurs at all levels of organizations in order to tap the full potential of every individual, and that more effective coalitions can emerge.

Leadership, New Technology, and New Skills

As technology advances, Americans, particularly youth, are overloaded with media and organizations vying for their attention and time. In particular, capturing the attention of the politically disenfranchised takes new innovation. As much as a third of the voting population is not affiliated with either major national party (Pollster, 2009). Phone calls and rallies are being quickly replaced by e-mails, text messages, Twitter "tweets," and YouTube videos aimed at reaching an increasingly digitally connected America. Some may recall that Obama announced Joe Biden as his running mate through a text message, and now the White House puts out regular Saturday morning addresses through YouTube.

And communicating is about more than the method. Racial equity leaders need to be conscious of how they frame issues. For example, calling immigrant integration the "new" civil rights issue might raise the hackles of some African Americans who see themselves as still waiting to realize their own civil rights—instead, using frames that stress the legacy and continuity of struggle rather than its reinvention can help.[11] Sometimes the racial equity movement needs to find new words to get free of tired, defensive conversations. For example, higher taxes that might improve inner-city schools or achieve other racially just ends could be framed as "investing in America" rather than taking from the pockets of hardworking citizens (Lakoff, 2004).

Finally, leaders must constantly acquire new skills and improve existing skills ones beyond technology per se. To fully understand their terrain, leaders should pursue a wide range of information sources, including experts—

both in the academy and in the field—formal training, and peer learning. Understanding the implications of the global economy does not come from local experience alone; grasping how systems function—and malfunction—requires broader study.

For the first time in decades, we live in a multipolar global community where no one nation is a superpower. A new responsibility for great leadership is to be able to develop strategies that respond to this increasingly interconnected and global society. More important, communities of color should not be left out.

Remaining in the global conversation may require today's youth to learn other languages and explore ways to partner with other countries to improve the environment and our communities. Representatives of the Los Angeles Urban League went to China in 2006 to learn about Chinese approaches to alleviating poverty. The Los Angeles Urban League has prioritized global networking, communicating, and language skills among its community members to enable new opportunities for minorities in America. The Committee of 100, an organization of influential Chinese American leaders, sponsored a Latino delegation trip to China in November 2008. One of the delegates, a Los Angeles Unified School District (LAUSD) member, proposed a Mandarin/Spanish and other world languages resolution in October 2008 to increase the public school foreign language requirement from a current two-year requisite to a six-year minimum.

The ability to collaborate at a global, or even local scale is a learned skill, and although collaborations among different sectors and even among peers are often difficult, they provide lessons that go-it-alone approaches simply do not. In the final analysis, such skills are tested in the cauldron of getting initiatives passed by electoral bodies, creating and implementing programs to address injustices, and mobilizing for positive changes for communities and groups.

Putting It Together:
New Capacities for Communities

While the current economic crisis affects everyone, much of the dire poverty is concentrated in minority and rural communities across the country. One set of institutions critical to racial equity are nonprofit community organizations. Nonprofits are often the only ethnic community voices, and they frequently are close to the ground and responsive to community concerns. They serve, advocate for, and mobilize these communities for important change. The challenge today is that these nonprofit organizations are being dramatically impacted by decreasing resources from government, foundations, corporate, and individual supporters while simultaneously the needs addressed by the organizations are growing at unprecedented rates.

Shifting inward, leaders need to learn to build organizational capacity. The challenge of leadership development and capacity building in our community in this economic downturn requires people in different nonprofit sectors to develop stronger, more efficient, and more connected movements for racial equity and progressive change. To passively wait for the economic recession to end will not produce the results needed and instead will further hurt communities of color.

Keeping these organizations strong in hard times will require different approaches to leadership; infrastructure building; mentoring and succession planning; increased fundraising; possible consolidation; skills building; good operating resources; and unrestricted resources for advocacy. In a 2008 article in *Diversity in Philanthropy*, Stewart Kwoh poses the question "What kind of deep capacity building, technical assistance, and leadership development will make an impact so that more organizations, especially small community-based agencies, can access resources to battle growing inequities?" (Kwoh, 2008).

The debate in 2008 around California Assembly Bill

624, which sought to require foundations to report on the racial composition of their staffs, boards, and grantees, raised important issues for all of us working in impoverished or struggling communities. Many community leaders and agencies are frustrated because of their inability to access resources to address growing economic inequities. On the other hand, foundations and community leaders saw it as problematic to have data-driven solutions through legislative oversight. While this bill was controversial and eventually withdrawn, it still elicited an important discussion about the role of leadership in strengthening capacities. At the same time, ten large foundations in California did agree to build the capacity of smaller nonprofit organizations, especially those focused on minority communities.

Kwoh suggests four leadership solutions for effectively building the capacity of nonprofit organizations. First, it is essential to utilize collaborative and multilayered methods to build deep capacity. It will not suffice to provide the executive director with a number of training classes. We should start with a holistic assessment of the capacity-building needs with the goal of building a stronger organization. Of course, training in skills such as finance and fundraising are important. But developing mentorship opportunities, partnerships between large and small organizations in similar communities or working on similar issues, peer-to-peer networking, and the use of intermediaries that focus on working with small agencies can make for significant and sustainable growth. Part of the assessment should look at staff development beyond the executive director. Too often, capacity building is simply centered on one individual.

Second, multifaceted leadership development should be seen as an organizational imperative. Many organizations suffer from a limited pipeline of well-rounded leaders. Too often, leaders are limited in either their ability or willingness to build broader collaboratives or coalitions. We can strengthen the development of leaders who have skills to collaborate across boundaries of race and geography, which can not only enhance programmatic goals, but can significantly advance learning and confidence building. Learning how to develop clear assessments and power analyses of communities as well as how to communicate effectively are all part of multifaceted leadership development. Many nonprofits in the state are now facing a wave of imminent retirements of executive directors. Multilayered leadership development must happen soon to make sure that the new wave of executives is well trained and diverse.

Third, there are few successful organizations without strong boards of directors. Yet, many community organizations run without such boards. Sometimes staff do not make space for talented board members who can shape the policies of the organizations. More often, organization leaders, both staff and existing board, simply cannot find talented and committed board members. Capacity building can include the development of pipelines of board members with the help of foundation affinity groups, large organizations that have a much larger resource pool, professional associations, and intermediaries.

Finally, the foundations themselves have a new opportunity to look within. They can learn from this debate by making sure that their own boards of directors are diverse, with people from different backgrounds and especially with community experience and involvement. The ten foundations who led the agreement in California can also reach out to other foundations that were not party to this compromise and educate them to see that we all benefit by building the capacity of our diverse communities and leaders.

Approaches to Developing Effective Leadership

Effective leadership requires support from and interaction with peers, mentors, and coaches. Many time-proven ways to develop leadership already exist. While we focus on three approaches, they are by no means exhaustive. For example, mentoring has long been one of the most direct ways of developing leaders. Through this type of relationship, one can develop important leadership qualities and often ascend to the leader's position. In this section we address (1) leadership networks; (2) leadership programs; and (3) ongoing leadership development within organizing campaigns, legal cases, and institutions. We believe that these three approaches may be the most accessible and scalable.

Leadership Networks. An important approach that builds and nurtures existing or emerging leaders is the formation of networks, particularly among those who are similarly committed to racial equality and inclusion. These networks should be multiracial and cross-sectoral, including nonprofit, business, religious, and academic leaders. Race and ethnic-specific networks, however, can play a positive role. The latter should be forward-looking in addition to being responsive to immediate issues.

Ideally, multiracial networks need to be in place before crises occur so that trusting relationships can be established. Relationship building is key: it can be the base from which true coalitions are built and new solutions developed. These networks can also form crucial channels of communication, not just dialogue or study circles. The multiracial character of these networks should not preempt ethnic-specific networks or avoid ethnic- or racial-specific issues. Having several leadership circles or networks is important.

Experiments are ongoing in building cross-sector networks in key social movements. For example, the Rockefeller Foundation in the 1990s developed a leadership program to allow civil rights, environmental, community-building, and labor leaders to build a network to explore overlapping interests and influence each other's work. In addition to building trusting relationships, investigating large-scale trends across sectors, permitting the exploration of shared interests and obstacles to collaboration, and enabling the ongoing communication of ideas, joint projects have been developed that model effective problem solving on specific race-related policy issues and foster collaboration among leaders from segmented social change movements.

Another example of a leadership network is the Digital Steppingstones (DSS) project, launched by The Tomás Rivera Policy Institute (Pachon, Macias, and Bagasao, 2000). The DSS project is investigating how access to advanced technologies in low-income and minority communities can best be achieved. Collaborating with knowledgeable librarians, educators, and community members, this issue-based leadership network has produced major policy recommendations through its research and findings that address the need to encourage partnerships between corporate sectors and public access centers. The recommendations also address the need to optimize resources by promoting cooperation among public access centers. This network has allowed member collaborators to avoid reinventing the wheel and to learn important lessons from each other in order to take a lead in reducing the digital divide in their communities.

With eighteen prominent leaders from business, academia, labor, and the media, the Business Enterprise Trust was an active business leadership network from 1991 to 1996. A national nonprofit organization, it sought to identify bold, creative leadership that incorporated a commitment to social justice and community as a pivotal part of its vision for business. These businesses, once identified, were upheld as exemplary, brought into the national spotlight by the network, and served as positive corporate responsibility models.

Business leaders have also fostered networks to confront racism directly. Project Change, first established in 1991 by Levi Strauss & Company through its corporate foundation, built local networks in four cities to address racial prejudice and institutional racism. Networks or task forces are created, and after an assessment of institutional racism, business, community, and other partners work on projects to alleviate such barriers and provide training in areas such as fair lending, hate crimes prevention, educational advancement, and improved law enforcement.

Collaborations of foundations are rare in cities. In the aftermath of the Los Angeles riots, however, over twenty-five foundations networked to create the Los Angeles Urban Funders to build leadership capacity and community revitalization efforts in three impoverished neighborhoods. Not only have the neighborhoods developed stronger leaders, but the foundations have gained valuable knowledge and insight from community partners and other foundations.

Leadership Development Programs. An abundance of literature on leadership development programs exists (see, for example, Meehan, 1999, and Campbell & Associates, 1997). Such programs can contribute significantly in developing skills, experience, networks, and personal relationships that strengthen the leadership capacity of individuals and organizations.

What makes leadership development successful? Claire Reinelt, director of research at the Leadership Learning Community, states: "In the process of our work together we have identified the need for a much broader and more culturally inclusive approach to cultivating and sustaining leadership that focuses on nurturing and supporting teams, networks, and communities; and prepares individuals to lead collectively with others whose leadership cultures and practices differ from their own" (Meehan, Perry, and Reinelt, 2009: 3).

So it follows that leadership development programs in any setting must deal with race and cultural awareness as a clear focus. Searching for common ground is important; alienating participants by exclusively focusing on racial differences is not productive. Yet race issues will surface or resurface, so it is better to plan for this discussion. John

Maguire and colleagues emphasize this point in the article "15 Tools for Creating Healthy, Productive Interracial/Multicultural Communities—A Community Builder's Tool Kit" (Maguire, Leiderman, and Egerton, 2000): "The time spent at the beginning [either of a community building project or leadership training program, according to John Maguire] working on race will be well-repaid later. When you avoid this painful, protracted conversation at the outset, proposed partnerships fall apart, leading to head-shaking—and sometimes finger pointing—over the intractability associated with race and the depth of animosities held by one group in relation to another" (Maguire et al., 2000).

The more leadership development programs deal with real situations and practical collaborations, the more likely it is that they will have a positive impact on participants' daily work and lives. The Leadership Development in Interethnic Relations program, cosponsored by the Asian Pacific American Legal Center, the Southern Christian Leadership Conference, and the Central American Resource Center, consists of three components in the six-month training class for adults and high school students: cultural awareness training, including personal, cultural, racial, and ethnic backgrounds and the role of stereotypes; skills building, including conflict resolution, team building, and violence prevention; and a community project completed in multiethnic teams working with local community leaders. It is this last component—the community project—that most tests collaboration skills. The bonds and trust resulting from these projects usually last well beyond the program.

In its examination of leadership development programs for youth that emphasize racial justice issues, the MultiCultural Collaborative found that practical involvement is a key component of effective programs. At the same time, it learned that successful programs also provide training and analysis of the larger causes and systems so that youth participants can understand their personal experiences in the context of broader societal trends and issues (MultiCultural Collaborative, 2001).

Finally, we agree with Deborah Meehan, executive director of the Leadership Learning Community when she writes:

> Unusual partnerships and strategic alliances within the community have catalyzed the most innovative and successful community revitalization and development initiatives. An understanding of the 21st century leadership challenges of globalization, disparities of wealth, complexity, interconnected systems, change, and diversity all call for strong cross-sectoral collaborations and solutions. Surprisingly, there are few established leadership development programs to foster the development of these teams. Business and civic leaders rarely sit at the table with grassroots community leaders engaged in collective problem-solving. (Meehan, 1999)

Support for the varied leadership development programs, particularly those that have an impact on racial justice, should be enhanced and expanded. Businesses need to be challenged to see these leadership development efforts as part of their corporate and social responsibility commitment and as a preferred way to do business. Competitive pressures have led to decreasing support for measures to address racial disparities both within companies and within communities, and yet, the success of most businesses depends on the vitality of the communities in which their customers live.

Some foundations have also taken a new or renewed interest in leadership development and organizational capacity building. For example, The California Wellness Foundation has significantly increased core operating support grants to build the capacity of nonprofit organizations and the leadership of those organizations. This kind of grant making acknowledges the importance of strengthening their partners rather than just focusing on program

grants. During the past ten years, foundations such as the
Ford Foundation, The W. K. Kellogg Foundation, The
California Wellness Foundation, The California Endowment, The James Irvine Foundation, and many others initiated leadership development programs to highlight the
contributions of new leaders to community revitalization in
many fields.

There is a danger in minimizing the importance of
leadership development programs at a time of economic
crisis. But in a time of hardship, we face the challenge of
addressing acute needs in order to strengthen important
social relationships. With shrinking resources, there is a
tendency to turn away from funding preventative, skill-
enhancing programs and community education initiatives
and instead to prioritize direct services. In fact, both are
critically needed.

Developing Leadership in Ongoing Organizing Work. Leadership comes from many sources. It should not be limited
to leadership networks and leadership development programs. What is essential is an ongoing commitment to
develop leadership as an integral component of achieving
racial justice. Training may occur within organizations: it
may arise during an organizing drive, may be required
during a civil rights lawsuit, or may happen as part of regular interactions in business. Opportunities for leadership
development are everywhere.

A case in point: during the civil rights lawsuit (1995–
2000) against the El Monte contractors—manufacturers
and retailers who were responsible for the enslavement
of more than seventy undocumented Thai garment workers in a sweatshop in Southern California—the garment
workers themselves were educated and trained to become
their own leaders, to speak out against exploitation in their
industry. The case was racially and geographically complicated by the fact that there were over twenty Latino workers in a front shop in a different location where workers

were not enslaved but certainly were exploited. Hundreds of hours of discussion, training, and nurturing led to many of the workers speaking at rallies and before the California legislature on behalf of stronger antisweatshop laws. Greater learning and understanding about each other led Latino and Thai workers to come together for mutual support of a unified successful campaign for stronger antisweatshop laws in California.

Penda Hair (2001) lifts up the emerging field of racial justice innovation as communities work with lawyers using a range of tools to challenge exclusion based on race and ethnicity. In the process, these advocates are buttressing local leadership and reinvigorating local democracy.

One case from Boston illustrates this practice. In 1993, when the city proposed developing a parking garage on one of Chinatown's last parcels of underdeveloped land, a coalition of residents and activists rallied to stop it. Taking democratic decision-making as its core principle, the coalition launched a relentless organizing campaign against approval of the garage. Teaming with a group of young legal service lawyers, the coalition mobilized residents for administrative hearings, conducted a community-wide referendum, and held news conferences and cultural events to stimulate public involvement among marginalized immigrant groups. The coalition made leadership development a priority. Activities organized by resident committees created repeat opportunities to develop public speaking skills, learn community outreach, communicate messages, and engage neighbors. In the process, the coalition opened the neighborhood's decision-making and won a decisive victory to preserve community open space.

Even with limited resources, nonprofits and others can advance staff and board development through a number of approaches that promote cross-racial and cross-sectoral organizational exchanges to share information and lessons. In addition, organizations can plan office training to understand other communities and their infrastructures

Box 5-4. Eight Questions for Leaders

Here are eight questions leaders should reflect on to guide them in facing the challenges of social justice leadership:

1. As a leader, do I understand the economic crisis and the harsh consequences for people of color? Do I understand the interconnectedness of issues and the multifaceted approach to solutions? Am I fighting for genuine equality and not just reacting to the symptoms?

2. As a leader, do I have a multiethnic and multiracial perspective? Can I fight for justice for my own group and at the same time build a broader coalition for justice?

3. As a leader, am I looking to take advantage of the opportunity to build a larger movement for change?

4. As a leader, do I understand that the fight for racial justice must complement and support the fight for the rights of those who face discrimination because of disability, sexuality, class, and gender?

5. As a leader, am I able to redefine the terms of debate to expand social justice analysis to create a new integrated social vision?

6. As a leader, am I able to persuasively get a message out to the public with the creative use of media?

7. As a leader, do I have a global understanding of change, the necessity to connect America's solution that is complementary to the efforts for change throughout the world?

8. As a leader, do I have a penchant for action, a commitment to reflection, and the ability to collaborate?

so that connections can be made easier in the course of their work and activities. Leadership development, especially concerning racial justice issues, must be ongoing. In that regard, we end with key questions presented in Box 5-4 to help nurture the next generation of social justice leaders.

Notes

[1] Figures taken from the U.S. Dept. of Labor, October 2009 Current Population Survey (CPS); see http://www.bls.gov/news.release/empsit.nr0.htm.

[2] "More or Less Equal?" *The Economist*, April 2, 2009.

[3] Meizhu Lui, "The Wealth Gap Gets Wider," *Washington Post*, March 23, 2009.

[4] Peter Wallsten and David G. Savage, "Conservatives invoke Obama in Voting Rights Act Challenge," *Los Angeles Times*. March 18, 2009.

[5] David Savage, "Supreme Court Narrows, but Preserves, Voting Rights Act," *Los Angeles Times*, June 22, 2009.

[6] Rubén Lizardo of PolicyLink. Phone interview with Stewart Kwoh, April 13, 2009.

[7] See http://www.cnn.com/ELECTION/2008/results/polls/#val=CAI01p1.

[8] Dan Savage, http://slog.thestranger.com/2008/11/black_homophobia. The Public Policy Institute of California found white voters were split (50–50) on Prop. 8. See http://www.ppic.org/content/pubs/jtf/jtf_Prop8JTF.pdf.

[9] See official API Equality-LA and APALC press release at http://apiequality.org/about/PressRelease-APIsAgainst8PanelPressRelease-Oct23.pdf.

[10] Interview with Stewart Kwoh, March 2001.

[11] The Opportunity Agenda's "African Americans and Immigrants: Moving Forward Together," http://opportunityagenda.org/files/field_file/African%20Americans%20and%20Immigrants.pdf.

References

Asian Pacific American Legal Center. 2005. *Leaders for Change: Boundary-Crossing Leadership Development in the Health Sector*. Los Angeles: Asian Pacific American Legal Center.

Asian Pacific American Legal Center. 2009. *Asian Americans at the Ballot Box: The 2008 General Election in Los Angeles County*. Los Angeles: Asian Pacific American Legal Center. October 27.

Campbell & Associates. 1997. "Lessons Learned About Grassroots Community Leadership." Report commissioned by the Kellogg Foundation.

Chang, Robert, and Karin Wang. 2009. *Democratizing the Courts: How an Amicus Brief Helped Organize the Asian American Community to Support Marriage Equality*. Los Angeles: Asian Pacific American Legal Center and UCLA.

Choi, Cindy, Ruben Lizardo, and Gary Phillips. 1996. *Race, Power, and Promise in Los Angeles: An Assessment of Responses to Human Relations Conflict*. Los Angeles: MultiCultural Collaborative.

Egan, Patrick J., and Kenneth Sherrill. 2009. "California's Proposition 8: What Happened and What Does the Future Hold?" New York: National Gay and Lesbian Task Force Policy Institute. January 6.

Gates, Henry Louis, Jr., 1999. "Backlash?" In Eric Brandt, ed., *Dangerous Liaisons: Blacks and Gays and the Struggle for Equality*. New York: New Press.

Hair, Penda D. 2001. *Louder Than Words: Lawyers, Communities, and the Struggle for Justice*. New York: Rockefeller Foundation.

Kwoh, Stewart. 2008. *Diversity in Philanthropy: An Opportunity to Build Communities*. Southern California Grantmakers. Accessible at http://www.diversityinphilanthropy.org/voices/clegislation/commentaries.php#link2.

Kwoh, Stewart, and Russell Leong, eds. 2009. *Untold Civil Rights Stories: Asian Americans Speak Out for Justice*. Los Angeles: Asian Pacific American Legal Center and UCLA Asian American Studies Center.

Lakoff, George. 2004. *Don't Think of an Elephant! Know Your Values and Frame the Debate*. White River Junction, VT: Chelsea Green Publishing.

Maguire, John, Sally Leiderman, and John Egerton. 2000. "A Community Builder's Tool Kit: 15 Tools for Creating Healthy, Productive, Interracial/Multicultural Communities." Claremont, CA: Institute for Democratic Renewal and the Project Change Anti-Racism Initiative.

Meehan, Deborah. 1999. "Leadership Development Opportunities and Challenges: A Scan of the Field of the Leadership Literature and the Field of Leadership Development." Woodland Hills, CA: California Endowment.

Meehan, Deborah, Elissa Perry, and Claire Reinelt. 2009. "Developing a Racial Justice and Leadership Framework to Promote Racial Equity, Address Structural Racism and Heal Racial and Ethnic Divisions in Communities." Leadership Learning Community.

Morgan, Carmen. 2009. *Intersectionality and the False Dichotomy of Proposition 8*. Los Angeles: Bilerico Project. Accessible at http://www.bilerico.com/2009/04/intersectionality_and_the_false_dichotom.php.

MultiCultural Collaborative. 2001. "The Future of Change." Los Angeles: MultiCultural Collaborative.

Pachon, Harry P., Elsa E. Macias, and Paula Y. Bagasao. 2000. "Minority Access to Information Technology: Lessons Learned" Occasional Paper No. 67, Latino Studies Series. East Lansing, MI: Michigan State University, Julian Samora Research Institute.

Pastor, Manuel, and Rhonda Ortiz. 2009. *Making Change: How Social Movements Work—and How to Support Them.* Los Angeles: Program for Environmental and Regional Equity (PERE).

Pollster. 2009. "National Party Identification." July 20. http://www.pollster.com/polls/us/party-id.php.

State of California, Department of Finance. 2007. *Population Projections for California and Its Counties, 2000–2050.* Sacramento, California, July.

Wang, Karin. March 2009. "The Real Threat of Prop 8 and Why It Must Be Overturned." Accessible at http://www.californiaprogressreport.com/2009/03/the_real_threat.html.

Weiser, John, and Simon Zadek. 2000. "Conversations with Disbelievers: Persuading Companies to Address Social Changes." New York: Ford Foundation.

Wright, Kai. March/April 2009. "A Fragile Union." *ColorLines.* Accessible at http://colorlines.com/article.php?ID=484.

6

The Way Forward: An Equity Model

In many ways, America has been here before, confronting an epic financial crisis with a charismatic new president known for his soaring rhetoric, admired First Lady, and bold promises to break sharply from the policies of his unpopular predecessor.

The epoch, of course, was the 1930s, the president was Franklin Delano Roosevelt, and the crisis, the Great Depression. In the midst of the deepest financial catastrophe the industrialized world has ever known, Roosevelt's response was nothing less than to reinvent America with a bold package of programs aimed at putting the country back to work, rebuilding its infrastructure, and protecting vulnerable persons and communities from the free-market's worst excesses.

But if Roosevelt's New Deal is a model for how this nation can recover from its worst economic collapse in eighty years, it also offers a profound lesson on how even the grandest plan can fall short of the mark if it doesn't specifically address the results of America's Original Sin: systematic racial injustice and exclusion.

As we noted in our first chapter, far from seizing an opportunity to reform long-standing disparities in the U.S. economy, parts of the New Deal reinforced and even deepened this enduring racial hierarchy. Today, with the nation hemorrhaging jobs, families losing their homes, climate change threatening the planet, and an integrated global economy that does not wait for stragglers, America needs another new deal—or a *new* New Deal—to rebuild our economic and environmental foundation, and strengthen it to better withstand any storm that comes our way in the future. But to be successful, this new New Deal will have to address the realities of racial inequality and inequity forthrightly and intelligently.

This is not a matter of altruism, or redeeming a historical sleight, but of identifying the pathway to get this country back on track, prepare the next generation to compete in the world's marketplace, and set the table for more balanced and sustainable growth. We can't afford to get it wrong this time—we must make sure that all policies and practices, in addition to whatever else they seek to do, also redress the historical legacies of racial exclusion and prepare for the future by investing in all members of an increasingly diverse population.

We wish racial inequity were a thing of the past. But all the data of Chapter 3 and the challenges reviewed in Chapter 4 suggest that it is not. Instead, the leadership task of the twenty-first century must involve understanding a terrain of new issues and developing a new repertoire of skills while bridging an old set of differences. This will require different capacities than in the past and a conscious effort on all our parts to develop leadership that can lead across constituencies.

Leading with Equity

In short, we urge the nation's leaders to embrace the idea that an economically vibrant and sustainable American future depends, almost wholly, on a broader vision for equity, one that recognizes that lifting up the least of us will lift up *all* of us.

To understand how this vision would play out in everyday life, take, as an example, the curb cutouts that are now commonplace on sidewalks all across America, enabling people in wheelchairs to maneuver on pedestrian walkways. This practice was developed in response to the demands from people with disabilities who, even though discrimination against them was prohibited, found it difficult to get to jobs or public facilities. It took the curb cutouts to make real for them the promise of equal opportunity.

But those cutouts have helped far more than just those in wheelchairs: women and men pushing strollers have eased from corner to corner without having to lift the heavy contraption just to cross the street; travelers have hurried across town, with suitcases in tow, never having to break stride to lift the bag; workers pushing carts and pulling wagons have had their labor made easier; and parents have had their nerves settled knowing that young bike riders were successfully traversing the neighborhood from sidewalk to sidewalk, not in the street.

Or consider the much-maligned affirmative action policies that helped African Americans enter law and medical school. The deliberate actions taken to open up the university admissions process not only cleared the way for African Americans, Latinos, Asians, and Native Americans, but also for white women, who have benefited more than anyone from demolishing the notion that careers in law, medicine and other professional fields were the domain of white men only.

Why do we insist on making racial disparity a key and explicit consideration in the overall commitment to equity? We understand that this is tricky in a time that poses as postracial, particularly when there are countervailing voices saying that lifting up race means that you are stuck in the past. We also acknowledge that the goals of equity are sometimes achieved through a universal approach such as providing Social Security payments to workers who reach retirement age, using government spending or tax cuts to jump-start a stalled economy, or imposing fuel economy and other standards on automakers to discourage air pollution and greenhouse gas emissions. This approach is just, fair, and reaches people of all races and ethnic groups.

But there are times when an equitable result cannot be obtained without specifically addressing the issue of race. Many immigrant children of color are given a chance to succeed because of bilingual services targeted at them. In other areas, reserving slots for "low-income" families in programs such as Head Start without considering racial or ethnic identity as an element of admittance can have the effect of squeezing out children who are most in need of early childhood development activities. Similarly, job-training programs for ex-offenders must deliberately seek to reach black and Latino parolees who are typically the most difficult to place in the labor force. The entire society benefits when these children and young people are able to learn, obtain skills, and thrive, just as we all benefit when older Americans are kept out of poverty. And we can't get there without considering and addressing specific circumstances and needs.

Of course, we recognize that race alone is not a full marker of disadvantage—nor is it always the most effective way to build political consensus. We are, for example, supportive of strategies such as requiring that a percentage of workers building a new stadium near a low-income community of color come from that neighborhood. In this case, place, not race, may be more salient to the economic and political realities—and we all benefit when workers land jobs that can lead to steady work and stable careers that pay enough to escape poverty. But we think that some have erred too frequently on the side of submerging race—we think that one needs to lead with racial equity.

Why do we need to go beyond simply lifting legal barriers and toward more—dare we say it—affirmative action? Consider one of the emblematic moments of the civil rights movement—when Rosa Parks refused to give up her seat and move to the back of the bus. A wave of mass protests, consumer boycotts, and legal action eventually brought an end to segregation on public transit.

But it did not bring an end to segregation in transit. Nearly a quarter of African American households—and one-fifth of Latino households—do not own cars, and the lack of adequate public transportation poses a forbidding structural barrier to employment. Under a full equity model, building a community in which everyone can participate requires a good transit network. You can't just have the right to be on a bus—you need a bus that is frequent, connects you to employment, and provides a platform for economic, social, and physical mobility.

Examples of these kinds of gaps abound: the right to an education is guaranteed, but its quality is not; the law treats everyone equally in theory, but racial profiling and ineffective policing have criminalized black and Latino youth; of course, some people have managed to overcome the odds and succeed, but this nation is at its best when it creates better odds for everyone.

Leading for Equity

Racial progress is not just a matter of policy. The civil rights movement was not just a matter of lawyers and politicians; it was about ordinary citizens, black, white, and others, rural and urban, coming together to challenge the strictures of Jim Crow. It was, in short, about the strength and connective tissue of social movements.

Social justice and movement building received a huge boost from Obama's presidential campaign. Americans found a more inclusive movement to achieve equality during the 2008 election. A report published by the Program for Environmental and Regional Equity (PERE) argues that there are complex layers to building a social movement:

> Social movements are the threads that string together efforts
> bubbling up across the nation, sparking people's aspirations
> and imaginations for a better America. . . . Social movement
> organizations and networks that fundamentally seek to chal-
> lenge the configurations of power that currently produce ineq-
> uity. Such organizations and networks can be distinguished
> from coalitions in several ways: they are sustained, not epi-
> sodic, multi-sector rather than special interest, wide-ranging
> rather than single issue, constituency-based rather than inter-
> mediary-driven, and focused on transforming people's lives
> rather than on just changing policy. (Pastor and Ortiz, 2009: 1)

Torie Osborn (2008) puts it this way: "[A] social movement is characterized by a widely-shared analysis and
vision, but is a multi-issue mosaic of different parts. A
full-blown social movement has the following: vibrant
grassroots organization with engaged members; effective
lobbying and advocacy groups; electoral engagement; public education; messaging and media capacity; think tanks;
legal/litigation groups."

Osborn further notes that "a social movement must
attract new recruits; sustain the commitment of current
members; build and sustain organizational infrastructure; generate media coverage and spread ideas; mobilize the support of allies; constrain the opposition; and
utilize electoral power to advance an agenda. . . . A movement is not the same as a single issue organizing or advocacy campaign."

But that requires both leadership and support. Osborn
says: "Foundations do not make history; they fund it. Just
the same, there have been funders that have stepped up
and funded social movements since the American Revo-
lution—through abolitionism, suffragism, early 20th century immigration and child labor struggles, the civil rights
movement, feminism, gay/lesbian equality and more. The
advantage today is that there is a wealth of knowhow from
three generations' worth of direct experience in social
movements residing in staff and board members within the

philanthropy, as well as in leaders of non-profit partners and allies in the public sector."

In their analysis, Pastor and Ortiz (2009) offer three specific ways foundations can help: provide operational and long-term funding, support network building and expansion, and develop metrics to assess movement success.

One contemporary example of such an approach is the Equal Voice for America's Families campaign. Sponsored by the Marguerite Casey Foundation with long-term funding, training, and infrastructure building, EVAF, in conjunction with one hundred community groups, organizes families across the nation—including in Alabama, Arizona, Arkansas, California, Florida, Georgia, Illinois, Louisiana, Mississippi, New Mexico, Texas, and Washington—to shift the national attitudes and policies affecting poor and working families on issues such as living wages, access to affordable health care, education, housing, child care, immigration, and criminal justice reform. The call to action and the desire of the families to organize was apparent when more than 16,000 people gathered across the nation in September 2008 in three cities—Los Angeles, Birmingham, and Chicago—to ratify a national platform for working families. The platform was then submitted to the 2008 presidential candidates.

The Marguerite Casey Foundation came to the idea after listening to many leaders and recognizing the poor infrastructure for movement building. In a 2001 interview with Stewart Kwoh, Luz Vega-Marquis, president of the foundation, said that there is "no money for general support, no spokespeople for low-income communities, no media training to shift public opinion." When the foundation formed in 2002, after extensive research, the founders focused on assisting with a new bottom-up movement that allows families to be engaged locally but makes changes nationally. And their strategy has worked. In February of 2009, 150 families from twelve states traveled to Washington to hand-deliver their national family platform to Congress. As Luz Vega-Marquis explains, "We understand that foundations alone cannot nurture a movement. Foundations can, however, as Marguerite Casey Foundation does, use grantmaking dollars to invest in cornerstone organizations that support family leaders and advocate collective action to solve universal issues."

Leading on Equity

The equity framework we propose wouldn't produce a utopia, but it would carve out space for more people to contribute to their communities, metropolitan regions, and the country. There would be broader access to jobs and lower rates of welfare use—all contributing to the labor productivity and fiscal probity needed to compete in a global economy. There would be more public transportation, fewer cars on the streets, more parks, cleaner air, more grocery stores in the low-income neighborhoods—all helping to address climate change.

With fewer prisons and more reentry programs, neighborhoods would be safer and productive talent would not go to waste. With more recreation and better food available, there would be less obesity and fewer health problems. With immigrants integrated rather than shunned, entrepreneurship and hard work would pay off in both individual gains and community revitalization. And with more skin in the game, ordinary people would have more at stake in the development of their community, and begin to engage their local policymakers and institutions differently, strengthening democracy.

How do we get there? Part of the path will involve a continuing commitment to the basic procedural fairness secured by civil rights law. Part of it will involve the development of new and innovative policy to make the promises of civil rights real and alive to those in distressed neighborhoods. And part of it will be the resuscitation of the nation's metropolitan economies and our broader macroeconomy.

But just as the earlier movement for racial equity was not

just a job for lawyers and judges, politicians and p.
ers, the new civil right challenges—addressing the i.
distressed neighborhoods, subpar schools, and imm.
isolation—is really the province of all Americans: we wi.
be tested and we must all be leaders.

We included our own stories in the first chapter, noting how we came to our commitments and how we came to
write this volume. We ask you, the reader, to consider your
own story, your own reasons for tackling this book, and
perhaps something much more important: your next step.
Will you be willing to engage in the difficult and uncomfortable conversations about race Americans have been so
eager to avoid? Will you work to develop the skills to lead
across communities and toward uncommon ground?

America is at a demographic, economic, and environmental crossroads. How we act today will determine
whether we embrace our multicultural future, forge an
economy that delivers for all, and save a planet threatened
by our wasteful consumption. Yet despite the multiplicity
of challenges, at the dawn of the twenty-first century, this
nation is tasked with answering one fundamental question:
what will America be?

We must capitalize on a renewed enthusiasm for change
to craft a bold vision for the country we want our children
to inherit, and back up that vision with an action plan
infused by our collective wisdom and creativity, and by the
fundamental American ideals of fairness and democracy.
There has never been a better opportunity to make good
on America's promise.

References

Osborn, Torie. 2008. "Social Movements." Memo to the California
Endowment, April 4.

Pastor, Manuel, and Rhonda Ortiz. 2009. *Making Change: How Social
Movements Work—and How to Support Them.* Full Report. Los Angeles:
Program for Environmental and Regional Equity (PERE).

Data Sources

Chapter 1 Figures

1-1: Data for 1970 and 1980 from *Statistical Abstract of the United States: The National Data Book*. Annual CD-ROM. Washington, DC: U.S. Department of Commerce, 1999. Section 1, Population. Data for 1990 and 2000 from U.S. Census Bureau, 1990 Census STF3 and 2000 Census SF3, respectively. Data for 2010 through 2050 from U.S. Census Bureau, Population Division, Table 4. "Projections of the Population by Sex, Race, and Hispanic Origin for the United States: 2010 to 2050" (NP2008-T4). Released August 14, 2008.

1-2: Tabulations by the Program for Environmental and Regional Equity (PERE) of IPUMS 2007 American Community Survey (ACS); data from Steven Ruggles, Matthew Sobek, Trent Alexander, Catherine A. Fitch, Ronald Goeken, Patricia Kelly Hall, Miriam King, and Chad Ronnander. *Integrated Public Use Microdata Series: Version*

4.0 [machine-readable database]. Minneapolis: Minnesota Population Center [producer and distributor], 2008. Available at http://www.ipums.org.

1-3: Ibid.

1-4: Data for 1980 and 1990 from the California Department of Finance, Demographic Research Unit. "Revised Race/Ethnic Population Estimates: Components of Change for California Counties, July 1970 to July 1990." http://www.dof.ca.gov/HTML/DEMOGRAP/ReportsPapers/Estimates/RaceEthnic/documents/MMRevisedTablesRace70–90.xls. Data for 2000 from State of California, Department of Finance. Population Projections for California and Its Counties 2000–2050, by Age, Gender and Race/Ethnicity. Sacramento, California, July 2007. http://www.dof.ca.gov/html/DEMOGRAP/ReportsPapers/Projections/P3/documents/CALIFORNIA.XLS. Data for 2005–2007 from U.S. Census Bureau. 2005–2007 ACS, 3-Year Estimates, B03002: Hispanic or Latino Origin by Race (total population).

1-5: U.S. Census Bureau. 2007 ACS, 1-Year Estimates, C03002: Hispanic or Latino Origin by Race. Map based on Census Bureau TIGER/Line® files.

1-6: Paul R Campbell. 1996, Population Projections for States by Age, Sex, Race, and Hispanic Origin: 1995 to 2025. U.S. Bureau of the Census, Population Division, PPL-47. Map based on Census Bureau TIGER/Line® files.

Chapter 2 Figures

2-1: U.S. Census Bureau. Data for 1990 from 1990 Census STF1, P010: Hispanic Origin by Race. Data for 2000 from 2000 Census SF1, P8: Hispanic or Latino by Race (Total Population). Data for 2007 from 2007 ACS, 1-Year Estimates, C03002: Hispanic or Latino Origin by Race.

2-2: U.S. Census Bureau. 2007 ACS, 1-Year Estimates, C03001: Hispanic or Latino Origin by Specific Origin.

2-3: U.S. Census Bureau. 2007 ACS, 1-Year Estimates, C02006: Asian Alone by Selected Groups; and C02007: Native Hawaiian and Other Pacific Islander Alone by Selected Groups.

2-4: Frank Newport. "Americans Today Much More Accepting of a Woman, Black, Catholic, or Jew as President." Gallup Organization-Princeton, March 29, 1999. http://www.gallup.com/poll/releases/pr990329.asp. Election results data from CNN Election Center 2008. http://www.cnn.com/ELECTION/2008/results/president.

2-5: Frank Newport. "Most Say Race Will Not Be a Factor in Their Presidential Vote." Gallup Organization-Princeton, June 9, 2008. http://www.gallup.com/poll/107770/Most-Say-Race-Will-Factor-Their-Presidential-Vote.aspx.

2-6: Federal Bureau of Investigation. Hate Crime Statistics, Table 1: "Incidents, Offenses, Victims, and Known Offenders by Bias Motivation, 2007." http://www.fbi.gov/ucr/hc2007/table_01.htm.

2-7: Ibid.

2-8: Building Resilient Regions comparative cities database. Analysis by the Program for Environmental and Regional Equity (PERE).

2-9: Ibid.

2-10: U.S. Census Bureau. 2000 Census SF4, PCT141: Ratio of Income in 1999 to Poverty Level. Data shown is for the City of Los Angeles.

Chapter 3 Figures

3-1: U.S. Census Bureau. Current Population Survey, Annual Social and Economic Supplements. Historical Income Tables—Families, Table F-5: "Race and Hispanic Origin of Householder—Families by Median and Mean Income: 1947 to 2007." http://www.census.gov/hhes/www/income/histinc/f05.html.

3-2: Ibid

3-3: U.S. Bureau of Labor Statistics. Seasonally Adjusted Unemployment Rate for Adults 16 Years and Over Who Are in the Labor Force. Series numbered LNS14000000, LNS14000003, LNS14000006, LNS14000009. http://data.bls.gov/cgi-bin/surveymost?ln.

3-4: Algernon Austin. 2009. "Among College-Educated, African Americans Hardest Hit by Unemployment." Economic Policy Institute: Research and Ideas for Shared Prosperity. http://www.epi.org/economic_snapshots/entry/snapshots_20090422.

3-5: U.S. Bureau of Labor Statistics. Unpublished tabulations from the Current Population Survey, requested by the Program for Environmental and Regional Equity. "Median Usual Weekly Earnings of Full-Time Wage and Salary Workers by Sex, Age, Race, and Hispanic or Latino Ethnicity, Annual Averages 1979–2007." Quarterly averages, not seasonally adjusted.

3-6: Ibid.

3-7: Gregory Acs and Pamela Loprest. *Job Differences by Race and Ethnicity in the Low-Skill Job Market*. Urban Institute Brief No. 4. February 2009. P. 3.

3-8: Ibid. P. 4.

3-9: Neil Bania and Laura Leete. *Income Volatility and Food Insufficiency in U.S. Low-Income Households, 1992–2003*. Madison, WI: Institute for Research on Poverty, April 2007. P. 14. http://www.irp.wisc.edu/publications/dps/pdfs/dp132507.pdf.

3-10: Lawrence Mishel, Jared Bernstein, and Heather Boushey. *The State of Working America, 2002/2003*. Economic Policy Institute. Ithaca: Cornell University Press, 2003. P. 269, Table 3.29. Original data from the 1993 and 1996 Survey of Income and Program Participation (SIPP) panel.

3-11: U.S. Census Bureau. Poverty, Historical Poverty Tables—Current Population Survey, People, Table 2: "Poverty Status, by Family Relationship, Race, and Hispanic Origin: 1959–2007." Where data was originally missing, rates for blacks are imputed as a straight line between 1960 and 1965. http://www.census.gov/hhes/www/poverty/histpov/perindex.html.

3-12: Ibid. Table 3: "Poverty Status of People, by Age, Race, and Hispanic Origin: 1959 to 2007." http://www.census.gov/hhes/www/poverty/histpov/perindex.html.

3-13: Ibid. Table 10: "Related Children in Female Householder Families as a Proportion of All Related Children, by Poverty Status: 1959 to 2007." http://www.census.gov/hhes/www/poverty/histpov/perindex.html.

3-14: U.S. Census Bureau. Families and Living Arrangements, Current Population Reports, Table CH-3: "Living Arrangements of Black Children Under 18 Years Old: 1960 to Present." http://www.census.gov/population/socdemo/ms-la/tabch-3.txt.

3-15: U.S. Census Bureau. Current Population Survey, 2008 Annual Social and Economic Supplement, Table HI08: "Health Insurance Coverage Status and Type of Coverage by Selected Characteristics for Children Under 18: 2007." http://pubdb3.census.gov/macro/032008/health/h08_000.htm.

3-16: National Center for Health Statistics. *Health, United States, 2007, with Chartbook on Trends in the Health of Americans*, Table 19: "Infant, Neonatal, and Post-Neonatal mortality Rates, by Detailed Race and Hispanic Origin of Mother: United States, Selected Years 1983–2004." http://www.cdc.gov/nchs/data/hus/hus07.pdf#summary.

3-17: Ibid., Table 27: "Life Expectancy at Birth, at 65 Years of age, and at 75 Years of age, by Race and Sex: United States, Selected Years 1900–2005." http://www.cdc.gov/nchs/data/hus/hus07.pdf#summary.

3-18: U.S. Census Bureau. Housing Vacancies and Home-ownership (CPS/HVS), Annual Statistics: 2007, Table 20: "Homeownership Rates by Race and Ethnicity of Household-holder: 1994 to 2007." http://www.census.gov/hhes/www/housing/hvs/annua107/ann07t20.html.

3-19: Association of Community Organizations for Reform Now (ACORN). *Foreclosure Exposure: A Study of Racial and Income Disparities in Home Mortgage Lending in 172 American Cities*. Washington, DC: ACORN 2007. P. 2, Table: "High Cost Home Purchase Loans." Based on 2006 Home Mortgage Disclosure Act (HMDA) data. Income brackets based on percentage of median income: low income (<50%), moderate income (50–79%), middle income (80–119%), upper income (120%+).

3-20: Manuel Pastor. "State of the Region: The New Demography, the New Economy, and the New Environment." Program for Environmental and Regional Equity (PERE) and the Bay Area Social Equity Caucus (SEC). Presented at the SEC 10th Anniversary State of the Region Conference, December 15, 2008. Data from foreclosureS.com, October 22, 2005, to October 22, 2008, for the San Francisco Bay Area 9-County Region. Foreclosure rates were estimated by dividing total foreclosures by the estimated number of owner-occupied housing units in 2008. http://www.foreclosureS.com.

3-21: U.S. Census Bureau. Wealth and Asset Ownership, Detailed Tables, Table 5: "Mean Value of Assets for Households by Type of Asset Owned and Selected Characteristics" for 1995, 2000, and 2002. http://www.census.gov/hhes/www/wealth/detailed_tables.html.

3-22: The Applied Research Center. *Race and Recession: How Inequity Rigged the Economy and How to Change the Rules*. May 2009. P. 33, Figure 11. http://arc.org/downloads/2009_race_recession.pdf.

3-23: U.S. Census Bureau. Current Population Survey, Annual Social and Economic Supplements. Historical Income Tables—Families, Table F-4: "Gini Ratios for

Families, by Race and Hispanic Origin of Householder: 1947 to 2007." http://www.census.gov/hhes/www/income/histinc/f04.html.

3-24: Tabulations by the Program for Environmental and Regional Equity (PERE) of IPUMS 2005–2007 American Community Survey (ACS) data. A pooled 2005–2007 data set was used to produce more statistically reliable results.

3-25: Gregory Acs, Katherine Ross Phillips, and Daniel McKenzie, In *Low-Wage Workers in the New Economy*. Edited by Richard Kazis and Marc Miller. Washington, DC: Urban Institute Press 2001. P. 77, Table 4.8. Based on Philip Moss and Chris Tilly, *Stories Employers Tell: Race, Skill, and Hiring in America*. New York: Russell Sage Foundation, 2001. P. 132, Table 4.7.

3-26: U.S. Dept. of Education. National Center for Education Statistics, Digest of Education Statistics 2007, Table 105: "Percentage of High School Dropouts Among Persons 16 Through 24 Years Old (Status Dropout Rate), by Sex and Race/Ethnicity: Selected Years, 1960 Through 2006." Prepared in August 2007, based on U.S. Department of Commerce, Census Bureau, Current Population Survey (CPS), October 1967 through October 2006. http://nces.ed.gov/programs/digest/d07/tables/dt07_105.asp?referrer=report.

3-27: Building Resilient Regions comparative cities database. Analysis by the Program for Environmental and Regional Equity (PERE).

3-28: State of the Nation's Cities Database. Analysis by the Program for Environmental and Regional Equity (PERE), using place-of-work data. Data download available at http://socds.huduser.org/Census/Census_Home.html.

3-29: Building Resilient Regions comparative cities database. Analysis by the Program for Environmental and Regional Equity (PERE).

3-30: U.S. Environmental Protection Agency's 2003 Toxic Release Inventory. Demographic and income data from

2000 Census SF3. Analysis by the Program for Environmental and Regional Equity (PERE), using Tele Atlas and Geographic Data Technology to check for location accuracy and possible errors in TRI facilities. http://www.epa.gov/triinter/tridata/index.htm.

3-31: Ibid.

3-32: California Department of Education's California Basic Educational Data Systems (CBEDS), 1981–2005. http://www.cde.ca.gov/ds/sd/cb.

3-33: Jeanne Batalova and Michael Fix. *Uneven Progress: The Employment Pathways of Skilled Immigrants in the United States*. Migration Policy Institute. October 2008. P. 19, Figure 2. Data includes all college-educated people twenty-five years and older in the U. S. civilian labor force. "Recent" immigrant refers to those who migrated in the past ten years, while "Long Term" immigrant refers to those who migrated eleven or more years ago.

Chapter 4 Figures

4-1: Tabulations by the Program for Environmental and Regional Equity (PERE) of IPUMS 1990 and 2000 Public Use Microdata Samples (5%) and 2007 American Community Survey (ACS). See Figure 1-2 for full citation.

4-2: U.S. Census Bureau. Current Population Survey: Annual Social and Economic (ASEC) Supplement, Table PINC-03. "Educational Attainment—People 25 Years Old and Over, by Total Money Earnings in 2007, Work Experience in 2007, Age, Race, Hispanic Origin and Sex." http://pubdb3.census.gov/macro/032008/perinc/new03_000.htm

4-3: U.S. Census Bureau. Current Population Survey, School Enrollment—Social and Economic Characteristics of Students: October 2007, Table 1: "Enrollment Status of the Population 3 Years Old and Over, by Sex, Age, Race, Hispanic Origin, Foreign Born, and Foreign-Born

Percentage: October 2007." http://www.census.gov/popu
lation/www/socdemo/school/cps2007.html.

4-4: U.S. Dept. of Education, Institute of Education Sciences, National Center for Education Statistics, National
Assessment of Educational Progress (NAEP), 1971–2004
Long-Term Trend Reading Assessments. http://nces
.ed.gov/nationsreportcard/lttdata.

4-5: Global Insight. *U.S. Metro Economies: Current and Potential Green Jobs in the U.S. Economy.* Prepared for the U. S.
Conference of Mayors and the Mayors Climate Protection
Center. October 2008. P. 17. http://www.usmayors.org/
pressreleases/uploads/GreenJobsReport.pdf.

4-6: U.S. Census Bureau. For Data before 1990, Foreign-
Born Population Data, Working Paper No. 29: Campbell
Gibson and Emily Lennon, "Historical Census Statistics
on the Foreign-Born Population of the United States:
1850–1990." http://www.census.gov/population/www/doc
umentation/twps0029/twps0029.html. Data from 1990
to 1999 from U.S. Census Bureau, Population Estimates
Program, Population Division, "Foreign-Born Resident
Population Estimates of the United States by Sex, Race,
and Hispanic Origin: April 1, 1990 to July 1, 1999."
http://www.census.gov/population/estimates/nation/nativ
ity/fbtab003.txt and http://www.census.gov/population/
estimates/nation/nativity/nbtab003.txt. Data for 2000 to
2004 from U.S. Census Bureau, The Foreign-Born Population, Data Tables, Annual Data Tables 2000–2004.
http://www.census.gov/population/www/socdemo/foreign/
datatbls.html. Data for 2005–2007 from American Community Survey 1-Year Estimates, Detailed Tables, Table
B05001: "Citizenship Status in the United States."

4-7: U.S. Census Bureau. Data for 1970 and 1990 from
Campbell Gibson and Emily Lennon, Working Paper
No. 29: "Historical Census Statistics on the Foreign-
Born Population of the United States: 1850–1990," 1999.
http://www.census.gov/population/www/documentation

/twps0029/twps0029.html. Data for 2005–2007 from IPUMS American Community Survey (ACS) data as analyzed by the Program for Environmental and Regional Equity (PERE). A pooled 2005–2007 data set was used to produce more statistically reliable results.

4-8: Demetrios G. Papademetriou and Aaron Terrazas. *Immigrants and the Current Economic Crisis: Research Evidence, Policy Challenges, and Implications*. Migration Policy Institute, January 2009. P. 16, Figure 5. http://www.migrationpolicy.org/pubs/lmi_recessionJan09.pdf.

4-9: Aaron Terrezas and Jeanne Batalova. The Most Up-to-Date Frequently Requested Statistics on Immigrants in the United States. "What Percentage of the Foreign-Born are Limited English Proficient (LEP)?" Migration Policy Institute. December 2008, http://www.migrationinformation.org/USFocus/display.cfm?ID=714#2.

4-10: U.S. Department of Justice, Bureau of Justice Statistics. BJS Publications: "Prison and Jail Inmates at Midyear 1999"; "Prison and Jail Inmates at Midyear 2000"; "Prison and Jail Inmates at Midyear 2001"; "Prison and Jail Inmates at Midyear 2002"; "Prison and Jail Inmates at Midyear 2003"; "Prison and Jail Inmates at Midyear 2004"; "Prison and Jail Inmates at Midyear 2005"; "Prison and Jail Inmates at Midyear 2006"; "Prison Inmates at Midyear 2007." http://www.ojp.usdoj.gov/bjs/prisons.htm.

About The American Assembly

The American Assembly, founded by Dwight D. Eisenhower in 1950, is affiliated with Columbia University. The Assembly is a national, nonpartisan public affairs forum that illuminates issues of public policy through commissioning research and publications, sponsoring meetings, and publishing reports, books, and other literature. Its projects bring together leading authorities representing a broad spectrum of views, interests, and backgrounds. Assembly reports and other publications are used by government officials, community and civic leaders, and educators. American Assembly topics examine both domestic and foreign policy and have included issues that concern arts and culture, philanthropy, health, business, the economy, education, law, race, religion, and security.

Index

Page numbers in *italics* refer to figures.